P9-CTO-955

The
Basic Manual
of
Fly-Tying

The Basic Manual of
Fly-Tying

fundamentals of imitation

Paul N. Fling

Donald L. Puterbaugh

Foreword by Phillip N. Wright, Jr.

 STERLING
PUBLISHING CO., INC.   NEW YORK

Published in 1981 by
Sterling Publishing Co., Inc.
Two Park Avenue
New York, N.Y. 10016

Library of Congress Cataloging in Publication Data

Fling, Paul N
    The basic manual of fly-tying.

    Bibliography: p.
    Includes index.
    1. Fly tying.   I. Puterbaugh, Donald L., joint
author,   II. Title.
SH451.F56   688.7'9   77-80194
ISBN 0-8069-8146-6
(previously 0-8473-1570-3)

Printed in the United States of America

To Tony Gross who gave us the impetus
to begin and whose enthusiasm wouldn't
allow us to quit.

contents

Chapter Seven

*Color plates illustrating materials
face pages 32 & 33.*

*Color plates illustrating flies
face pages 64 & 65.*

Foreword

Montana's fishing season opened here this weekend with a perfect illustration of the need for Don Puterbaugh's and Paul Fling's book. Their book will fill a gaping hole for the novice fly-tyer and fly fisherman, and will pique the interest of experts.

An ardent and enthusiastic fisherman stopped by my place to compare fishing notes. While we talked he showed me with pride two cane rods that he had wrapped himself and a number of adequately tied flies. Adams, Royal Wulffs, Humpies, and Lt. Cahills were the major patterns in his box.

To my question of why he had so many of those particular patterns, he responded, "Well—they work!" And so it is with so many fishermen—they tie or buy flies *only* because "they work." It is of course *perfect* logic—as far as it goes. There is another question that should be asked: "Why do they work?" Is it a caddis? a mayfly? a stone fly? a terrestrial? What is the fly doing? Why is it working? When a fly fisherman asks these questions, he is on the road to becoming a better fisherman. It is the realization that trout do not feed on hatches of "Adams" or "Royal Wulffs," but do feed on caddis flies and terrestrial insects.

My new friend and I started discussing the impending salmon fly hatch and the feeding orgy it causes for the trout. At my mention of the Latin name, Pteronarcys californica, of the insect, he blanched and said he had a couple of the better known books on the subject but had never bothered to wade through all of that "technical garbage" as he put it. "Why can't someone come up with a book for guys like me? Something simple that *I* can understand." He went on with more of the same: "tired after a day at the office"—he didn't have time to become an entomologist. I had heard it all many times, and I sympathized.

When I told him about Don's and Paul's forthcoming book, his eyes lighted up like a kid with a new toy. Despite a propensity for being as tight as the bark on a tree, he exclaimed, "I'll buy it!" It was an auspicious start for the fishing season, and should prove to be an equally auspicious portent for a fine book.

Phillip N. Wright, Jr.
Wise River, Montana
May 21, 1977

9

Preface

This book evolved from a need: we have taught more than fifteen hundred beginners to tie flies and have continually been dismayed by the large number who return at some time after completing the course to ask about a particular method or technique. We needed a text for our classes, and after searching through all of the available basic books couldn't find one that was fundamental enough for the true beginner.

Additionally, the whole philosophy of fly-tying and fishing has changed in the last few years as a result of the outstanding work of such people as Schwiebert, Swisher and Richards, Whitlock, Caucci and Nastasi, and others who have done the necessary research to develop a firm association between the aquatic insects and the trout. The knowledgeable angler no longer uses the old standard patterns in a searching attempt to find what will work on a given day. Instead, he is more involved with the stream, its insects, and their relationship to the trout. Flies are now tied to be representative of a particular group of insects and indeed, in some cases, to represent a certain species of that group. A new approach is needed in the learning process so that this new philosophy is developed along with the necessary mechanical skills.

In the past, the approach to teaching fly-tying was to select a group of standard patterns that would require a variety of methods and techniques to tie and lead the student through them. Very little, if any, attempt was made to teach the student the "why" of what he was doing, and in his mind there was no doubt—he was learning to tie an Adams or Lead-wing Coachman or whatever. The fallacy of this method and its result was pointedly brought to our attention recently: Don was teaching an advanced class and had just finished demonstrating how to tie a white caddis larva imitation when one of the students asked if he would show them how to tie a *green* caddis larva imitation. This gentleman was an experienced tyer and had the necessary skills to tie any pattern but was having real difficulty trying to relate what he was tying to the insects that trout feed on.

This book is intended to fill the need for a basic self-instruction manual as well as a text for classroom use, and was written to serve as a direct prelude to the excellent intermediate and advanced books that have inspired the new philosophy of insect imitation.

We wish to thank our students who, as a group, have taught us much

11

more than we've taught them. To the many tyers that we have associated with over the years we owe a great debt of gratitude; being gentlemen all, they have shared their "secrets" and ideas, many of which we are passing along in this manual. The entire group at General Fishing Tackle deserves an accolade for their assistance and support during the preparation of the material herein. Especially deserving of our thanks is Bob Damico who acted as the sounding board for our ideas and who wasn't too "kind" to criticize the areas that were in need of more work. It takes a very special woman to endure the "creative process," and we are fortunate to each have such a lady; to them we owe a very special thanks.

The
Basic Manual
of
Fly-Tying

Chapter One

Introduction

Fly-tyers will list all sorts of reasons to support their contention that you should learn to tie your own flies. They'll tell you that it's cheaper than purchasing them, that you'll always have the flies that you need or at least the ability to have them much quicker than waiting for the mailman to deliver your back-ordered order. They will be sure to explain that your flies will be better constructed than you can buy, and certain to tell you of the time that their tying ability saved the trip or allowed them to take that really big one.

Well, these are all facts, but they are only the justifications for tying your own—not the reasons. The reason that we tie flies is for the pure joy of it. We know tyers who haven't cast a line in years, and yet their "reasons" would still follow along the lines of the preceding list. Fly-tying is a pursuit that takes you back to a favorite pool—in the dead of winter, it is a contemplative thing that can be done with your pipe in your mouth. Fly-tying leads naturally into the study of the stream, of insects, and invariably you gain a greater appreciation for the trout. You may draw freely from the list of justifications to convince your wife that a few dollars spent to get started would be a wise investment or to persuade your buddy to start tying *his* own. The reasons are better kept to ourselves to savor and enjoy.

The method we use to instruct in this manual is as close to the approach we use in our classes as we have been able to make it. There is a tremendous number of techniques and methods that may be used to tie a given fly or even to perform a single step in the tying process; we are not teaching *the* way to tie, but rather *a* way. In fact, we would be rather disappointed if you didn't adopt other techniques and even develop some of your own in the future. The methods that we have chosen to use were selected because they are the easiest for the beginner to learn and are sound basic techniques. There is no "best" way to tie, and after you have mastered the basic steps in the tying process you should be open-minded to all ways of assembling a fly.

Throughout this manual we have tried to maintain a very fundamental presentation. There are many very good intermediate and advanced books that will take you as far as you want to go into materials, insects, patterns, and tying procedures; our goal is to help you develop a level of skill and understanding that will allow you to fully benefit from these books. We have included a bibliography to assist you in making your initial selections from the works available.

The illustrated instructions have been arranged and the patterns selected so that you will get the necessary repetitions of each step in the tying process. Whenever possible we have repeated each step in its entirety three times, as we have found that the average student in our classes requires about three repetitions before a step is firmly grasped. We recommend that you tie two or three of each pattern before progressing to the next, but several trips through the entire series will have the same result. It is very important that you read the main text prior to starting the tying process.

In the text we refer to the barb of the hook, and it is shown in the illustrations; this is because we use it as a reference point for proportion during the tying process. This is the *only* purpose for that barb in today's fishing. Barbless hooks are available (Mustad 94845—dry fly and Mustad 3257B—wet fly/nymph), but because they are more expensive, harder to find, and available in only one shank length we recommend that you develop the habit (forced, if necessary) of flattening the barb with pliers before using the fly. You will lose very few (if any) fish as a result, and it will allow you to return the trout unharmed to the water. *Please* . . . do that so we will all continue to have a reason to teach our sons and daughters to tie flies.

Chapter Two

The Tools and Work Area

The Work Area

The tying area may be anything from the kitchen table to a highly refined, efficient bench built expressly for the purpose of tying flies. Whatever the size or location of the area, however, there are a few points to consider that will make your fly-tying easier and more pleasant.

Rigidity: The desk, table, or whatever is used must provide a rigid support for the vise. Some steps in the tying process (spinning deer hair, for example) place a good deal of force on the hook, and this is transmitted to the table through the vise. Tying a difficult pattern is challenging enough without the handicap of a moving hook.

Convenience: The fly-tying materials should be readily available to the tyer. Compartmented parts storage boxes are sufficient for the beginner who hasn't accumulated a large quantity of materials.

The plastic sewing boxes that are available at most discount houses are very good, as they have built-in thread holders on one tray, large compartments on another, and a deep storage area in the bottom.

New on the market is a large tackle box that opens on the side to reveal five drawers. Each drawer is divided differently to hold varying types of materials, and the bottom drawer is sufficiently deep to hold vise, necks, and other bulky items.

Also available are portable tying benches that are made to sit on a table or desk top. They have a support for the vise to mount on; spool holders for threads, flosses, and tinsels; bottle holders for head cement and lacquers; and some include storage for a few necks. These are really handy for the apartment dweller or anyone who hasn't room for a permanent tying area.

The important thing is for the tyer to have his tools, and at least the materials needed for immediate use, conveniently at hand. Nothing is quite as disconcerting as having to stop in the middle of a fly and go rummaging through shoe boxes to find the material that you need to finish the fly.

Lighting: The fly-tying area *must* be well lit, not only to prevent eyestrain but so that subtle shades of color can be readily detected. Many tyers use a high-intensity light directed on the vise, but unless the surrounding area is also well lit, you will find that your eyes tire from adjusting each time you look away from the vise to the bench and back again.

An old-fashioned gooseneck lamp provides a good strong light and diffuses over a large area, but it also radiates a lot of heat and can make tying uncomfortable, particularly if the back of your hand accidentally brushes the shade. A combination of a gooseneck lamp and a high-intensity light is nearly ideal. Place the gooseneck well away from the vise and focus the high intensity light on the fly; this provides a well-lit background with the fly slightly highlighted.

An inexpensive photoflood also works very well. The one that I use has an adjustable ball and socket arrangement attached to a spring clamp similar to oversized hackle pliers. It can be clamped in any position, although directly over the tying bench seems to give the best results and illuminates the entire area with a strong, nonglare light.

The area behind the fly is important and is often overlooked as the cause of eyestrain. A very dark background makes colors appear brighter than they are and gives a misleading interpretation of the shades of materials. A white or very light background reflects a lot of glare into your eyes. The best background that we have found is space. A bench removed from the traditional "facing-the-wall" position to the center of the room allows for a very diffused background which makes good lighting of the tying area much easier, with no problems of glare or reflection. Unfortunately, it seems difficult to convince the women that we need our bench in the middle of the room.

The Basic Tools

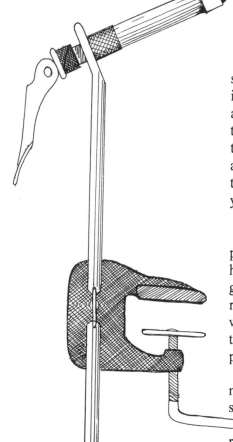

The basic tools required by the fly-tyer are simple, relatively inexpensive, and although most of us have accumulated a drawer full, really few in number. A very few extra dollars spent to buy the best quality available will not only promise long life but will make the tying process the joy it should be. The best tyer around can't do a good job and certainly can't enjoy tying on a shaky vise, or using hackle pliers that slip or a bobbin that frays his tying thread. For the most part, the price of the tools available is directly proportional to the quality—buy the best that you can afford.

Vises: The vise is the tool used to hold the hook during the tying process. It may have a clamp base for the edge of the tying table or a heavy pedestal base for setting on the work area. The pedestal base is great for the occasional tyer using the thick-edged kitchen table and is a real boon to the tyer on a fishing trip who is tying in the camper or motel where a table with a top of the right thickness may not be available. For the serious tyer with a permanent tying area, the clamp-type base provides for a more rigid mounting.

The jaws of a good vise will be of hardened steel and the locking lever must be sturdy. Check particularly the hinge pin on the locking lever; it should be fairly large in diameter and firmly seated in place. To the tyer in the market for a quality vise at a modest price we highly recommend the Thompson Model "A." We have used this vise for eight years in our tying classes with perfectly satisfactory results. If a survey were conducted of all the tying benches in the country, there surely would be more "A's" found than all others combined. Also available are beautiful, functional, special-design vises from many sources (Leonard, Orvis, HMH Tools, etc.), and although more expensive than the "A," they are worth every penny of their price. If your taste and budget agree, any one of these would be a good choice. Veniard, of England, exports some very good, modestly priced, vises to this country also. Beware of any vise selling for much less than the Model "A," as we have found none that are acceptable at a much lower price.

Bobbin: The bobbin is the tool that is used to hold the tying thread. The thread passes from the spool out through a tube allowing us to place the thread exactly where we wish, and since we don't handle the thread, the problem of rough hands fraying it is eliminated. The greatest advantage of the bobbin though is its weight, which serves to maintain tension on the thread between steps in the tying process.

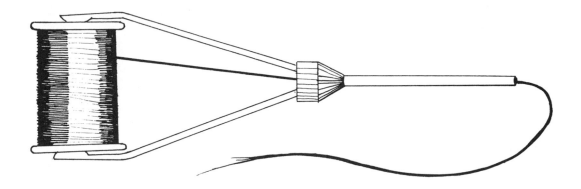

The bobbin is found in many shapes and descriptions, and all that we have seen and used will adequately do the job. We use the open type that holds the thread spool between two legs of spring steel. It allows for quick changing of the thread, quick retrieval of excess thread, and an easy means for adjusting tension by slipping a wrap of thread from the spool onto one of the legs. We don't feel that this type has any *great* advantage over the others—it's just what we use. Bobbins in this style are available from all tying suppliers. The Chase bobbin is another good performer and is very popular.

Many tyers still tie, as we learned to do, without a bobbin, but not only is this more difficult and slower, but the resulting fly will probably not be as well constructed because of the difficulty of maintaining an even thread tension throughout the tying process.

A good bobbin will be nicely finished, the tube will be perpendicular to the spool, and the knobs that the spool rests between will be small enough to fit well inside the spool and yet large enough to hold the spring wires clear of the spool edge. Tube length is a matter of personal preference; Don prefers a long tube, and I prefer a short one. Although every manufacturer tries to get the tip of the tube perfectly smooth, we have found it worth a few seconds time to polish the inside of the tip with emery paper.

Bodkin: The bodkin is simply a needle in a handle. It is used to fluff up a dubbed body by picking, to help position a wing case, to split out the desired size of quill section for wings, and to do a myriad other things. For placing the drop of head cement on a finished fly it is indispensable. Bodkins are made with plastic handles like a small screwdriver, with handles having a small eye on the end for hanging them on a hook at the edge or back of the tying bench, with metal handles of all shapes, and with wooden handles, but the fact remains—a bodkin is just a needle. My present one is a large sewing needle that I glued into a small piece of one-half inch wooden dowel with a drop of epoxy; I guess it's adequate since I can't remember to buy a new one. We're talking about a very small sum of money, from the do-it-yourself model for pennies to the fanciest available at only a couple of dollars, so splurge and get whatever you want, as the quality of needles is pretty consistent—you're paying for the handle.

Scissors: There are still tyers who "tie in the hand"—no vise. It's quite possible to get along without a bobbin, and a bodkin is really not indispensable, but I can't conceive of tying without scissors. Maybe someone has had his dentist do some special design work on his front teeth so they would work as scissors (that could have its use on the stream, too), but short of that, you have to have scissors to tie a fly.

The tyer really needs two pairs, one heavy pair for cutting wire, lead, rubber, and so on and a smaller pair for the more delicate work. The quality of the heavy pair is not critical, and they need not be expensive. The fine pair should be the very best that you can afford. Some of the good quality manicure scissors are fine, but *they* are not cheap and generally the finger holes are rather small. Expect to pay a fair amount of money for a good pair of scissors, and don't buy any other kind. This is an item where quality is commensurate with price.

The basic scissor types for fly-tying are straight blade and curved blade. Other variations are length and size of the finger holes. Straight blade or curved is a matter of choice, although each is better suited for some particular tasks. The straight-blade scissors are most useful for cutting quill sections and cutting off the butts of tied-in material, whereas the curved type are better for close trimming of thread and for shaping wings and hair bodies. A pair of each is ideal, but one good pair of either is a better purchase than a cheap pair of each.

Don uses a pair called corneal section scissors. The blades are very fine, they are of superb quality, and they cost a small fortune. They are available from medical supply houses.

I use straight and curved bladed iris scissors, also available from medical supply houses and most tying material suppliers. They are of very good quality with fine tips and comfortable finger holes. I have several pairs, but the pair on the bench is four years old and functions as flawlessly as the new ones.

Hackle Pliers: Hackle pliers are used to grasp the end of a hackle so that it can be wound on the hook. They are used occasionally in the same manner for winding body material and to clamp on the tying thread to maintain tension after you have inadvertently cut the wrong thread and released the bobbin from this task.

We have found vises that work perfectly, bobbins that are flawless, and scissors of the same high standard, but the best hackle pliers that we have found still slip sometimes, and occasionally cut the hackle. Undoubtedly, this is the reason that so many types are available.

Basically, there are two styles of hackle pliers, the English style and the duplex. The English pliers are made of spring wire and have overlapping tips of the same material in a flattened shape. The duplex pliers are made of flat spring steel with attached pads. The pads may be of grooved metal or one of metal and one of rubber, or both of rubber. Perhaps we just haven't found the right pair, but we've never seen a duplex style that worked well.

We both use the miniature size English hackle pliers and haven't found anything that they won't do that a larger pair will—the reverse is not true. Don ties a lot of large streamers and stone fly nymphs in the #2 to #8 size range, and the miniatures work fine; on the other hand, I tie mostly #16 to #22 dries, and the miniatures are practically a must.

On one jaw of his pliers Don puts a piece of shrink tubing—(available from electrical supply dealers, it is a rubber-like tubing that shrinks about 30 percent when subjected to heat)—and advocates it strongly. It works great, and I have a pair that I fixed this way, but the pair that I use most is a pair that I took the time to smooth down to a perfect fit by running a doubled sheet of emery paper through the closed jaws.

The tension of the pliers can be changed by unhooking the jaws and springing the wire in either direction as needed. The pliers will last longer and require less adjusting, and glazing (one drawback to shrink tubing) will be reduced, if the jaws are unhooked and the tool is allowed to remain open between tying sessions. Sure wish I would remember to do that!

Other Tools

If you are gadget prone, you have a whole new world open to you as a tyer. In the next few paragraphs we will discuss some of the "auxiliary" tools that are available. All of them work, but none is really a necessity. If there is one particular step in the tying process that you are having trouble with, by all means try the tool designed for that step; it may be just what you are looking for. To assist you in evaluating the need for each, we will describe what the tool is for and how it works.

Hackle Guards: Hackle guards are small, funnel-shaped pieces of metal with a hole in the center to slip over the eye of the hook and a slot to slip the thread through. They are used to hold the hackle away from the eye to facilitate easier forming and tying-off of the head of the fly. They work well although they are time consuming to use. Most tyers seem to abandon using them after a short while.

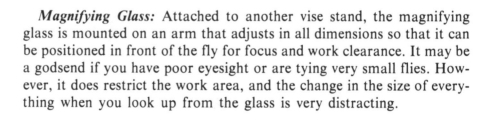

Magnifying Glass: Attached to another vise stand, the magnifying glass is mounted on an arm that adjusts in all dimensions so that it can be positioned in front of the fly for focus and work clearance. It may be a godsend if you have poor eyesight or are tying very small flies. However, it does restrict the work area, and the change in the size of everything when you look up from the glass is very distracting.

Mirror: Similar in design to the magnifying glass, the tying mirror is positioned behind the fly to allow you to see the back side of the fly as you tie. Like the magnifying glass, it tends to restrict the work area. I used one for a long time before I realized that if the front side of the fly was right, t'other side had to be.

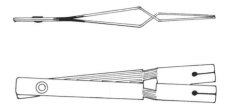

Winging Pliers: Getting the knack of putting upright wings on a fly is one of the most exasperating lessons in learning to tie. This tool is designed to hold the wings in position until they have been sufficiently anchored to remain there. It works pretty well, but we'll show you an easy way to accomplish the step without using the tool.

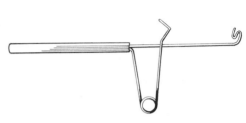

Whip-Finisher: Want to get a good knockdown argument going among a group of tyers? Just bring up the subject of whip-finishers and state an opinion, pro or con. This, like the half-hitch tool, is designed to assist in tying a knot to finish the head of the fly, although in this case, to tie the much superior whip-finish. The whip-finisher is a peculiarly shaped spring wire on a small handle. It is placed behind the eye of the hook, strung with tying thread, and rolled between the fingers. It works and a lot of very good tyers use them. The whip-finish can be tied easily without the tool, although this knot has been the impasse of many a beginner. Neither of us uses one, primarily because it is slower than whip-finishing by hand, and also when finishing by hand we can lay each wrap *exactly* where we want it and better control the shape of the finished head. If you just can't get the knack of the whip-finish from the descriptions and illustrations in this manual you may want to give the tool a try.

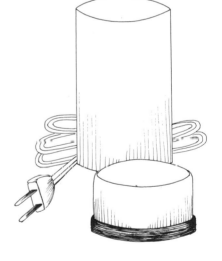

Fur Blender: The fur blender is a real "luxury" tool. A small blender about the size of a soup can, it works just like the big kitchen model. For blending furs to achieve different shades of dubbing, you throw in the furs you want blended, hold the top down (that turns it on), and in just a few seconds it is blended smoothly and evenly. It is especially useful where hard-to-dub fur such as seal is being blended with a softer fur. The blender mixes small amounts easily and the resulting dubbing is ready to use immediately.

Hair Stacker: The hair stacker is a tube that can be opened on one end by removing a cap of some sort. It is used to even the ends of a bunch of hair by inserting the hair, replacing the cap, and tapping on the tying table. It is really a great help when tying patterns that use hair for the wing or tail. We use a small glass test tube with a rubber stopper, and although it does the job, sometimes static electricity builds up on the glass and its efficiency is somewhat reduced. There are a couple of commercially available models now on the market that we're sure will work very well. If you get into tying a lot of hairwing flies, one of these will be a real time saver and will also improve the appearance of the finished product. An old lipstick case or an empty cartridge case will serve the purpose for the occasional tyer of this type of fly.

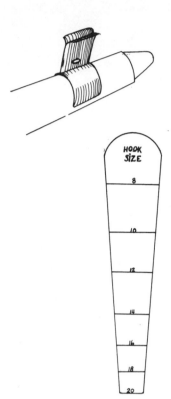

Material Clip: Mounted just behind the head of the vise by means of a spring clip, the material clip is used to hold tied-in material out of the way until the tyer is ready for the step requiring that piece of material. Material clips fall into the category of tools that work for the purpose for which designed but are certainly not required. For the beginner, they may be a worthwhile aid, and since their cost is quite small you may want to give one a try.

Hackle Gauge: A hackle gauge is a piece of metal or plastic that has been inscribed with lines to show the proper size of materials to be used for the parts of a given size fly. The one that I have shows hackle length, tail length, wing size, and body length for flies from size #4 to #24. The tool is a little awkward to use and it is much faster to attain the proportion directly from the hook as will be shown in the tying instructions.

There are many other tools that you may find useful to have on the bench although they are not specifically made for fly-tying. Tweezers are helpful for picking up small hooks and are worth their weight in jungle cock for sorting the #20 and #22 hooks that got spilled or dumped together. A small pair of needle-nosed pliers are useful for working with wire that is being used for body material. A razor blade or scalpel has many uses, and a rubber eraser is an aid in stripping peacock herl. This list is limited only by your ingenuity and bench space.

Chapter Three

The Materials

Nearly every creature that walks or flies is a source of material to the fly-tyer. Our discussion will be limited to those that are readily available and most frequently called for in the standard patterns. The most important lesson that we hope the beginner will learn from this section is the substitution of materials. There are those who will not tie a pattern with anything but the materials originally used. Our greatest desire is that you will become a fly-tyer, not just a pattern reproducer. Surely, many of the patterns presently used are effective, but that effectiveness need not be reduced because you have substituted a different kind of thread or hook or even type of wing. Fish feed on insects, *not on artificial flies*, and as long as the fly that you are producing is an accurate reproduction of that insect it is going to work.

With this in mind, our approach will be to describe the materials available to you for use in the various parts of a fly, so that you may have some idea of which materials may be substituted in a recognized pattern and, more importantly, so that you will have the basic knowledge of the characteristics of the materials and can develop your own patterns based on the insect life of the streams that you fish.

Hooks: We are forever dismayed by the list of hooks recommended in most tying manuals. Hooks are the most expensive part of the finished fly, and to imply to the beginner that he must have twenty or thirty different types of hooks and a range of all sizes of each serves not only to discourage him but is out and out foolish. At least 90 percent of all flies can be tied, with no loss of fish-taking ability, on five types of hooks. Again, the point is, is there a *reason* for using a particular hook, or does the pattern call for it just because that was what the originator happened to use? As long as the hook that you use is of the right length to accurately represent the insect and is of the right type (wet or dry), we can assure you that the fish doesn't care about the number on the box it came out of. As an example, the tackle shop where we work and run our classes sells more than 1,000 dozen flies a year and carries a stock of more than 150 different patterns; we use a total of seven hook types.

In our discussion of hooks and particularly hook designations, we are referring to Mustad brand. We use Mustad as an example because they are by far the most readily available tying hooks and are of good quality. In other brands the sizing may be somewhat different but the general designations (long, short, fine, stout) will be roughly the same. Unfortunately, there is no industry standard.

Wet Hooks: The hook used for wet flies and nymphs is made of heavier wire than that used for dry flies so that the additional weight will help to sink the fly. The Mustad 3906 and 3906B are commonly used for wet flies and nymphs, as are the 3399 and 3399A. The 3906B and 3399A are 2X long hooks and are used for imitations that require a little longer body length.

Dry Hooks: To aid in allowing the fly to float, the hook used for dry flies is made of finer wire and is, therefore, lighter. So that as much strength as possible an be retained, the bend area is forged flat. The Mustad 94840 is our standard dry fly hook and the Mustad 9671 and 9672 are used for patterns that require a longer hook shank. The 9671 and 9672 also work well as streamer hooks and for the really long-bodied nymphs such as stone flies.

There are many other makes and types of hooks that you may use just as well as these, and again, that is the point: you are not restricted to any particular make or type. Just be sure that the hook you are using will give you a finished fly of the right size and will complement the way the fly is to be fished.

Hook sizes are designated by numbers, with the size of the hook decreasing as the number grows larger; i.e., a size 20 is smaller than a size 14. The size of the hook *only* refers to the width of the gap of the hook, the distance from the shank to the point. Hooks used for freshwater flies are normally in the size range from #4 to #28 although they are available in both larger and smaller sizes; usually hooks are only available in even-numbered sizes. Remember, hook size is only an indicator of the gap width of the hook.

Hook length is designated by X's; a #14-2X long is a number 14 with a shank length of a hook two sizes larger (#12). A #14-2X short is a number 14 with a shank length of a hook two sizes smaller (#16).

Wire size is designated in basically the same way; a #14-2X fine is a number 14 made from wire normally used for a hook two sizes smaller (#16). A #14-2X stout is made from the same wire as a standard #12. As you can see, there is a really great number of variations available for a hook of a given size.

Another variable among hooks is the shape of the eye. The most common is the turned-down-eye (TDE) in which the eye is bent down from the shank of the hook. The turned-up-eye (TUE) is another commonly used hook and is of some advantage for very small hooks, as the eye is turned away from the gap and gives more clearance for hooking the fish. The ringed eye, with the eye of the hook parallel to the shank, is the least common and is normally seen only on streamer hooks, although this type has recently become available in very small sizes where it offers the advantage of the TUE (increased gap clearance) with a better hooking characteristic, as the direction of force is in line with the hook shank.

The shape of the bend is the least important variable among hooks. The most common bend shapes are the perfect bend, the sproat bend, and the limerick bend. The perfect bend has the bend as a part of a circle while the sproat bend is slightly parabolic and the limerick has a very pronounced parabolic bend.

As you can see by now, the variety of hooks available to the fly-tyer is staggering. The only thing of importance, though, is the finished product, so don't become too concerned about using a particular hook as long as the finished fly is of the proper proportion for the size of the insect that you are attempting to imitate.

Thread: The tying manuals really get carried away here. One pattern book that I have lists approximately sixty patterns, and you would need eighteen different spools of thread to follow the instructions for tying these sixty patterns. HOGWASH! On a properly tied fly the only thread that is visible to the fish is the head, and we have no evidence that the color of the head has any effect on the fish-attracting ability of the fly. If it is more aesthetically pleasing to you for the thread to be of the same color as the major portion of the fly, by all means use it, but don't feel that you have to do without a particular pattern because you don't have any primrose thread on hand.

Thread sizes are indicated by letters of the alphabet, with *A* being the smallest. Sizes *A* through *E* are used for rod wrapping but are of no use to the fly-tyer. Sizes smaller than *A* (I lied, there are smaller sizes) are designated by "oughts" with two-ought (00) being one size smaller than A and three-ought (000) the next smaller, and so on, down to nine-ought (000000000). Instead of listing six-ought as 000000, the common method is to use the designation 6/0 or 4/0 or whatever. For most tying, thread of 3/0 to 6/0 is used although it is available as small as 9/0 and as large as *A*. *A* would only be used for large flies such as bass bugs, large streamers, and salt-water patterns.

We use Monocord (3/0) for nearly everything that we tie. Don does use a fine twisted nylon (7/0) for the smaller patterns. I use Monocord for everything down to and including #22's. Monocord is formed as a flat ribbon and therefore it ties flat, and if you keep the number of wraps to a minimum, as you should on these small ones, it doesn't bulk. As to color, we use two colors for at least 90 percent of the flies we tie, black and green. We use green when we tie a weighted fly so that we can iden- tify it in our fly boxes, since we tie many patterns in both weighted and unweighted versions.

We don't use waxed thread, although we seem to be in the minority. We feel that the use of waxed thread presents many disadvantages that outweigh the small advantage of easier dubbing which waxed thread gives. The bobbin is always clogged when using waxed thread, head ce- ment can't penetrate waxed thread readily, the thread tends to pick up any materials floating around the bench, and in the case of dry flies, it adds unnecessary weight. We will discuss the process of dubbing later and recommend that you try it without wax (as we have taught all our classes to do), and if you just can't get it to work, use wax to coat only the portion of the thread that is to be dubbed.

Tailing Materials: The traditional material for use as tails on flies is hackle fibers, although in the West you are more likely to find hair being used. The best hackle fibers for tails are from large neck hackles or sad- dle hackles. For dry flies, a very stiff hackle is needed, so the fibers are taken from near the upper end of the hackle feather. For a wet fly or nymph, a softer hackle is desirable and it is selected from a soft hackle or from further down the stem of a dry fly hackle, where it is softer and has more web.

There is no end to the types of hair that may be used for the tailing of a fly. Here in the West we use more hair for tails than hackle because of the heavier water we have to fish and the additional support that is needed. The heavier water also means that we needn't be quite so delicate in our imitations. Elk hair and javelina are exceptionally good tailing materials as are the coarse guard hairs of many of the water dwellers such as muskrat. In the selection of hair for tails, keep in mind what you want as a finished product. If you are tying a dry fly, you want the stiffest hair that you can find, and if you are tying wets or nymphs you want something softer so that you get a "swimming" action from the tail.

For a well-defined tail on nymphal patterns we often tie in two sections of turkey quill which are separated with wraps of tying thread and lacquered. Sections of any quill material may be used in a like manner. For a separated tail on dry flies such as the Swisher-Richards "no-hackle" patterns, face whiskers from a rabbit or groundhog are ideal, as they are very stiff and are of sufficient length to be used easily. The material itself is of no great importance so long as the desired imitation is obtained. Calf tail (also called kip and impala), squirrel tail, and bucktail are also used on some patterns.

Body Materials: Practically every material used by the tyer can be used for the formation of the body of the fly.

The center quill of a hackle is used by stripping off all the fibers and wrapping the quill around the hook, which gives a highly segmented appearance to the finished body.

Stripped peacock herl is used in the same manner, and if the herl has been selected from the eyed portion of the peacock feather, it will give a segmented effect due to the longitudinal coloring of the quill. This is the technique normally meant when a pattern calls for a "quill" body.

The hollow hairs from members of the deer family (elk, moose, deer, etc.) are used for making "hair" bodies. Bunches of hair are tied in, and as the thread is tightened the hair is allowed to spin around the hook and will flare away from the hook shank. Succeeding bunches are tied in, in the same manner, until the desired body length is obtained; it is then clipped into the desired shape. This type of construction produces a dry fly with outstanding floating characteristics because the hair used is hollow.

There are many man-made materials that are used for bodies on flies. Polypropylene is a substance with a specific gravity of less than water (it floats) that is available in many forms—including yarn, loose dubbing material, and pressed sheets from which fibers are teased—to be used as dubbing material. Latex sheet material is just now starting to be used extensively for the bodies of nymphs, larva, and pupa.

Textiles provide a wide selection of body materials, including floss, thread, tinsel, Mylar, and wool yarn. The finest body material for most uses, however, is dubbing.

Dubbing is the process of spinning a fur onto the tying thread to form a fur "yarn" which is then wound on the hook to form the body of the fly. A dry fly with a dubbed body floats extremely well if treated with a dry fly flotant, and a wet fly or nymph sinks equally well when the dubbing soaks up water. A dubbed body's greatest asset though is that it produces a translucent body due to the fine fibers of fur extending from the edges of the body. The furs used for dubbing come from the soft underfur of many animals, including rabbit, muskrat, mink, fox, and seal. The synthetic dubbing materials are used in the same manner, and the soft down from waterfowl may be handled the same way.

If you are tying a standard pattern, the directions will tell you what type of body material to use, and if you are trying to duplicate an insect that you have found, keep in mind that the type of body material you use should be the one that best represents the "natural."

Experiment with all of the materials that you can gain access to, so that logical substitution will become second nature to you.

Winging Materials: Basically, there are four types of wing construction: quill wing, rolled wing, hairwing, and hackle-tip wing.

A quill wing is made from sections of a quill feather tied in on each side of the hook in an upright position; this type of wing is often called an "upright." Duck quill feathers are the most commonly used, although goose and the flight feathers from many smaller birds may be used also.

A rolled wing is made from a bunch of soft body feathers tied in on the top of the hook shank as a clump and then divided with the tying thread or sometimes trimmed to shape. The rolled wing has the advantage of being more durable than the quill wing. Mallard side feathers are the most commonly used material, but soft hackle fibers work well, as do the body feathers of many of the pheasants. Many of the standard patterns that you may come across will call for a rolled wing to be constructed of "lemon wood duck." This is the flank feather from a wood duck and is the premium feather for this type of wing construction, but, unfortunately, it is in extremely short supply, and therefore quite expensive. Mallard flank feathers dyed to this shade are the common substitution material. If you or any of your friends are duck hunters, you should have no trouble getting mallard feathers and perhaps even a "woodie."

The hairwing is the most durable type of wing construction and is commonly used as the wing on streamers and wets and to a lesser extent on dry fly patterns. Calf tail, bucktail, squirrel tail, and mink tail are the most commonly used, although the body hair of deer, elk, bear, and many other animals are used also.

As the name would imply, hackle-tip wings are tied using hackle tips. This is a great place to use up some of those hackle feathers that are too large for most of the flies that we tie. Two matched hackles are chosen, and a tip of each, of the right length for the fly we are tying, is cut from the hackle stem. These are tied in on either side of the hook to form the wings. The hackle-tip wing makes a very attractive fly with a fair durability rating.

The quill wing, rolled wing, and hackle-tip wing are most often used for representing mayflies while the hairwing is more commonly used to suggest the "over-the-back" wing of the caddis flies and stone flies.

Hackle: Hackles (hackle feathers) may be purchased loose by the package but more commonly are purchased as a "neck"; the hackles are still attached to the neck skin of the chicken. The latter method gives the tyer a selection of all sizes of hackles and makes the sorting of sizes easier, as Mother Nature has provided the ultimate packaging method. Buying hackles by the neck also offers a cost savings. There is no prouder possession to a fly-tyer than a superb neck.

Necks come in several grades of quality from "wet" (very soft), to "super" (very stiff). The type of neck that the tyer needs is dependent on the type of fly that is being assembled. A wet fly hackle should be very soft to give a more enticing action to the finished fly, whereas a dry fly requires the stiffest hackle available, as the hackle is the prime support for keeping the fly afloat.

Other than their intended uses, the main difference between a "wet" neck and a "dry" neck is cost. A very good wet neck may cost from two to four dollars while a super dry neck will run from five to as much as fifty dollars in the rare colors. We all probably use too much hackle of dry fly quality because there is a tendency to buy only dry fly necks. The reason for this may well be that all of the qualities that we look for in a good dry fly neck are absent in a good wet neck, and it is just not very impressive. Occasionally, feathers other than from a chicken are used as hackle, but only for the soft hackle found on flies other than dry flies.

Although not true hackle by definition, we call the long, slim feathers from the rump of a rooster "saddle hackles." They have many of the characteristics of neck hackle and are used in many of the same ways—maybe *that's* why we call them hackles. For tying flies #10 and larger, they lend themselves particularly well, as the feathers are quite long while maintaining a narrow width for their entire length. Occasionally, a really superb saddle will be found that will tie all the way down to #14's; these are most common in a grizzly saddle. For tying a palmered fly (hackle wound the full length of the hook) a nice saddle hackle is unrivaled. This is one of the materials that is underused by nearly all tyers. It is less expensive than neck hackle, especially in the really good grades.

The basic colors of hackle should not give the beginner too much trouble, but these are not the most often used.

Black is found as a natural color but generally the hackle tends to run soft. A dyed black neck will not only be less expensive but will usually be of better quality.

A very dark brown shade of hackle is called "coachman," and this color tends to run somewhat soft although good quality is available for a price.

Dark ginger is somewhat lighter than coachman and has a reddish cast. This is probably the most used color and is available in very good quality.

Ginger is the color of that spice, a medium brown with a definite reddish tint. It is readily available in good quality but is more expensive than dark ginger (sometimes listed as just "brown").

Light ginger is about the color of a weak cup of tea. It is available in very good quality although rather costly in the really good grades.

Cream hackle ranges from just darker than white to a honey color; it is inexpensive but tends to run rather soft.

White is very common but quality is generally poor, and one of good quality is rare enough to be expensive. Fortunately, true white is not called for in many imitations, and a light cream can often be substituted with better effectiveness resulting.

Hackle is also categorized according to markings: furnace, badger, cock-y-bondu, and variant being the most common.

A "furnace" hackle is a hackle in the color range from dark ginger to coachman with a black center stripe.

A furnace hackle with the addition of black edges (called a "list") is a "cock-y-bondu."

A hackle in the color range from cream to ginger with a black stripe is called a "badger."

A variant, in its strictest defintion, is any hackle with more than one color present. In the venacular of the fly-tyer though, it generally means a barred hackle. It is found in the entire color range from white to coachman and is too often overlooked by nearly all tyers. This may be because it has no absolute definition and, therefore, is difficult to describe in a pattern. The quality is always better for the money than can be obtained in the standard colors, and it will usually tie a better-looking fly because of the breakup of the color, which is more natural appearing.

A variant that is black or grey with white bars has a special name—grizzly. Grizzly (also called Plymouth Rock because it comes from a rooster of that breed) is one of the most used hackles. This hackle has become very expensive in the really good grades and there is nothing else that approaches the quality of a "super" grizzly; the hackles are very stiff and wiry, very long in proportion to their width, and have a sheen like a mirror. For all of this you pay, boy do you pay.

The other prima donnas of hackles are the "duns." A dun neck is a very nondescript grey, usually with an overtone of blue, bronze, olive, or some other shade, but one thing is always consistent: they cost a fortune. Fortunately, a good imitation of these colors can be obtained by dyeing, and they are nearly always of good quality since the supplier doesn't want to waste time and materials in dyeing poor quality necks.

1. Polypropylene yarn
2. Floss
3. Wool yarn
4. Chenille
5. Silver tinsel
6. Gold tinsel
7. Polypropylene dubbing
8. Deer hair
9. Muskrat
10. Rabbit
11. Hare's ears
12. Javelina
13. Squirrel tail
14. Bucktail
15. Calf tail
16. Elk hair
17. Moose mane
18. Marabou plume section
19. Peacock eye

1. Duck quill
2. Goose quill
3. Turkey quill
4. Turkey tail
5. Ostrich herl
6. Pheasant tail
7. Saddle hackle
8. Mallard
    body feather
9. Grey partridge
10. Brown partridge
11. Cream hackle
12. Light ginger hackle
13. Ginger hackle
14. Brown hackle
15. Coachman hackle
16. Dark blue
    dun hackle
17. Black hackle
18. Furnace hackle
19. Badger hackle
20. Variant hackle
21. Variant hackle
22. Grizzly hackle

Life Cycle of the Caddis Fly

The caddis flies go through a complete metamorphosis—egg, larva, pupa, and adult.

The larval stage of most of the caddis species is spent inside of a case constructed by the insect of either pieces of sand or vegetable matter. The case of the larva is open at one end, and the insect can extend its head and thorax from the case; in some instances the larva can transport its case with it as it moves around to feed on microscopic vegetable matter on the stream bottom.

When the caddis goes into pupation, it seals up its case except for a very small hole that allows just a trickle of water to flow through. During this pupation, the wings, legs, and antennae develop and the insect attains the adult form. When this stage of development is complete, the caddis rises to the surface, breaks through the surface film, and flies immediately away from the stream.

The adult caddis mates while at rest away from the stream. The females then return to the stream and deposit their eggs either by dropping the eggs to the surface, alighting on the surface and releasing the eggs, or by crawling down into the stream and leaving the eggs attached to sticks, stones, or stream debris.

Life Cycle of the Mayfly

The mayflies have an incomplete metamorphosis consisting of egg, nymph, and adult. They are unique, however, in that there are two forms in the adult stage. The dun (subimago) stage is seen just after emergence, while the spinner (imago) stage is seen during the mating flight; this final moult occurs away from the stream, normally in the surrounding brush.

Nymphs of the mayflies are categorized by the type of water they are found in, as each group has particular physical characteristics that are adapted for that type of aquatic environment. The "crawlers" are found in the moderate stretches of the stream, the "clingers" are found in the fast stretches, the "swimmers" are found throughout the range from fast to slow, and the "burrowers" are found most often in the slow stretches of water. As the nymphal stage draws to a close, the nymph's wing case darkens and swells as the wings mature inside. It is during this time that the nymph starts its migration to the surface to hatch.

At the surface, the wing case splits open and the adult dun emerges. This is the stage that we are imitating with all of the upright-wing dry flies. Once the wings dry, the insect flies from the surface into the nearby brush where sexual development continues and the final moult into the spinner stage occurs.

The spinners then return to the stream where they can be seen in swarms above the water. The females seek out partners; the pairs leave the swarm and mate in flight. The females then deposit the eggs into the stream; some drop them from above the stream, some species lay prone in the surface film and release the eggs, and some species crawl back into the water to leave the eggs. Both the females and males then perish and fall onto the surface of the water in the spent position.

Life Cycle of the Stone Fly

The stone flies develop through an incomplete metamorphosis—egg, nymph, and adult.

The stone-fly nymphs are nearly all fast-water dwellers where they may either feed on the aquatic vegetation or prey on smaller nymphs and larva. The type of feeding varies with different species as does the length of time spent in the nymphal stage. Most species take one year to develop from egg to adult, but some species may be in the stream for as long as three years. The stone fly nymph does not hatch in the water but crawls out of the stream and then sheds its nymphal husk.

Nearly all species of adult stone flies leave the stream immediately after hatching and fly to the surrounding brush where they mate. The adults return to the stream (usually three or four days later) to lay their eggs. The eggs may be dropped while flying, deposited by the female by dipping her abdomen in the water while flying, or by swimming in the surface film to wash the eggs free.

Life Cycle of the Midge

The midges have a complete life cycle—egg, larva, pupa, and adult. Not a whole lot is known about the details of their development, partly because of the large number of species and their diverse habits, and partly because the necessary research just hasn't been done to answer all of the questions concerning these tiny insects.

Most of the midge larva are found in the slow, silt-laden stretches of the stream, although a few species are found in fast water. They may be either herbivorous or carnivorous.

The pupal stage often develops in a cocoon attached to rocks or sticks on the stream bottom. Prior to emerging, the pupal ascends to the surface where it floats, suspended in the surface film by the gills surrounding the throax, until the adult emerges.

The adult crawls out of the top of the pupal skin and flies low across the water. Occasionally, you will see small fish jumping clear of the water to capture the midge adults "on the wing." The details of mating and egg laying are not clearly understood, and probably vary with the many species.

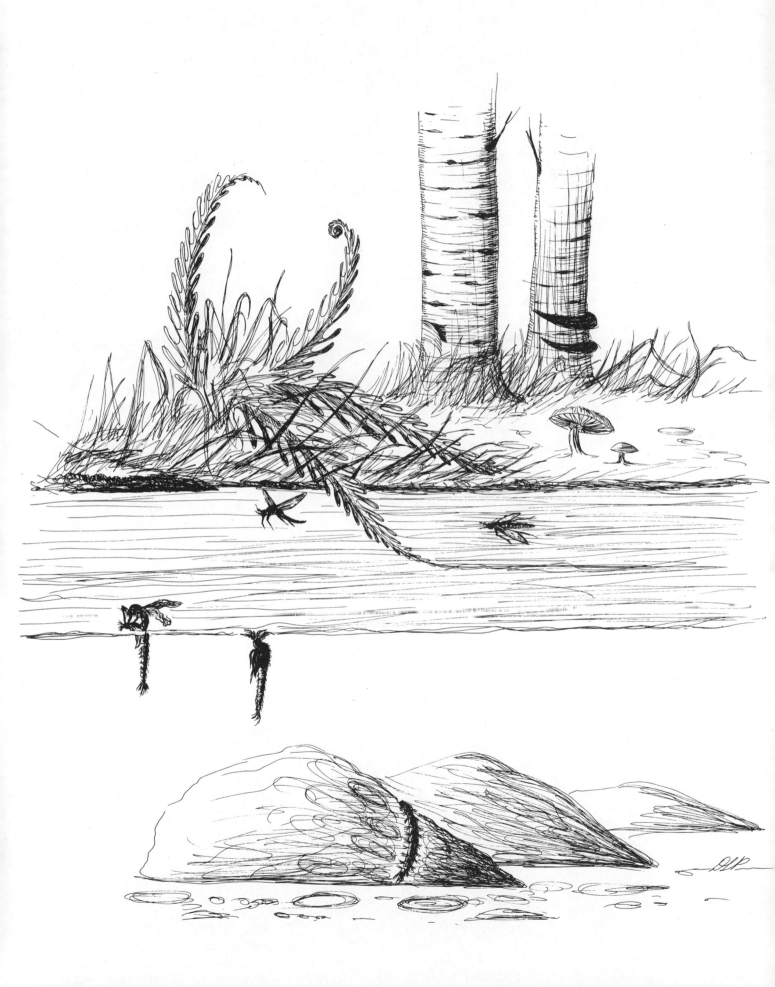

Chapter Four

The Insects
That We Imitate

To the fly-fisherman, the four important groups (called orders) of insects are the mayflies, the caddis flies, the stone flies, and the midges. Other insects that trout feed on may be of occasional importance, but these four orders account for the bulk of his diet. We will look briefly at the others later.

Aquatic insects progress through several stages during their life cycle (metamorphosis) and, depending on the insect, this metamorphosis may be complete or incomplete. A complete metamorphosis consists of egg, larva, pupa, and adult, while an incomplete metamorphosis has only three stages: egg, nymph, and adult. The mayflies and stone flies have an incomplete metamorphosis while the caddis flies and midges progress through all four stages of development.

These stages in the life of an insect are what we are trying to imitate with a fly and are the reason that we use wet flies, nymphs, and dry flies. Regardless of the type of metamorphosis, all but the adult stage is spent in the water; wet flies and nymphs are used to imitate these forms while dry flies are meant to be representative of the adult stage.

Nymphs and Larva

Mayflies (Ephemeroptera): With its incomplete metamorphosis, the mayfly has only a nymphal stage between the egg and the adult. When we tie and use a nymph we are imitating this stage. Many of the standard wet fly patterns are probably effective because they are also imitative of this stage.

The mayfly has either two or three (most commonly three) tails, a slim abdomen, and a large thorax with a hump on top which is called a "wingcase," as it is the storage area for the wings that are developing.

The tail is usually tied with hackle fibers or, as is becoming more common, with two or three heavy pieces of hair. The abdomen section is often tied with a quill body or floss to maintain the proper slim shape. The thorax area is commonly a dubbed section with a hackle wound through it to represent the legs. The wingcase is most often represented by a section of quill tied in at the rear of the thorax, laid forward over the dubbed section, and tied down at the head. A section of turkey quill is the traditional wingcase material although any type of quill section may be used and a bunch of hair is utilized on some patterns.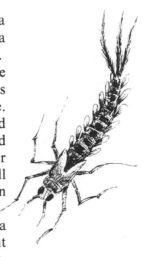

Remember, your goal is to represent the insect; so long as you tie a slim body, a full thorax, and an imitative wingcase—all of the right color and proportion—then the type of material used is of no importance. We are not implying that you must have the insect "in hand," or an illustration to work from. You may be tying from a pattern, but you are not limited to using exactly the same materials.

Caddis Flies (Trichoptera): The caddis has no nymphal stage, so what we are imitating is the larval stage. The larva all have the same general appearance—they look like worms. They have a short tail (actually a hook for securing themselves in their case), a highly segmented abdomen (a little fatter than the mayfly), and a head that is slightly larger and darker colored than the body.

Most caddis larva imitations leave off the tail. The body is sometimes floss with a wrap of tinsel or fine wire to give the segmentation, or a narrow strip of buckskin, or latex, or even just brass wire wound on the hook. The enlarged head may be thread wrapped to a diameter larger than the body, a dubbed area, or a few wraps of ostrich herl of the appropriate color.

Stone Flies (Plecoptera): Incomplete metamorphosis, remember? This means that we are tying a nymphal imitation. The stone fly nymph spends its time clinging to the underside of rocks or debris on the stream bottom and becomes food to the trout when dislodged by heavy water or other underwater disturbances.

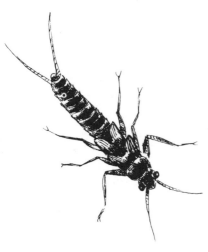

The stone fly nymph has two prominent tails, a highly segmented abdomen of fairly large diameter, a muscular thorax, and two wing cases that house the *two* pairs of developing wings.

Two sections of turkey quill, tied in and separated, make a good tail. Any type of quill could be used in a like manner, but the insect has a mottled coloring and the turkey matches it nicely; on the other hand, so does pheasant, grouse tail, and many others. Starting to get the picture? Only the final product is important, not the means. The heavy abdomen may be tied with several layers of floss, with a quill body wrapped over floss (to achieve the desired fullness), with latex strips, or as Don does, with a rubberband. The thorax is nearly always dubbed, although chenille can be used, and a hackle is usually palmered through either. The wing case may be a quill section, latex, or hair. Keep in mind that there are two wing cases, though. I wonder, can trout *really* count?

Midges (Diptera): This order includes the crane flies as well as the midges, but the gnats, mosquitoes, and other small members are of the most importance to the angler. Since they have a complete life cycle, we want to imitate the larval stage. Their enlarged head and slim body closely resemble the caddis larva, but the midges have wing pads that hang on either side of the thorax area, giving them a slightly different profile.

Artificials are tied generally the same as the caddis, although the thorax may be tied a little fuller to simulate the wing pads. The big difference is their smaller size. Have you ever been standing in a stream, turned to say something to your buddy, and inhaled half a zillion gnats? If so, you are acquainted with the Dipterans. They are commonly tied in sizes #22, #24, and #28. A quill body and a dubbed thorax are about all that you need for this imitation.

Emergers

Mayflies (Ephemeroptera): As the mayfly nymph starts its trip to the surface to emerge as an adult (this trip may be repeated several times before the adult emerges), it is basically the same shape as the nymphal stage; however, the wing case will usually be enlarged and somewhat darker. During this period the nymph is considerably more active that it has been in its hiding place among the stream-bottom debris. This stage of increased activity is probably what we are imitating with the wet fly. Tied with soft hackle, the wet fly has a slim appearance in the water, and since it is most often worked upstream with some action imparted by the rod tip, it duplicates the increased activity of the soon-to-emerge nymph.

Patterns are usually tied with a small tail, a slim body of floss, quill, etc., and a soft hackle that sweeps back along the body when wet. As you can see, this is a reasonably good imitation of the insect, although its realism could probably be improved with the addition of a wing case. Make your selection of materials with these facts in mind.

Caddis Flies (Trichoptera): The pupal stage of the caddis is spent in a case as was the larval stage. When hatching time arrives, the pupa has transformed into the adult within the pupal husk and will swim to the surface and emerge, or as with some species, the pupa will crawl out of the stream and emerge.

This stage may be imitated by a wet fly having an enlarged thorax region and, perhaps, wing pads on either side of the thorax. Again, a standard dressed wet fly with a throat hackle is a reasonable imitation and this probably speaks for the success of this type of fly on occasion. The short, over-the-back wing often seen on a wet fly also imitates the emerging wing quite well.

Stone Flies (Plecoptera): The stone fly nymphs do not hatch in the water; they crawl out of the stream onto stones or branches near the water and escape from the nymphal skin as adults. It is doubtful that any of the wet flies are effective as emerger imitations, since this form of the insect is not normally available to the trout.

Midges (Diptera): These tiny fellows have a complete metamorphosis, so there is a pupal stage prior to the appearance of the adult. Most of the Diptera pupa have a slim body, a larger thorax, and wings held on either side of the thorax. There is a circle of filaments surrounding the head, and the body of the pupa hangs vertically in the surface film, suspended by these filaments.

There are a few imitations tied in this manner: a slim quill body is formed, then a dubbed thorax is formed with either the dubbing picked out or a circle of hackle wound at the head to represent the filaments.

As you can see, except for the mayfly nymph moving to the surface to hatch and the caddis pupa making the same type of journey, there is really not much for us to imitate in this stage of an insect's life. Most successful wet flies are probably taken by the trout to be nymphs. The materials that you use to imitate the emerging mayfly nymph and the caddis pupa should be "soft" so that good motion is produced by movement through the water. A slim body, enlarged thorax, and swollen, darkened wing cases are the most important points to be remembered.

Adults

Mayflies (Ephemeroptera): The newly emerged adult mayfly is known by the fisherman as a dun, while the entomologist calls this stage a sub-imago. During a "hatch" we are trying to duplicate this stage.

The mayfly dun ranges in length from 3mm to 34mm (#2 to #28 hooks) with three tails (occasionally two), a very delicate abdomen, an enlarged thorax, four wings (two of which are quite small and generally not imitated), and a small head. Their most distinguishing feature is that the wings are carried upright like a sail. Most of the popular dry fly patterns are imitative of the mayfly dun.

The tail may be a group of hackle fibers, a few pieces of hair tied in as a bunch, or two widely separated hairs as used in the Swisher-Richards "no-hackle" patterns. The slim body is often imitated by a quill wrapped on the hook, although dubbing has better floating qualities. Floss may be used in the same manner as quill. The thorax is usually tied of the same material as the body, and here is another advantage of dubbing—the thorax region can easily be enlarged by simply dubbing a little heavier in that area. Wings may be represented by paired quill segments, hackle tips, a bunch of hair, or a rolled wing. Color and size are critical for a successful imitation, but the type of body construction, type of wing, and method of tying the tail are not important as long as a good imitation of the adult insect is the result.

After leaving the stream, the dun moults again. The fisherman calls this stage a spinner, and the scientist uses the term imago. Following this final moult, the insect is more brightly colored, with a slimmer, more delicate appearance and a longer tail. The mayflies return to the water to mate, and as copulation is completed and the eggs are deposited, the insects fall to the water and lie expired in the surface film with wings outstretched (spent).

An artificial spinner is tied much the same as the dun imitation except for the following: colors may be brighter; a longer hook is used to represent the longer, slimmer body; the tails are longer; and the wings are tied in perpendicular to the sides of the thorax. Hackle-tips are most commonly used for the wing, although hair and shaped polypropylene yarn are very effective.

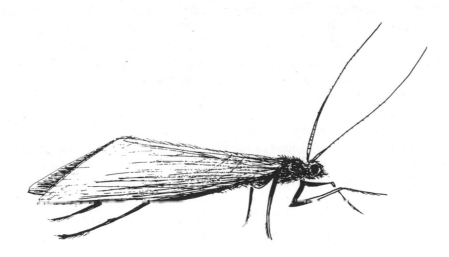

Caddis Flies (Trichoptera): The caddis fly adult has no tail, has a fairly heavy body, and carries its wings over its back in an inverted "V." Although the adult has no tail, it does carry its legs out behind it when at rest, and since a tail on our fly serves the important mechanical function of supporting the heaviest part of the hook (the bend), patterns are usually tied with a tail. The body can be of any of the materials that we have previously mentioned (and many that weren't), but dubbing is hard to beat, not only because of the excellent floatation properties, but because of the subtle shades that can be obtained by mixing different colors. The wing is most often imitated by a bunch of hair tied in over the back. Don often uses a lacquered piece of mallard side feather sloping over the back, while my favorite pattern uses a piece of mallard that has been reversed (by sweeping the tips back to the stem) and tied in in the same manner.

Stone Flies (Plecoptera): The stone fly adult crawls out of the water to hatch on a nearby stick or stone. Their frequent appearance on the water may be the result of a gust of wind, or perhaps just plain clumsiness: it fell in (like me, sometimes). Two tails, a heavy body, muscular thorax, and wings carried in a flat position over the back are the most recognizable characteristics of the stone fly adult. Many of the caddis fly imitations may be taken by trout as a stone fly since their shape is much the same. However, the stone fly is usually tied on a longer hook than a caddis fly of the same size.

Midges (Diptera): The adult midges are very hard to categorize with a simple description as they are so numerous. The basic point is that they are generally very small and mosquito-like. The wings are carried most often in a spent position, although a flat "V" shape is not uncommon.

Because of their small size, a detailed imitation is not only extremely difficult to tie but, fortunately, doesn't seem to be required. Most patterns are tied using just a tail, a dubbed body, and a hackle. Ostrich herl is also a good choice for a body material, and since the hooks used are quite small, a hackle may not be needed as the fibers of the herl can float the fly nicely.

We have intentionally left out any reference to the hackle used for tying the adult stages. Since the hackle is the prime support for the fly, it must be of good quality. Chose a hackle first of all by color—it must be right for the insect that you are imitating. It must be of the right size, both to look right to you, and to support the fly properly. Its quality must be sufficient to float the fly: stiff, resilent fibers, long enough to tie easily, with a good sheen. You will find that your quest for good hackle will become a passion, and you will probably develop guilt feelings as you lust after your neighbor's prime roosters.

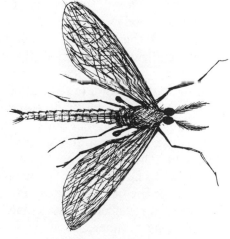

There they are—the most important insects to the fisherman and how we go about imitating them. Basically, it's just having a knowledge of the materials available to you and the skill to use those materials. The knowledge of the insects is readily available in many fine books (see the bibliography), and the common patterns are effective because they are representative of the actual insects. Keep in mind that you are trying to duplicate the insect and not the pattern, and learn to keep your mind open for logical, workable, substitutions of materials and methods. A wing is a wing regardless of the method used to tie it.

Chapter Five

Other Flies

Streamers: Most of the modern streamer flies are tied as baitfish (minnow) imitations and might be defined as flies that use the wing as the bulk and mass of the body material. Generally the material wound on the hook shank is quite sparse, commonly just a layer of floss or tinsel, and serves to represent the lower portion of the minnow's body. Wing material is then tied in at the head of the fly so that it will lie on top of the hook to form the main body shape. Often, several colors of material are tied in to form layers of color that when wet will suggest the coloring of a particular type of small fish. An example would be an imitation of a small rainbow trout tied in this manner: silver tinsel wrapped on the hook shank to represent the shiny belly, pink hair or marabou tied in on top, with yellow above that to suggest the main body color, and green hair or marabou or, perhaps, peacock on top to imitate the dark green dorsal area.

The materials used for streamers are usually chosen for their ability to move in the water and imitate the swimming action of a minnow. Soft hackle, bucktail, marabou, and peacock are most commonly used.

The hooks used for streamers are generally long shanked (3X to 6X), of heavy wire (2X stout), and are often ring eyed. The added length is needed to represent the body of a minnow, the extra stout wire aids in getting the imitation "down," and the ring eye gives the streamer a more realistic movement as it is worked in and out of the pockets and eddies of the stream.

Terrestrials: Terrestrials are forms of insect life that are not normally part of the aquatic scene: ants, grasshoppers, beetles, flies, and any other land-based insects that find themselves in the water are examples.

Terrestrials are nearly always tied as dry flies, and the same materials and techniques are used that we discussed earlier for tying drys. The number of patterns to work from is greatly reduced though, and the tyer must be more inventive. Grasshoppers seem to be a preferred trout food, and the ability to tie a good "hopper imitation" is important. Beetles and ants are very effective at times and should be a part of any tyer's repertoire. Just as in tying aquatic imitations, the tyer should be observant while on the stream so that when he returns to the tying table he knows what he needs to have ready for the next trip. What terrestrials are available to the trout depends on the time of the year and many local influences, so close observation is important.

Attracters: Attracter flies are those that appeal to some instinct other than hunger. They are not a realistic imitation of any particular creature and are often of very bright colors. A good example is the Royal Coachman; there isn't any insect that the trout sees that looks like this red, green, and white fly, and yet this pattern is still probably the single most popular dry fly. Why do trout take it? No one is sure, but the trout may be striking out of curiosity, playfulness, or maybe he's *really* hungry and it looks like something that *may* be edible. In the case of the attracter type streamers, territorial possession is perhaps the most logical reason for the trout's interest, although the other mentioned instincts may well be involved on occasion. Whatever the reasons, attracters do work at times. The only difference between tying the attracters and the flies that we have already discussed is the colors or arrangement of materials, and no special techniques are required.

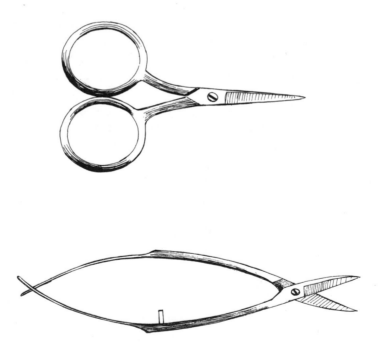

Chapter Six

Before You Begin

Fly-Tying Classes: It is possible to learn to tie without attending a fly-tying class and this manual is meant to make that easier, but we know that even though we have duplicated our classroom presentation as closely as possible, we could teach you more and you would learn faster if we were watching over your shoulder.

Classes are offered at many schools, in community recreation programs, by sportsman's clubs, and by many tackle shops. Ferret one out and enroll. Don't feel that because you can already tie there is nothing to learn or that you will have to start all over. A good instructor will not change your basic methods (if they are sound) although he will, in all likelihood, show you other ways of achieving the same result and leave it to you to determine which works best for *you*. Classes are kept small so that the student can receive individual attention, which means that the instructor can introduce you to the more advanced techniques that the true beginner in the class won't get to see. Do get into a class if at all possible and above all keep an open mind to what is taught. We all tie differently (even Don and I) but that doesn't mean that someone is doing it wrong—only differently. The only pitfall to avoid is the instructor (or book) that insists on teaching "THE" way to tie.

Fly-Tying Kits: The price of decent quality tools needed for tying runs around thirty dollars. There is no way, repeat—*NO WAY*, that a kit can sell for less without being junk.

At the shop where we work we sell a kit, primarily for our students, that goes for about fifty bucks, which is our cost plus a couple of dollars for labor. The retail price for the items in the kit is about eighty-five dollars. Now, we are in the business to make money, so why the big give-away? If you never start tying or start with poor equipment and give up, we can't sell you any tying materials, right? Besides, when you come in for a spool of thread you just might fall in love with a new rod, or reel, or vest, or ———. And we're not alone in our devious scheme; many of the mail order suppliers offer tying kits of quality, and so do many tackle shops, particularly if they also offer classes.

In judging the quality of a kit, look first at the tools; if they are of good quality, you can be reasonably sure that the kit is a good one, because the merchant has most of his cost represented there. The materials are relatively inexpensive because of his volume buying and are but a small part of his expenses, so he can afford to be generous with them.

Now that you have found a kit that contains good tools and a nice variety of materials, meeting the criteria we have outlined, you are ready to tie anything, right? Wrong. The variety of materials used in fly-tying is unlimited, and a kit that included some of *everything* would have to be transported home in a truck. If it included all *colors* of everything, a boxcar wouldn't be adequate. A good kit will contain some of each of the most often used materials so that the beginner can learn to handle these materials.

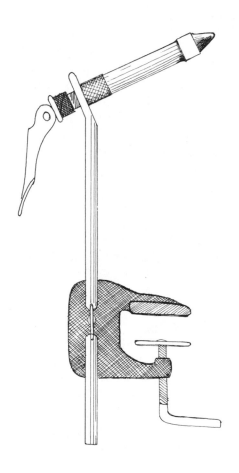

Chapter Seven

Having Problems?

This section is intended as a reference, should you have difficulty with a particular step in the tying process. We have listed the most common problems and their solutions under two headings: "Tools" and "Parts of the Fly." Rather than cross-referencing between problems that have the same solution, we have given the solution with each problem so that you will not have to spend a lot of time looking for the answer to your difficulty.

Tools

Vise

Hook slips. The most likely problem is that the vise is improperly adjusted; check the manufacturer's instructions for proper adjustment. The same difficulty may be experienced if you have the bobbin tension too tight; remove the spool of thread and spread the legs of the bobbin apart.

Hook breaks. You may have gotten a batch of bad hooks; check each one as you mount it in the vise by tweaking the eye with your fingernail. It should spring back to shape. If the hooks seem to be good, you may be setting the hook back too far in the vise jaws and destroying the temper of the steel; only the bend of the hook should be clamped in the vise.

Hackle Pliers

Cutting hackle. There is a sharp edge on the pliers; work a doubled piece of fine emery paper between the closed jaws to smooth them, or put shrink tubing over the jaws.

Slipping. Either the hackle pliers don't have enough tension or the jaws are glazed (if using shrink tubing on the jaws); to increase the tension, unhook the jaws and spread the pliers' legs apart; to eliminate slipping due to glazing, rough up the jaw surfaces with emery paper.

Scissors

Not cutting. Make sure that the joint where the two blades are fastened together is tight; all good quality scissors have a screw that secures the blades together. Perhaps the scissors need sharpening; check with your barber to see where he gets his done. For a temporary sharpening you may be able to get by with cutting a piece of emery paper a few times. If the scissors seem to be tight and sharp, you have probably sprung the jaws; the only solution is to buy a new pair, but keep these for cutting wire, rubber, and other tough things so that the new pair won't suffer the same fate.

Bobbin

Cutting thread. The bobbin has a rough edge at the end of the tube; cut a triangular piece of emery paper, roll it into a cone, and polish the inside of the tip.

Slipping. The bobbin tension is set too loose; remove the spool of thread and bend the legs of the bobbin toward each other. For a slight increase in tension, slip a couple of wraps of thread from the end of the spool onto one of the legs of the bobbin.

Breaking thread. The bobbin tension is set too tight; remove the spool of thread and spread the legs of the bobbin apart a small amount.

Threading. The quickest and easiest way to thread the bobbin is to pull off five or six inches of thread, start the thread into the end of the tube and then suck on the other end of the tube to pull the thread through.

Parts of the Fly

Tail

Rolls around the hook as it is tied in. After tying the butts of the tail material down, hold the tail slightly towards you as you wrap to the back of the hook and allow the thread to carry the tailing material to the top center of the shank.

Tipped down. The angle of the tail is determined by how far you wrap back on the tailing material; if you wrap too far back you will tip the tail down as you start around the bend of the hook.

Ribbing

Breaks. If the problem is with tinsel, there is probably a kink in the tinsel; be certain that the tinsel is smooth before tying it in. A quill that is being used for a ribbing material will break if you try to wrap it too tight.

Body

Quill

Breaking. A quill being used for a body must be handled gently. If you are not applying too much pressure and are still experiencing the problem, the quill may be dry; all stripped quill will soften if soaked in water.

Floss

Fraying. Fraying is the most common problem when using floss, and the problem is increased if your hands are rough; keep a bottle of hand lotion on the bench for use when your hands are rough. Keeping the floss wet as you wrap will help to alleviate the problem.

Separating. Most of the floss used for tying is made of four strands, and the strands will have a tendency to separate as the floss is wrapped; keeping the floss wet will help to keep the strands together, and holding the floss close to the hook shank assists in overcoming this problem.

Dubbing

Separating from thread. You are probably trying to either dub too long a piece of thread at a time or trying to put too much fur on the thread; you should dub the thread rather lightly and only dub one or two inches of thread at a time. If a longer piece is needed, you should dub a section, wrap it, dub another, and so on until the desired length of body is obtained.

Body not tapered. Trying to dub too heavily may be the problem; the thread should be dubbed rather lightly. Another common problem is wrapping all of one piece of dubbing on the hook before dubbing the next section of thread. When you dub a small section of thread you will notice that the dubbing is thicker in the center of the dubbed area and tapers at each end; if you will stop wrapping when this taper is above the hook shank and then dub the next section, the two tapers will overlap and give you a section of dubbing of equal diameter for its full length.

Spun Hair

Not flaring properly. This is most often the result of having thread wrapped under the area where you intend to spin the hair; the hook shank must be bare at this point. Attempting to spin too much hair at a time will result in the same problem.

Not smooth after trimming. The secret of a perfectly smooth body after trimming it to shape is to singe it: hold a match *above* the body and use the underside of the flame to smooth the body. You can actually shape the trimmed body by this method, and it also seals the ends of the hair and makes the fly more buoyant.

Rubber

Body too bulky or too thin. The shape of a wrapped rubber body (heavy latex or rubber band) is determined by the amount of tension that is applied during the wrapping process; when starting the wrap, stretch the material tightly, and as you wrap the hook shank loosen the tension slightly with each wrap. This allows the material to thicken with each wrap and will produce a nicely tapered body.

Wing Case

Rolling off top of hook. You must use the "soft loop" technique to tie in the wing case so that it will remain in position as the thread is tightened. Use at least two soft loops to anchor the material before continuing with normal wrapping.

Splitting. The wing case material is probably too wide if you are having problems with it splitting; the width of the wing case should be about one-fourth the length of the hook shank. Do not trim the top of a palmered hackle before bringing the wing case forward, as the stiff hackle fibers that are left will puncture the wing case material and cause splitting.

Wings

Quill Wing

Splitting. This problem is normally the result of using too wide a piece of quill for the wing or not holding the wing firmly in place during the tying-in step; each quill section should have a width equal to about one-fourth of the length of the hook shank, and you must make at least two "soft loops" to anchor the wing before continuing the wrapping process.

Rolling. Holding the wings firmly in place until anchored with at least two "soft loops" will solve this problem; a base of thread on the hook shank where the wing is to be mounted will also help.

Rolled Wing

Rolling off of top of hook. This problem is most commonly caused by not holding the wing firmly in place while using the "soft loop" for the tie-in; you must have at least two wraps using the "soft loop" before letting go of the wing material to continue wrapping.

Hackle-tip Wing

Twisting. Often the lower part of a hackle stem is oval in cross-section and the hackle will tend to twist as it is tied in. Softening the tip by gently chewing it is the most expedient solution; by selecting the hackle-tip from nearer the tip of a larger feather, the stem is more likely to be round.

Hairwing

Uneven tips. Using a hair stacker or its equivalent is the best solution to this difficulty, an empty rifle shell casing may be used by inserting the hair (tips first) and tapping lightly on the desk.

Rolling. This is the most difficult problem when tying a hair wing; you must be certain that you have at least three wraps (using the "soft loop") before letting go of the winging material.

Pulling out. To mount the wing so that it will stay firmly in place, make sure that you have a layer of thread under the area where the wing will be tied in, and after tying it in put a couple of drops of head cement on the windings.

Hackle

Breaking. If the hackle is breaking at the end of the hackle pliers, the problem is normally with the tool; there is a sharp edge that is cutting the hackle. If the stem is breaking at the point where it is tied in, the cause is probably that the hackle is too dry; steaming it over a tea kettle will soften the hackle stem without harming the hackle fibers. If the hackle is breaking somewhere between the butt and the hackle pliers, you have a bad neck; the hackle has been damaged by either disease or insects. Occasionally you can salvage some hackles by steaming to soften the stems and wrapping very carefully.

Doesn't flare properly. The hackle on some necks has very pronounced oval stems and is very difficult to wrap edgewise; you can steam the neck to soften the stems, but once in a while you will get a neck that you just can't use for hackling because of this problem.

Head

Tying down hackle tips. Usually this problem started when you mounted the wing. You set it too far toward the eye of the hook, and by the time you wound the hackle there just wasn't room for the head; check the proportion illustration for proper wing position. If you had room for the head and are still experiencing this problem, you are not keeping the hackle back out of the way with the left hand while forming the head; if you just can't get the knack of this technique you might consider using hackle guards.

glossary

abdomen The rear body portion of an insect.

adult The last stage in the life cycle of an insect; the stage spent out of the water.

badger Body hair or dubbing from that animal; a cream to ginger hackle with a black center streak.

barb The rear tip of the hook point.

bend The curve at the rear of the hook that establishes the gap; the shape of the bend; perfect bend, sproat bend, etc.

bobbin A tool designed to hold a spool of tying thread under tension.

bucktail The hair taken from the tail of a white-tailed deer.

caddis fly Order Trichoptera; complete metamorphosis; the adult carries its wing over its back in an inverted "V."

calf tail The hair from a calf's tail, also called impala or kip.

cape Another term for a neck.

coachman A hackle of very dark brown with just a tint of red.

cock-y-bondu A hackle in shades from dark ginger to brown with a black center streak and edges.

cream A color of hackle from just darker than white to a pale yellow.

Diptera An order of insects commonly called midges; complete metamorphosis; generally very small.

dry fly A fly tied to represent the adult stage of an insect.

dubbing The process of spinning fur onto the tying thread to form a "yarn" of fur for the body of the fly; a material used for dubbing, either natural fur or a synthetic material.

dun A hackle of a neutral grey color; may have undertones of blue, olive, bronze, etc.; rare in nature and expensive; readily available dyed.

Ephemeroptera An order of insects commonly called mayflies; incomplete metamorphosis; the adult has an upright wing.

eye The loop at the end of the hook shank to which the leader is attached; the painted dots or feathers at the head of some streamer patterns that are meant to imitate a minnow's eyes.

fine A relative measurement of hook wire diameters, e.g. a #14 2X fine is a number 14 hook made from wire normally used for a hook two sizes smaller (#16).

floss A heavy silk or rayon thread used primarily as body material.

furnace A hackle ranging in color from dark ginger to brown with a black center stripe.

gap The distance from the shank to the point of the hook.

ginger A color of hackle ranging from light to medium brown with a tinge of red.

guard hair The coarse, long hair on an animal's pelt.

grizzly A black or dark grey hackle with white bars, sometimes called Plymouth Rock after the breed of chicken that produces it.

hackle A feather from the neck or rump of a chicken; a feather wound on a hook edgewise; the act of putting a hackle on a fly.

hackle gauge Small funnel-shaped tool for holding the hackle away from the head area while the head of the fly is being formed and tied off.

hackle pliers A tool used to grasp a hackle for winding.

hackle-tip wing A type of wing construction using two hackle tips to form the wing.

hair stacker A tool used to even the ends of a bunch of hair.

hair wing A method of wing construction in which an evened bunch of hair is tied in to form the wings.

half-hitch An easy, although inferior, method for tying off the head of a fly.

half-hitch tool A tool designed to aid in the forming of half-hitches.

herl A long, thin feather with many short barbules which creates a "fuzzy" appearance when wrapped on the hook, as: peacock herl, ostrich herl, and emu.

impala Another name for calf tail.

jungle cock The feather from the breast of a grey jungle fowl that was commonly used for the eye on streamer flies; no longer available due to a ban on their importation.

kip Another name for calf tails.

larva The second stage in a complete metamorphosis, it comes between the egg and the pupa; generally wormlike in appearance.

long A relative measurement of hook length, e.g. a #14 2X long hook is a #14 hook that is as long as a hook two sizes larger (#12).

marabou A very soft, long-fibered feather from a white turkey. Dyed to desired colors, it is used primarily for streamers as it has a "breathing" action when moved through the water.

material clip A device that attaches just behind the vise jaws to hold tied-in material out of the way while performing other steps in the tying process.

mask The face skin of an animal, most commonly a rabbit or hare.

mayfly The common name for insects of the order Ephemeroptera: incomplete metamorphosis; adult has an upright wing.

metamorphosis The form changes occurring in the life cycle of an insect, i.e., larva to pupa to adult, or nymph to adult.

midge The common name for insects of the order Diptera; complete metamorphosis; generally very small; also called gnats, smuts, or snow flies.

Mylar A flexible plastic-like material with a metalized finish, available as a braided tube, in flat sheets, and in tinsel widths.

neck The neck skin of a bird, usually a chicken, with the feathers (hackles) attached.

nymph A stage in the incomplete metamorphosis of an insect which comes between the egg and the adult; an artificial fly fished as an imitation of a nymph, larva, or pupa.

palmered A fly with a hackle wound the full length of the hook shank in a spiral.

Plecoptera An order of insects commonly called stone flies; incomplete metamorphosis; the adult carries its wings flat over its back.

Plymouth Rock The chicken which produces grizzly hackle; another name for grizzly hackle.

point The sharp tip of the hook.

pointer The feathers at the very tip of a bird's wing, e.g. duck pointer, goose pointer; used as the source of quill segments for tying quill wings.

polypropylene A synthetic material used as dubbing or for wings; available in pressed sheets, as yarn, or as loose dubbing, it is very effective as a body material as it has a specific gravity of less than one.

pupa A stage in the complete metamorphosis of an insect that comes between the larva and the adult.

quill A feather from the wing of a duck or goose.

quill body A type of body construction in which stripped peacock herl, stripped hackle, or two or three quill fibers are wrapped around the hook shank to achieve a segmented effect.

quill wing A wing made from paired segments of quill feathers.

ribbing A thin strip of material wound over the body of a fly in a spiral to give the appearance of segmentation. Wire, tinsel, Mylar, and thread are commonly used ribbing materials.

rolled wing A type of wing construction in which a bunch of feather fibers is tied in as a clump and divided with the tying thread.

saddle hackle The long, slim feathers from the rump of a rooster.

shank The straight section of a hook from the eye to the bend.

short A relative measurement of hook length, e.g. a #14 2X short hook is a number 14 hook the same length as a hook two sizes smaller (#16).

spent Lying with wings outstretched.

spent-wing A fly tied with wings in the spent position.

stone fly An insect of the order Plecoptera; in-

complete metamorphosis; the adult carries its wings flat over its back.

stout A relative measurement of hook wire size, e.g. a #14 2X stout hook is a number 14 hook with the wire diameter of a hook two sizes larger (#12).

streamer A type of fly that is tied to represent a baitfish.

tail The tail of a fly; the act of attaching the tail material to the hook.

terrestrial An insect whose life cycle is completed outside of the aquatic environment.

thorax The area between the head and the abdomen of an insect; the wings are attached to this section.

throat hackle A small bunch of hackle fibers tied under the hook extending from just behind the eye to near the point of the hook.

tinsel A thin metal strip, usually of gold or silver, used for ribbing a fly.

Trichoptera An order of insects commonly called caddis flies; complete metamorphosis; the adult carries its wings over its back in the shape of an inverted "V."

variant Any hackle with more than one color present, most commonly barred.

vise The tool used to hold the hook during the tying process.

wet fly An artificial fly that is fished beneath the surface, probably taken by the fish to be a nymph or emerging nymph.

whip-finish The preferred method for finishing the head of a fly.

whip-finish tool A tool designed to assist in tying the whip finish.

wing case An enlargement on the top of an insect's thorax that houses the immature wings prior to the adult stage.

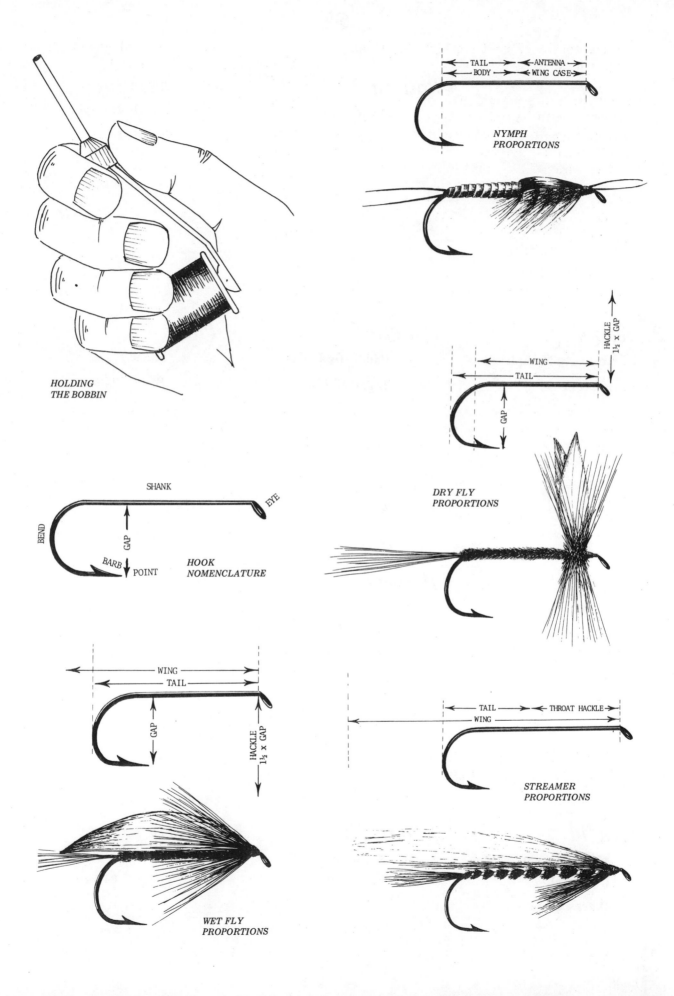

HOLDING
THE BOBBIN

NYMPH
PROPORTIONS

TAIL — ANTENNA
BODY — WING CASE

HACKLE
1½ x GAP

WING
TAIL
GAP

DRY FLY
PROPORTIONS

SHANK

EYE

BEND

GAP

BARB POINT

HOOK
NOMENCLATURE

WING
TAIL

GAP

HACKLE
1½ x GAP

WET FLY
PROPORTIONS

TAIL — THROAT HACKLE
WING

STREAMER
PROPORTIONS

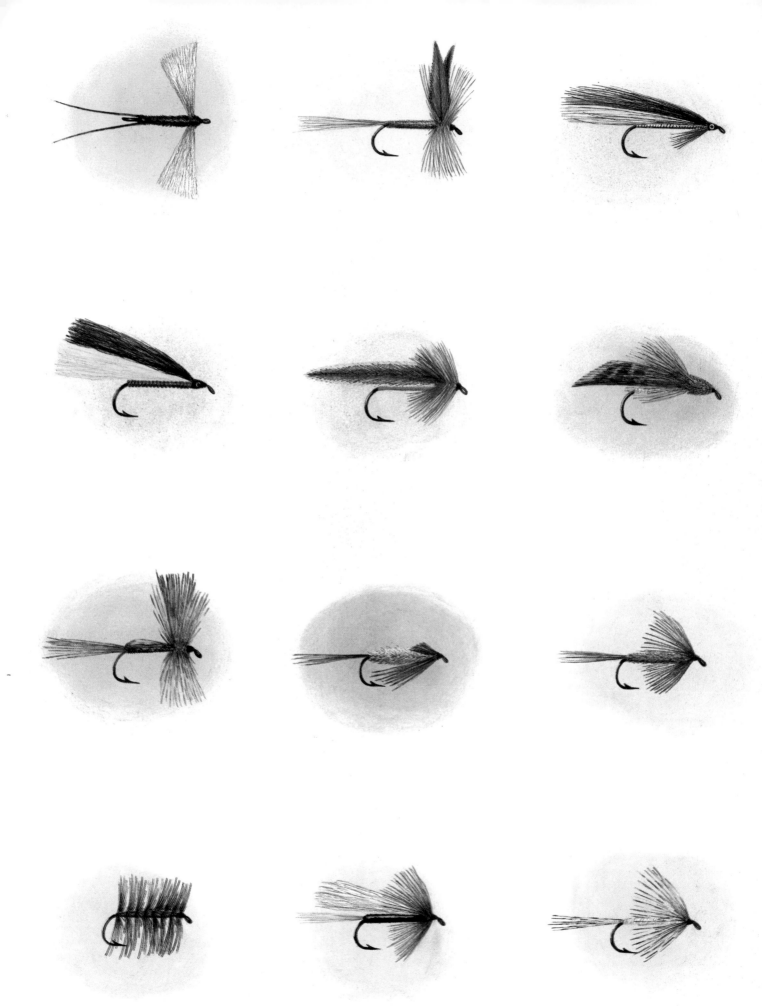

Pattern 1

The first fly that we are going to have you tie is a simple caddis (Trichoptera) larva imitation. Caddis larva vary greatly in size, from about a #10 hook to a #20, and, of course, the imitation should be tied on a hook that will give the correct size for the natural that you are trying to imitate. For the purpose of instruction, however, we suggest that you begin tying on a #10 or #12 hook. Since the insect is found near the bottom of the stream, you should use a wet-fly hook.

We have illustrated this fly being tied with a wool body, ribbed with fine brass wire, and with a thorax area of peacock. For the body you could substitute dubbing, ostrich, peacock, or any material that would give the desired fuzzy appearance. The ribbing might be thread, tinsel, or a quill. Dubbing or ostrich would be good alternatives for the thorax area. The most common colors are olive, grey, white, and tan, but certainly your choice will depend on the insects that are present in the streams that you fish.

Pay particular attention to the technique shown in steps 5, 9, and 23—the "soft loop." This may well be the most important single step in all of fly-tying. The soft loop is used to attach *all* material to the hook and will become critically important in some of the later patterns.

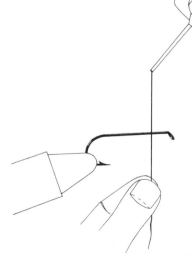

1. Start wrapping two eyewidths back from the eye. The thread should be on the near side of the hook.

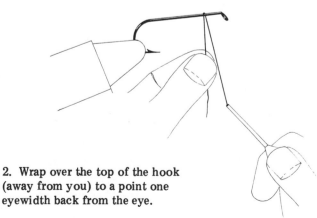

2. Wrap over the top of the hook (away from you) to a point one eyewidth back from the eye.

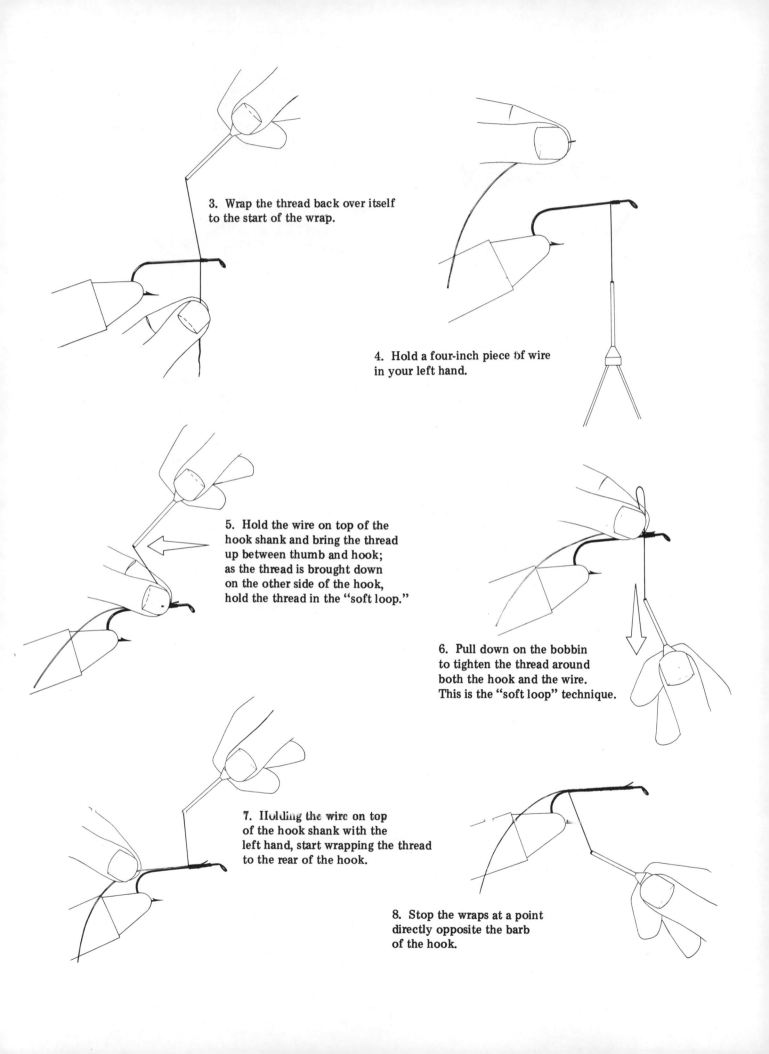

3. Wrap the thread back over itself to the start of the wrap.

4. Hold a four-inch piece of wire in your left hand.

5. Hold the wire on top of the hook shank and bring the thread up between thumb and hook; as the thread is brought down on the other side of the hook, hold the thread in the "soft loop."

6. Pull down on the bobbin to tighten the thread around both the hook and the wire. This is the "soft loop" technique.

7. Holding the wire on top of the hook shank with the left hand, start wrapping the thread to the rear of the hook.

8. Stop the wraps at a point directly opposite the barb of the hook.

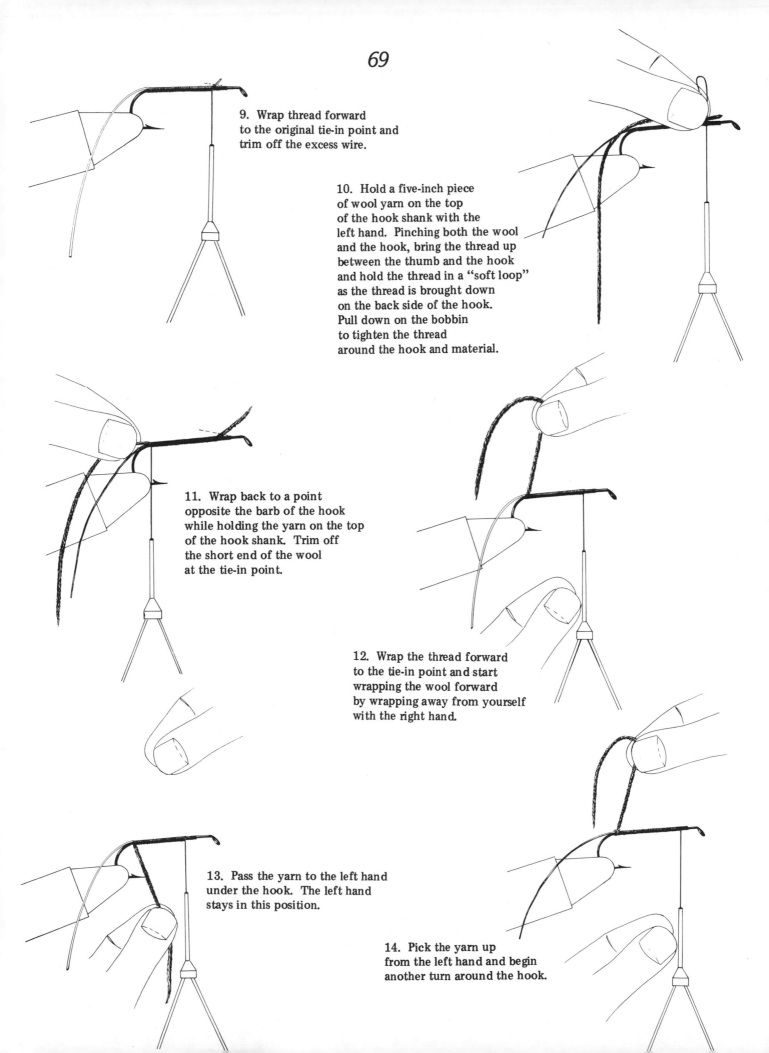

9. Wrap thread forward
to the original tie-in point and
trim off the excess wire.

10. Hold a five-inch piece
of wool yarn on the top
of the hook shank with the
left hand. Pinching both the wool
and the hook, bring the thread up
between the thumb and the hook
and hold the thread in a "soft loop"
as the thread is brought down
on the back side of the hook.
Pull down on the bobbin
to tighten the thread
around the hook and material.

11. Wrap back to a point
opposite the barb of the hook
while holding the yarn on the top
of the hook shank. Trim off
the short end of the wool
at the tie-in point.

12. Wrap the thread forward
to the tie-in point and start
wrapping the wool forward
by wrapping away from yourself
with the right hand.

13. Pass the yarn to the left hand
under the hook. The left hand
stays in this position.

14. Pick the yarn up
from the left hand and begin
another turn around the hook.

15. Pass the yarn to the left hand under the hook.

16. Pick the yarn up with the right hand and begin another wrap.

17. Note that the left hand remains under the hook at all times and that the right hand does the actual wrapping.

18. Continue wrapping in this manner until the original tie-in point is reached.

19. Hold the yarn as shown with the right hand; pick up the bobbin with the left hand and pass it over the top of the hook and allow it to drop on the other side. Continue wrapping the thread over the yarn using this method for three turns.

20. Hold the end of the yarn up with the left hand and cut off the excess.

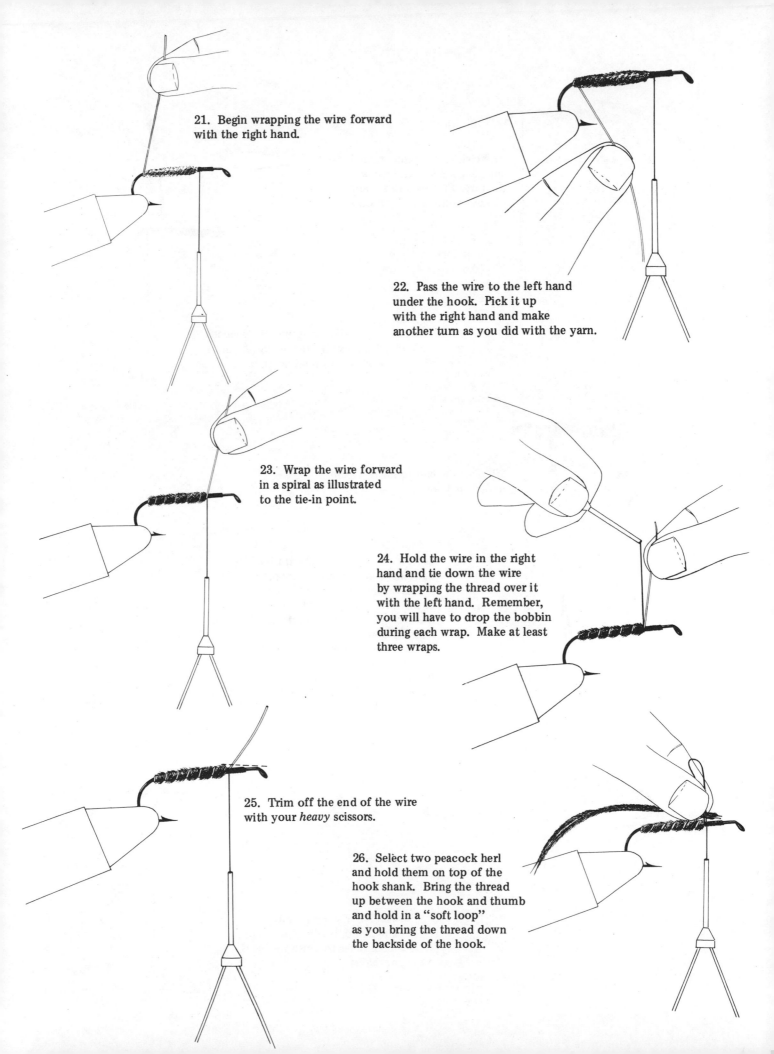

21. Begin wrapping the wire forward with the right hand.

22. Pass the wire to the left hand under the hook. Pick it up with the right hand and make another turn as you did with the yarn.

23. Wrap the wire forward in a spiral as illustrated to the tie-in point.

24. Hold the wire in the right hand and tie down the wire by wrapping the thread over it with the left hand. Remember, you will have to drop the bobbin during each wrap. Make at least three wraps.

25. Trim off the end of the wire with your *heavy* scissors.

26. Select two peacock herl and hold them on top of the hook shank. Bring the thread up between the hook and thumb and hold in a "soft loop" as you bring the thread down the backside of the hook.

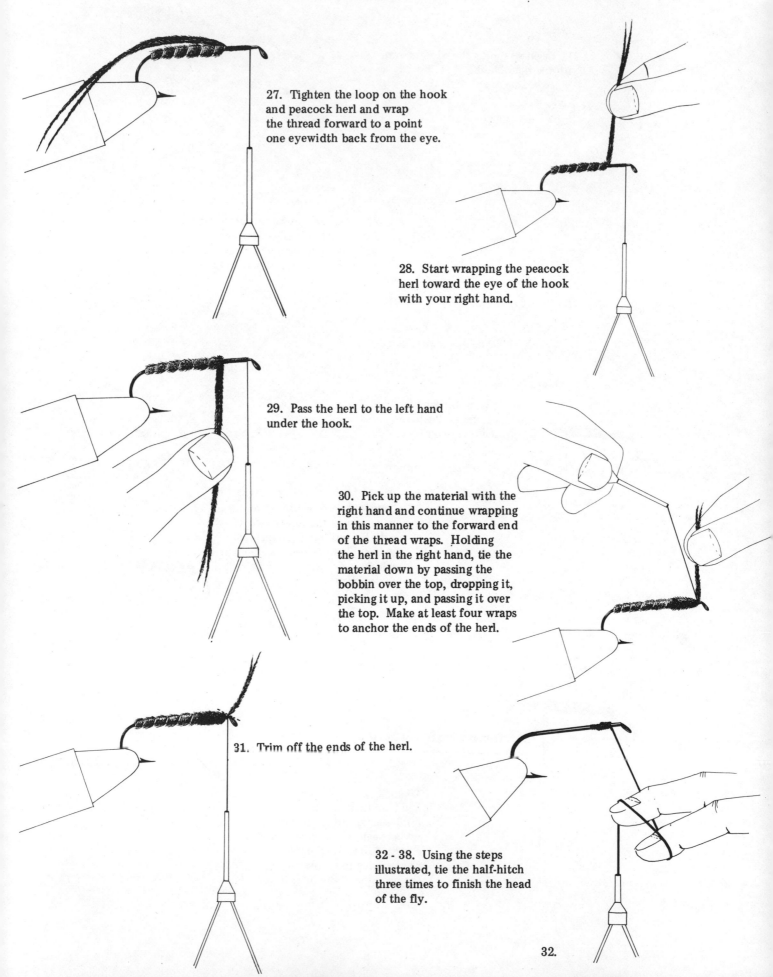

27. Tighten the loop on the hook and peacock herl and wrap the thread forward to a point one eyewidth back from the eye.

28. Start wrapping the peacock herl toward the eye of the hook with your right hand.

29. Pass the herl to the left hand under the hook.

30. Pick up the material with the right hand and continue wrapping in this manner to the forward end of the thread wraps. Holding the herl in the right hand, tie the material down by passing the bobbin over the top, dropping it, picking it up, and passing it over the top. Make at least four wraps to anchor the ends of the herl.

31. Trim off the ends of the herl.

32 - 38. Using the steps illustrated, tie the half-hitch three times to finish the head of the fly.

32.

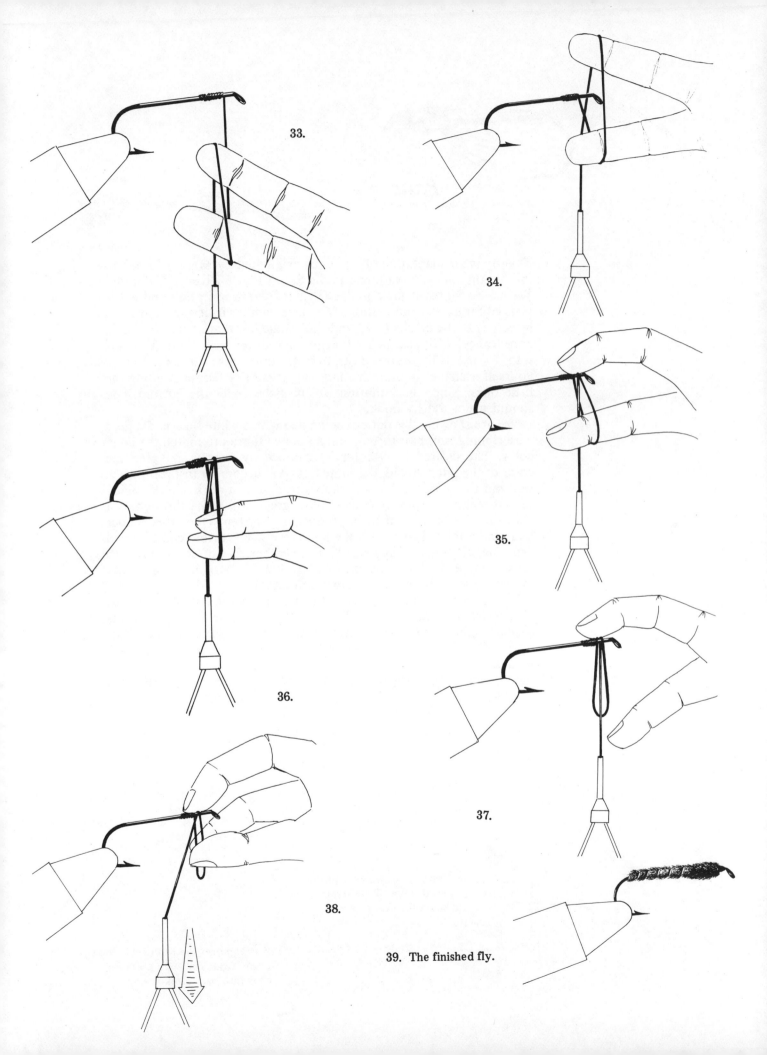

33.

34.

35.

36.

37.

38.

39. The finished fly.

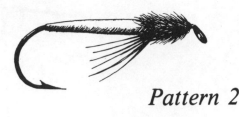

Pattern 2

This fly is an adaptation of a pattern originated by Mr. Ed Marsh to imitate the caddis larva found in the South Platte River in Colorado. We have adapted it for a midge (Diptera) larva imitation and it has worked for us very successfully. You'll remember from the chapter on insects that the caddis larva and the midge larva are very similar in appearance, with size being the primary difference. Later you will want to tie this fly in sizes down to #24, but for now use a #12 to give yourself a chance to gain the necessary dexterity before tackling the little ones. Since the imitation will be fished near the bottom, you should use a wet-fly hook.

We are showing this pattern being tied with a white floss body, gold wire ribbing, soft hair throat, and a dubbed thorax to match the body color. The desired body color is obtained by simply changing the color of the tying thread; the white floss will become translucent when wet and the thread color will show through as a dark streak. Black thread will give a nice blue dun color, green will come through as a delicate olive, and orange will produce a rusty tan. Thin latex rubber body material will give much the same result. The throat could be tied using hackle fibers or any soft hair or feather. We often tie this with no throat or dubbing; instead, we use ostrich herl of a color that matches the body for the entire thorax area.

The main learning objective in this pattern is the dubbing process. Take particular care with it. Use a soft fur for the dubbing, as it is easier to learn with. (Rabbit, muskrat, or mink is suitable.) Try spinning it directly onto the thread first; if you have trouble that way, wet your fingers just before spinning the fur. As a last resort try waxing the portion of the thread that you are going to dub. If you still have trouble, you are probably trying to spin too much fur at a time.

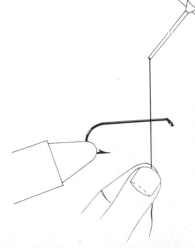

1. Start wrapping two eyewidths back from the eye. The thread should be on the near side of the hook.

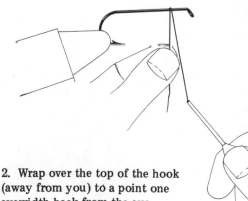

2. Wrap over the top of the hook (away from you) to a point one eyewidth back from the eye.

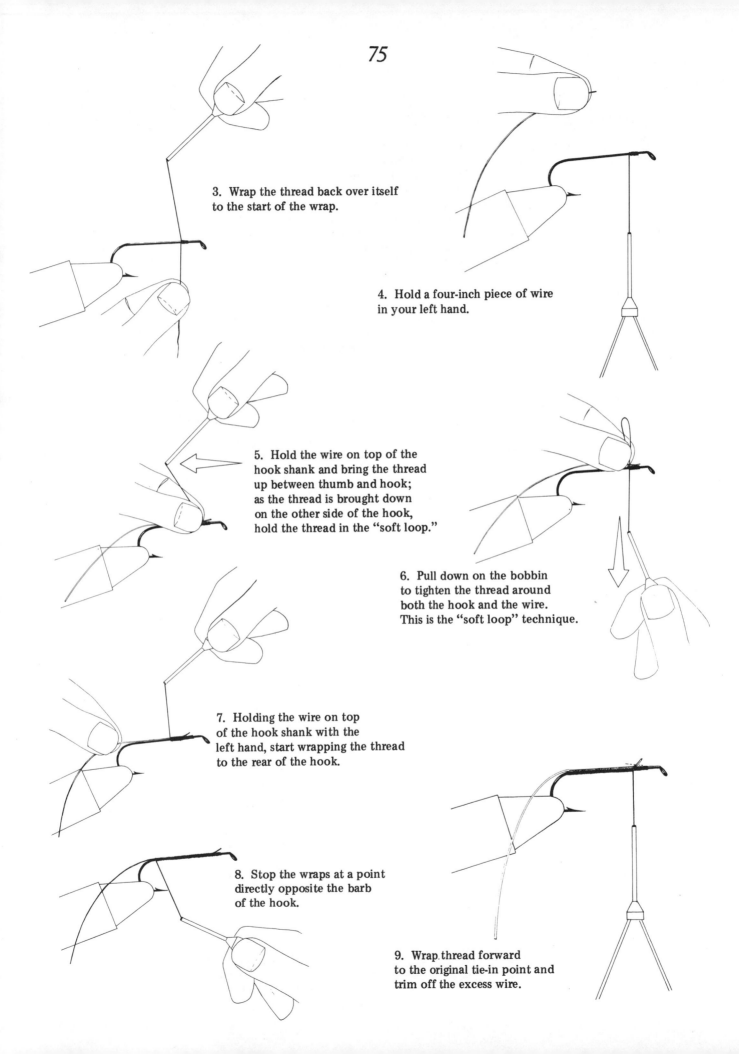

3. Wrap the thread back over itself to the start of the wrap.

4. Hold a four-inch piece of wire in your left hand.

5. Hold the wire on top of the hook shank and bring the thread up between thumb and hook; as the thread is brought down on the other side of the hook, hold the thread in the "soft loop."

6. Pull down on the bobbin to tighten the thread around both the hook and the wire. This is the "soft loop" technique.

7. Holding the wire on top of the hook shank with the left hand, start wrapping the thread to the rear of the hook.

8. Stop the wraps at a point directly opposite the barb of the hook.

9. Wrap thread forward to the original tie-in point and trim off the excess wire.

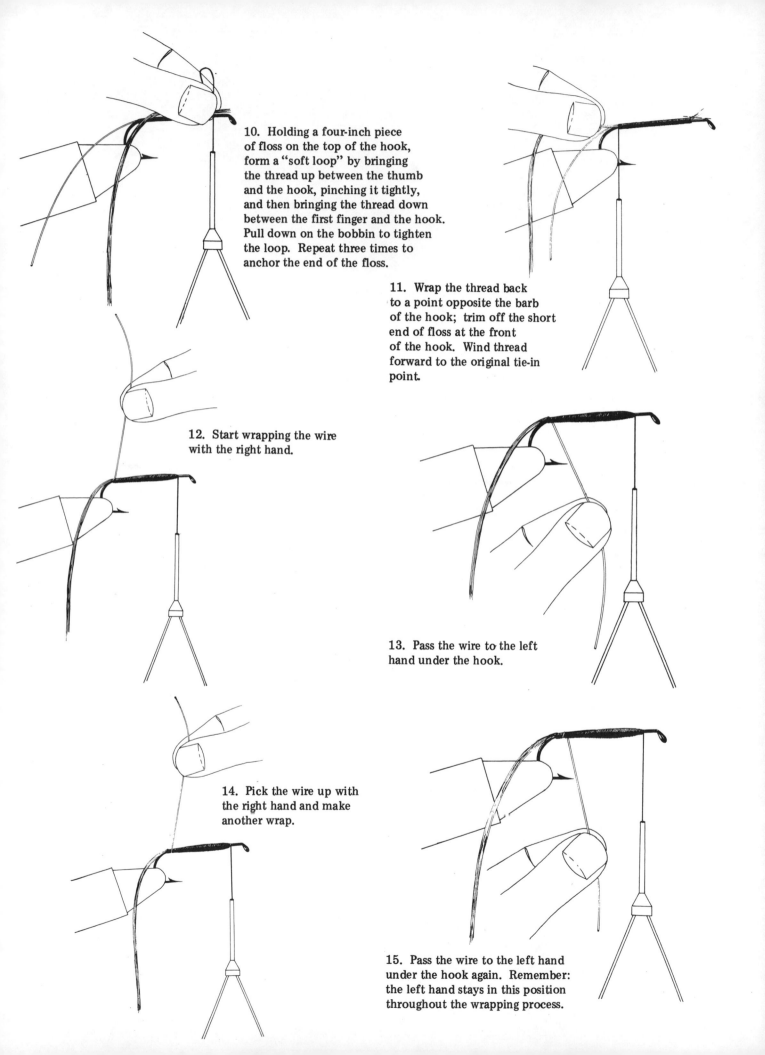

10. Holding a four-inch piece of floss on the top of the hook, form a "soft loop" by bringing the thread up between the thumb and the hook, pinching it tightly, and then bringing the thread down between the first finger and the hook. Pull down on the bobbin to tighten the loop. Repeat three times to anchor the end of the floss.

11. Wrap the thread back to a point opposite the barb of the hook; trim off the short end of floss at the front of the hook. Wind thread forward to the original tie-in point.

12. Start wrapping the wire with the right hand.

13. Pass the wire to the left hand under the hook.

14. Pick the wire up with the right hand and make another wrap.

15. Pass the wire to the left hand under the hook again. Remember: the left hand stays in this position throughout the wrapping process.

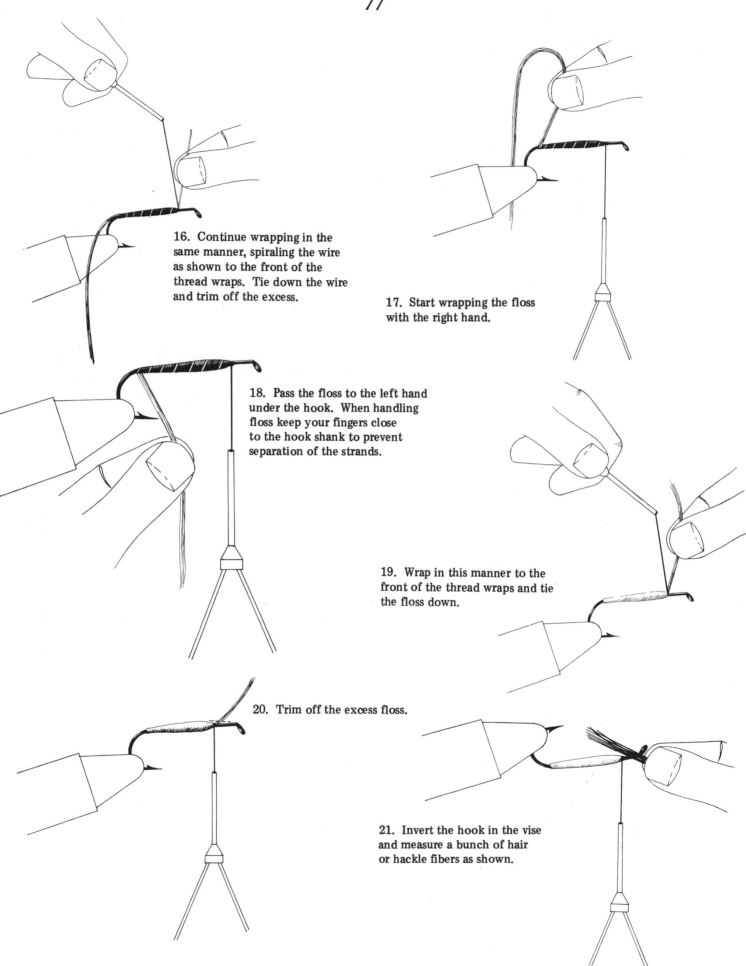

16. Continue wrapping in the
same manner, spiraling the wire
as shown to the front of the
thread wraps. Tie down the wire
and trim off the excess.

17. Start wrapping the floss
with the right hand.

18. Pass the floss to the left hand
under the hook. When handling
floss keep your fingers close
to the hook shank to prevent
separation of the strands.

19. Wrap in this manner to the
front of the thread wraps and tie
the floss down.

20. Trim off the excess floss.

21. Invert the hook in the vise
and measure a bunch of hair
or hackle fibers as shown.

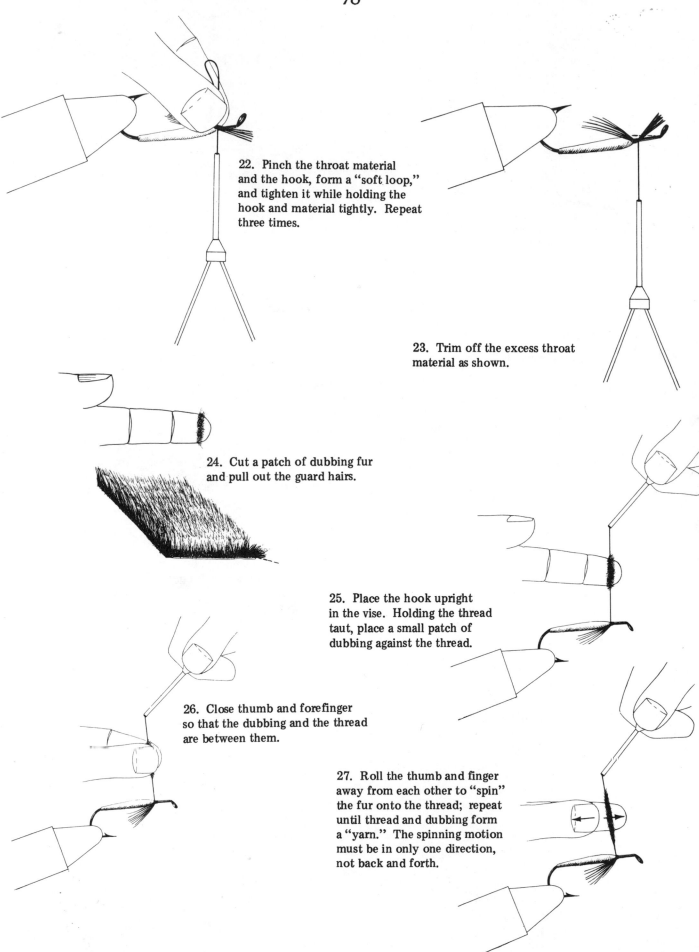

22. Pinch the throat material
and the hook, form a "soft loop,"
and tighten it while holding the
hook and material tightly. Repeat
three times.

23. Trim off the excess throat
material as shown.

24. Cut a patch of dubbing fur
and pull out the guard hairs.

25. Place the hook upright
in the vise. Holding the thread
taut, place a small patch of
dubbing against the thread.

26. Close thumb and forefinger
so that the dubbing and the thread
are between them.

27. Roll the thumb and finger
away from each other to "spin"
the fur onto the thread; repeat
until thread and dubbing form
a "yarn." The spinning motion
must be in only one direction,
not back and forth.

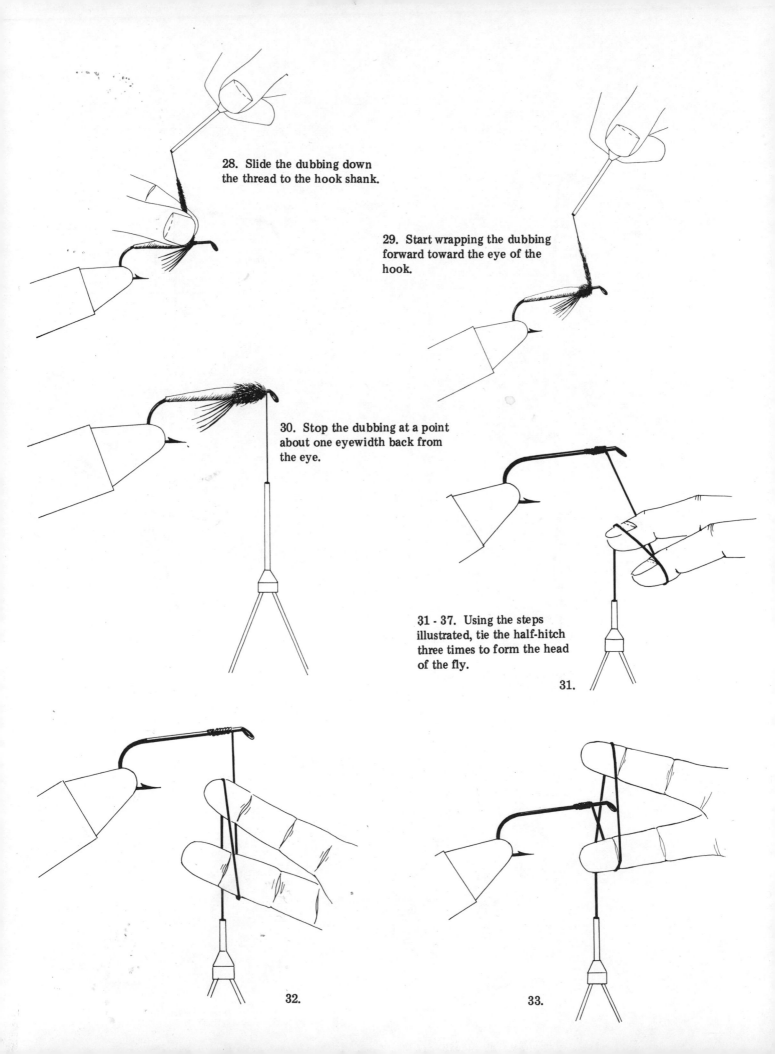

28. Slide the dubbing down the thread to the hook shank.

29. Start wrapping the dubbing forward toward the eye of the hook.

30. Stop the dubbing at a point about one eyewidth back from the eye.

31 - 37. Using the steps illustrated, tie the half-hitch three times to form the head of the fly.

31.

32.

33.

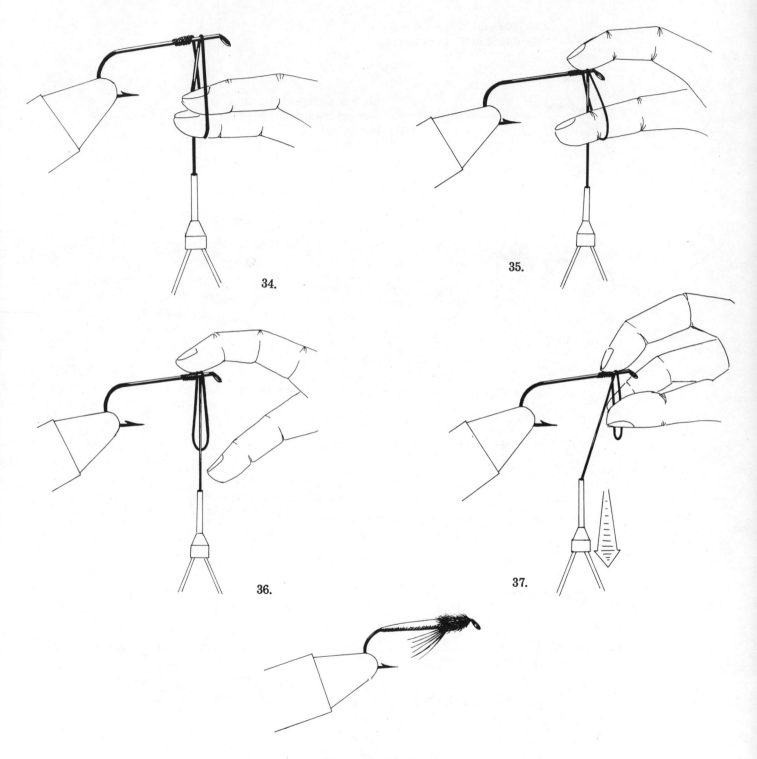

34.

35.

36.

37.

38. The finished fly.

Pattern 3

This is a simple mayfly (Ephemeroptera) nymph imitation. Since you are going to fish it deep, you should tie it on a wet-fly hook. Some of the Ephemeroptera nymphs are rather long-bodied, and for these you will want to use a 1X or 2X long hook.

We show the tail as soft hackle fibers, but soft hair or soft body feather fibers would work equally well. The dubbing can be any soft underfur such as rabbit, mink, fox, or muskrat. The throat should be of the same material as the tail. The wing case that we illustrate is cut from a small mallard body feather that has been lacquered with head cement, but a piece of lacquered turkey quill or pheasant tail or many other materials could be used.

When dubbing for a body, you generally won't be able to dub a section of thread long enough to wrap the whole body. A good method is to dub a relatively short section, wrap until all but one-half inch or so is on the hook and then dub another section. The advantage of this method is that when you spin the dubbing, it will be thicker in the center of the section and will taper at each end. By dubbing another section before the first is completely wrapped, the two tapered ends will overlap and the junction of the two sections will be the same diameter as the center area.

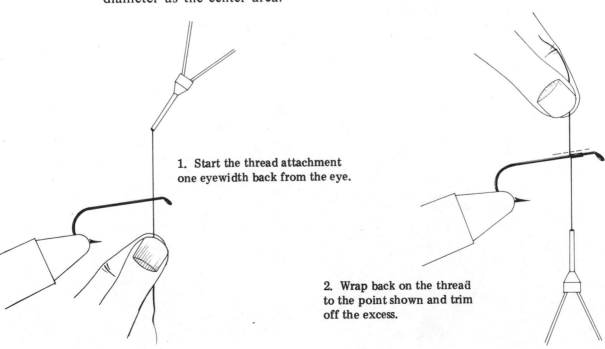

1. Start the thread attachment one eyewidth back from the eye.

2. Wrap back on the thread to the point shown and trim off the excess.

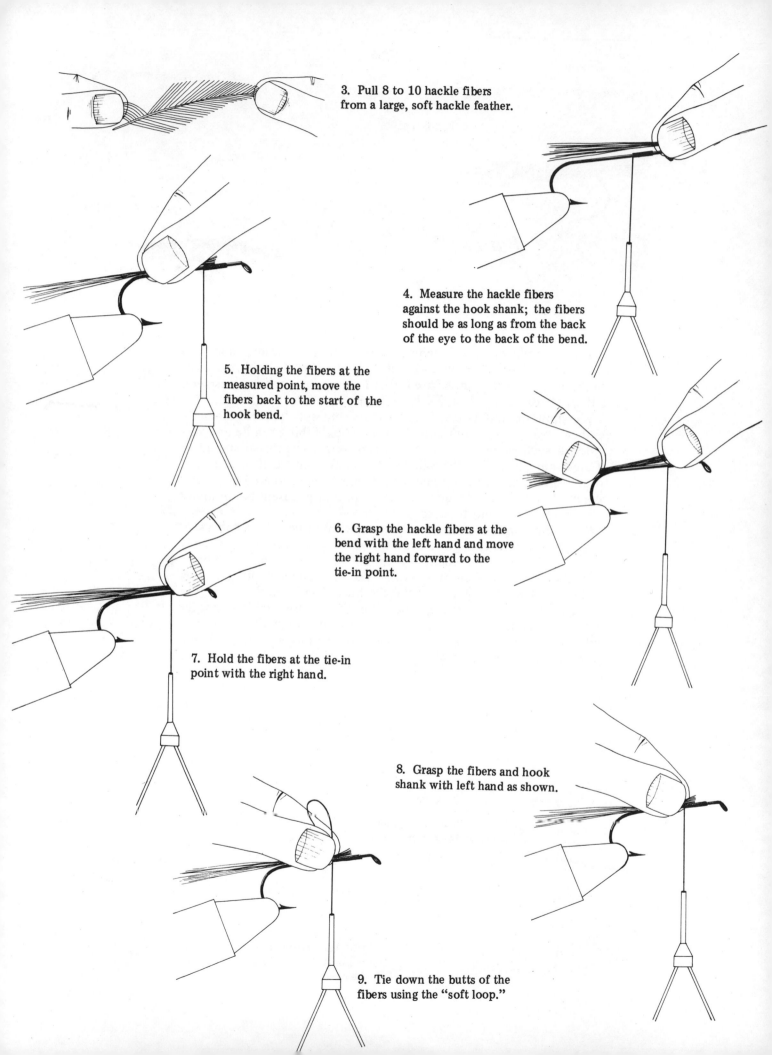

3. Pull 8 to 10 hackle fibers from a large, soft hackle feather.

4. Measure the hackle fibers against the hook shank; the fibers should be as long as from the back of the eye to the back of the bend.

5. Holding the fibers at the measured point, move the fibers back to the start of the hook bend.

6. Grasp the hackle fibers at the bend with the left hand and move the right hand forward to the tie-in point.

7. Hold the fibers at the tie-in point with the right hand.

8. Grasp the fibers and hook shank with left hand as shown.

9. Tie down the butts of the fibers using the "soft loop."

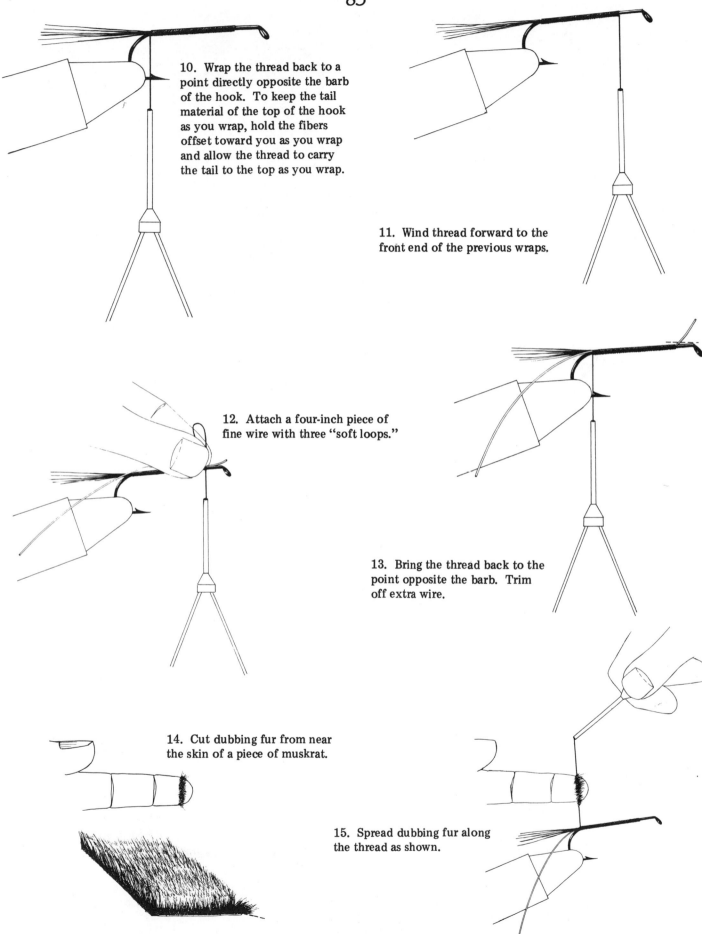

10. Wrap the thread back to a point directly opposite the barb of the hook. To keep the tail material of the top of the hook as you wrap, hold the fibers offset toward you as you wrap and allow the thread to carry the tail to the top as you wrap.

11. Wind thread forward to the front end of the previous wraps.

12. Attach a four-inch piece of fine wire with three "soft loops."

13. Bring the thread back to the point opposite the barb. Trim off extra wire.

14. Cut dubbing fur from near the skin of a piece of muskrat.

15. Spread dubbing fur along the thread as shown.

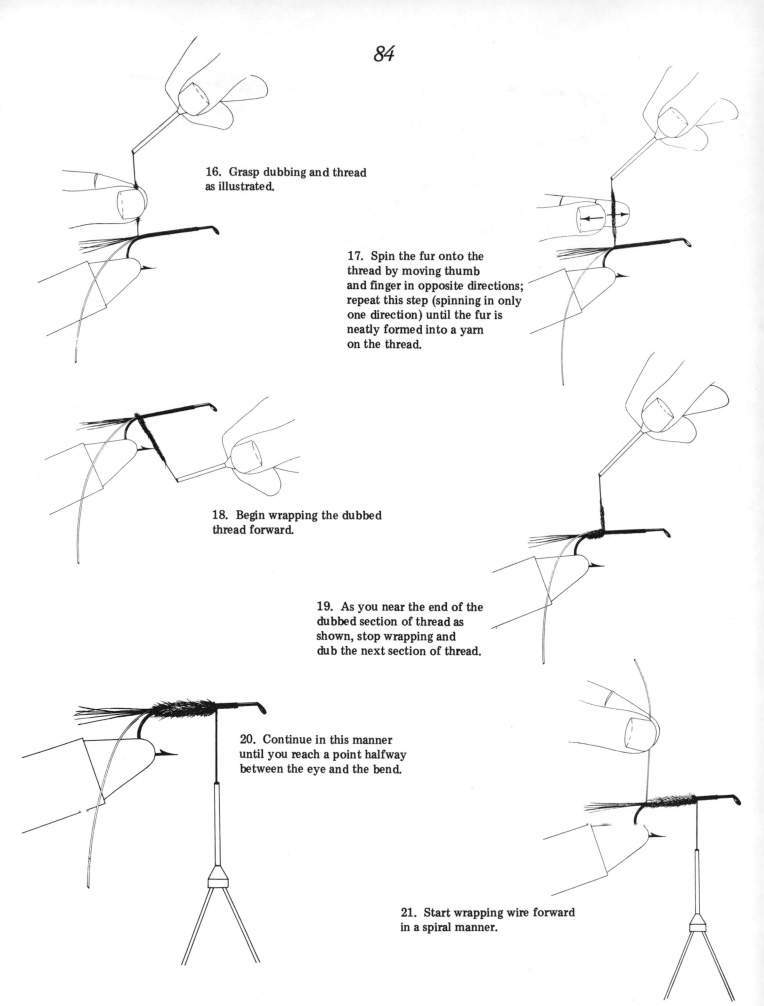

16. Grasp dubbing and thread as illustrated.

17. Spin the fur onto the thread by moving thumb and finger in opposite directions; repeat this step (spinning in only one direction) until the fur is neatly formed into a yarn on the thread.

18. Begin wrapping the dubbed thread forward.

19. As you near the end of the dubbed section of thread as shown, stop wrapping and dub the next section of thread.

20. Continue in this manner until you reach a point halfway between the eye and the bend.

21. Start wrapping wire forward in a spiral manner.

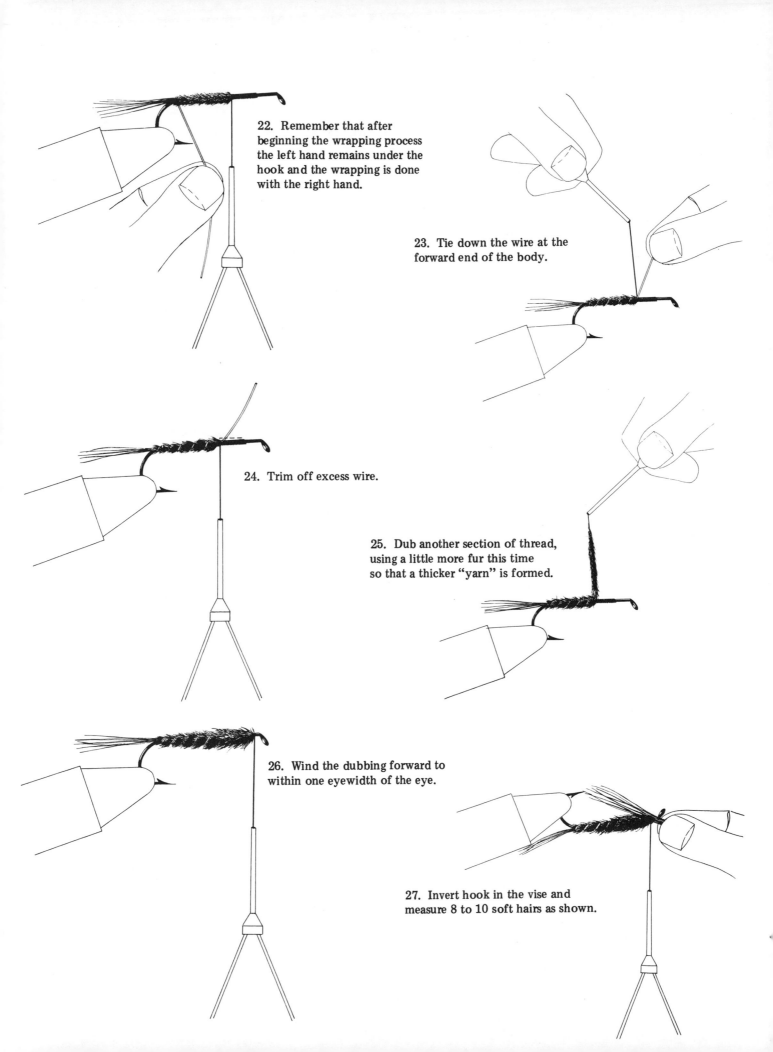

22. Remember that after beginning the wrapping process the left hand remains under the hook and the wrapping is done with the right hand.

23. Tie down the wire at the forward end of the body.

24. Trim off excess wire.

25. Dub another section of thread, using a little more fur this time so that a thicker "yarn" is formed.

26. Wind the dubbing forward to within one eyewidth of the eye.

27. Invert hook in the vise and measure 8 to 10 soft hairs as shown.

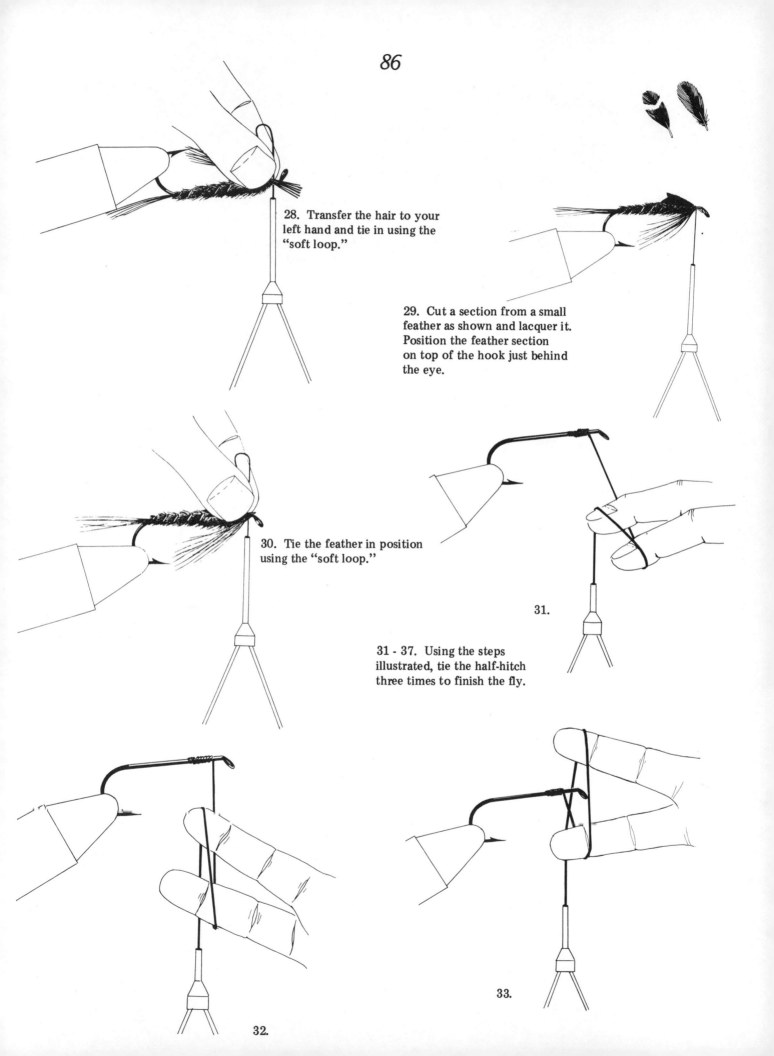

28. Transfer the hair to your left hand and tie in using the "soft loop."

29. Cut a section from a small feather as shown and lacquer it. Position the feather section on top of the hook just behind the eye.

30. Tie the feather in position using the "soft loop."

31.

31 - 37. Using the steps illustrated, tie the half-hitch three times to finish the fly.

32.

33.

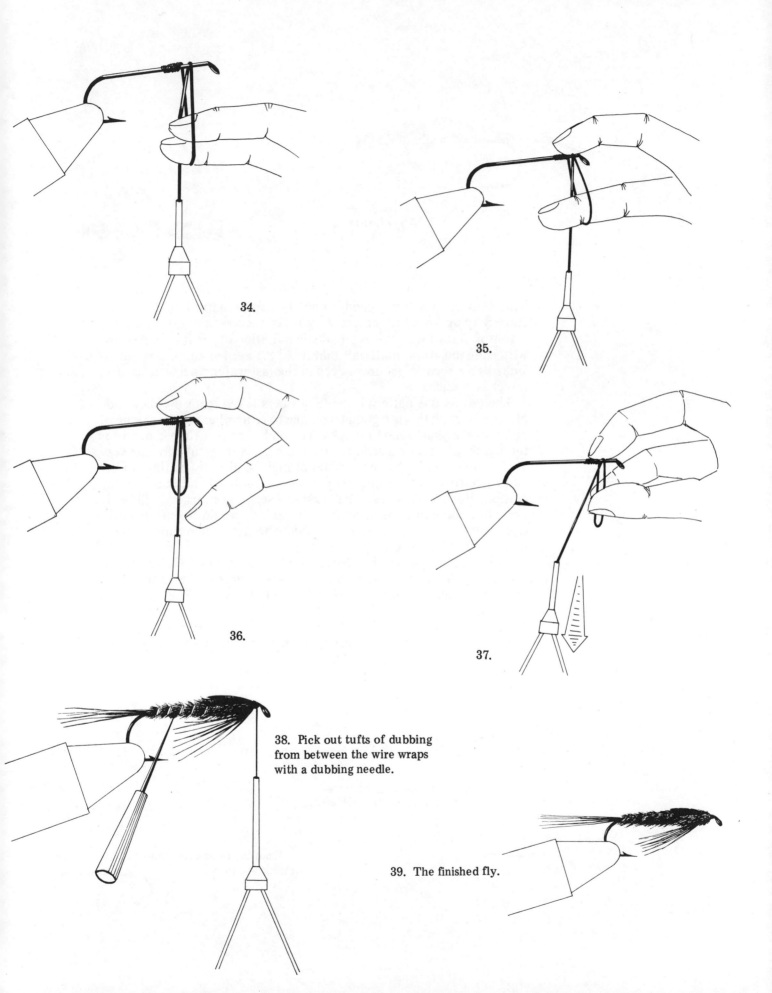

34.

35.

36.

37.

38. Pick out tufts of dubbing from between the wire wraps with a dubbing needle.

39. The finished fly.

Pattern 4

This pattern is a very good stone fly nymph imitation that Don started tying about eight years ago. Its success is most likely the result of many factors; it is a realistic imitation of the insect, it is tied with enough natural materials that it has the needed animation, and it sinks like a rock to get down deep in the fast water where the natural insect is found.

The tail on this pattern is made of fibers taken from the short side of a goose quill; this is a good technique to remember for the tailing of many of the short-tailed nymphs. The abdomen is a rubber band for the lighter colors, or a strip cut from a bicycle innertube for the very dark imitations. Latex sheet material may be used by cutting rubber band-size strips from it, but why not use a rubber band and save the cutting? For the wing case we illustrate a section of turkey quill being used, but goose quill or pheasant tail sections would be just as effective. The thorax area is heavily dubbed with a hackle wound through it to imitate legs and to provide animation.

Although this pattern involves a lot of steps, it is not difficult to tie. The only thing that is likely to give you problems is the wrapping of the rubber band so that a nicely tapered body results. The key to this step is to stretch the rubber band when you start wrapping and then decrease the tension with each wrap as you go forward. Each wrap should overlap the previous one by about one-third of the width of the rubber band.

1. Start attaching the thread at the center of the hook shank.

2. Wrap the thread forward four or five turns.

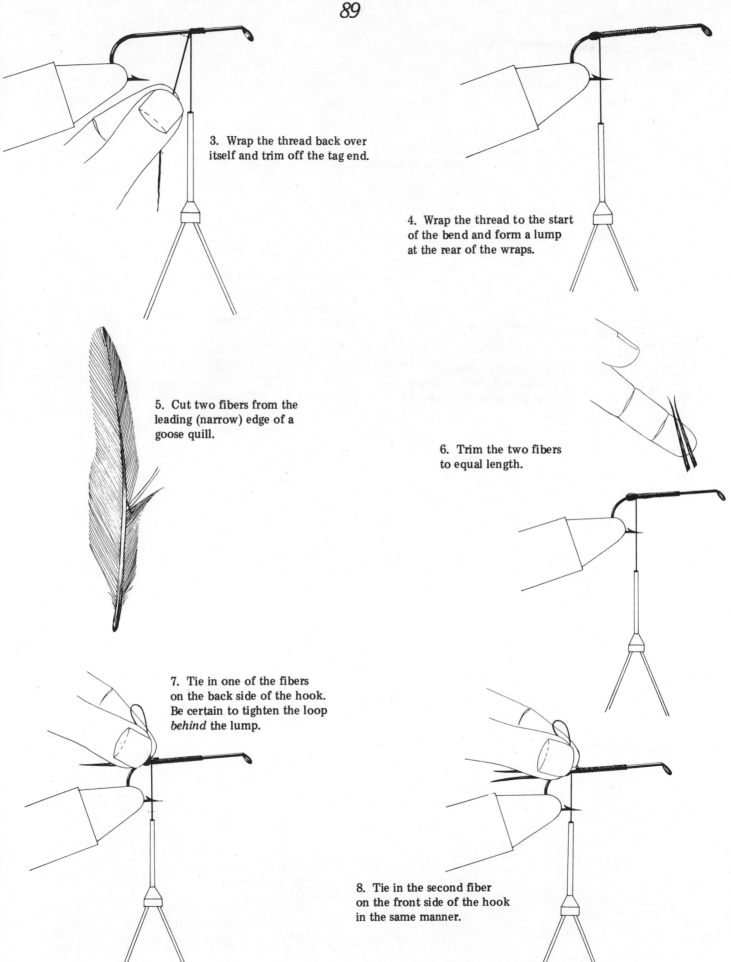

3. Wrap the thread back over itself and trim off the tag end.

4. Wrap the thread to the start of the bend and form a lump at the rear of the wraps.

5. Cut two fibers from the leading (narrow) edge of a goose quill.

6. Trim the two fibers to equal length.

7. Tie in one of the fibers on the back side of the hook. Be certain to tighten the loop *behind* the lump.

8. Tie in the second fiber on the front side of the hook in the same manner.

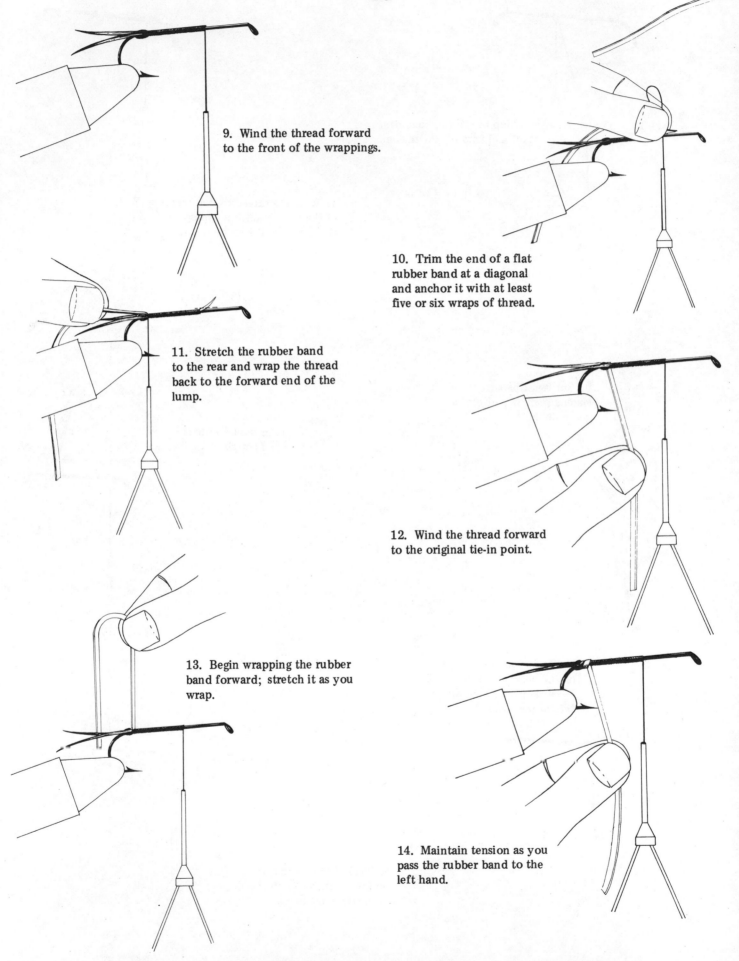

9. Wind the thread forward to the front of the wrappings.

10. Trim the end of a flat rubber band at a diagonal and anchor it with at least five or six wraps of thread.

11. Stretch the rubber band to the rear and wrap the thread back to the forward end of the lump.

12. Wind the thread forward to the original tie-in point.

13. Begin wrapping the rubber band forward; stretch it as you wrap.

14. Maintain tension as you pass the rubber band to the left hand.

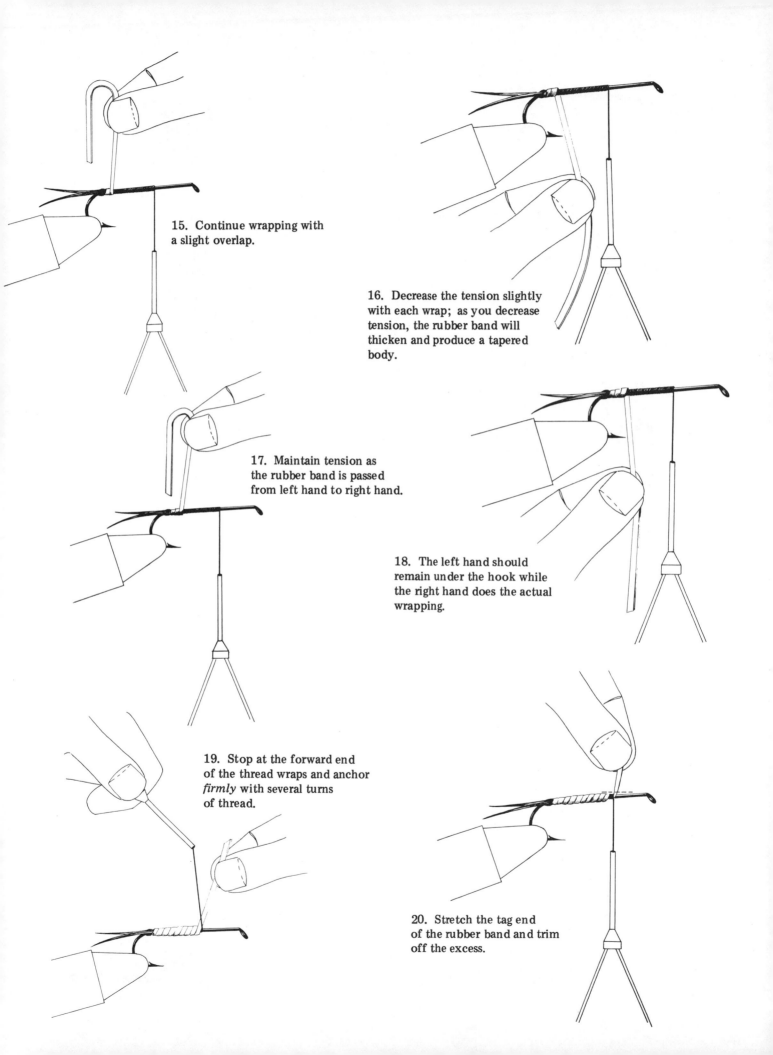

15. Continue wrapping with a slight overlap.

16. Decrease the tension slightly with each wrap; as you decrease tension, the rubber band will thicken and produce a tapered body.

17. Maintain tension as the rubber band is passed from left hand to right hand.

18. The left hand should remain under the hook while the right hand does the actual wrapping.

19. Stop at the forward end of the thread wraps and anchor *firmly* with several turns of thread.

20. Stretch the tag end of the rubber band and trim off the excess.

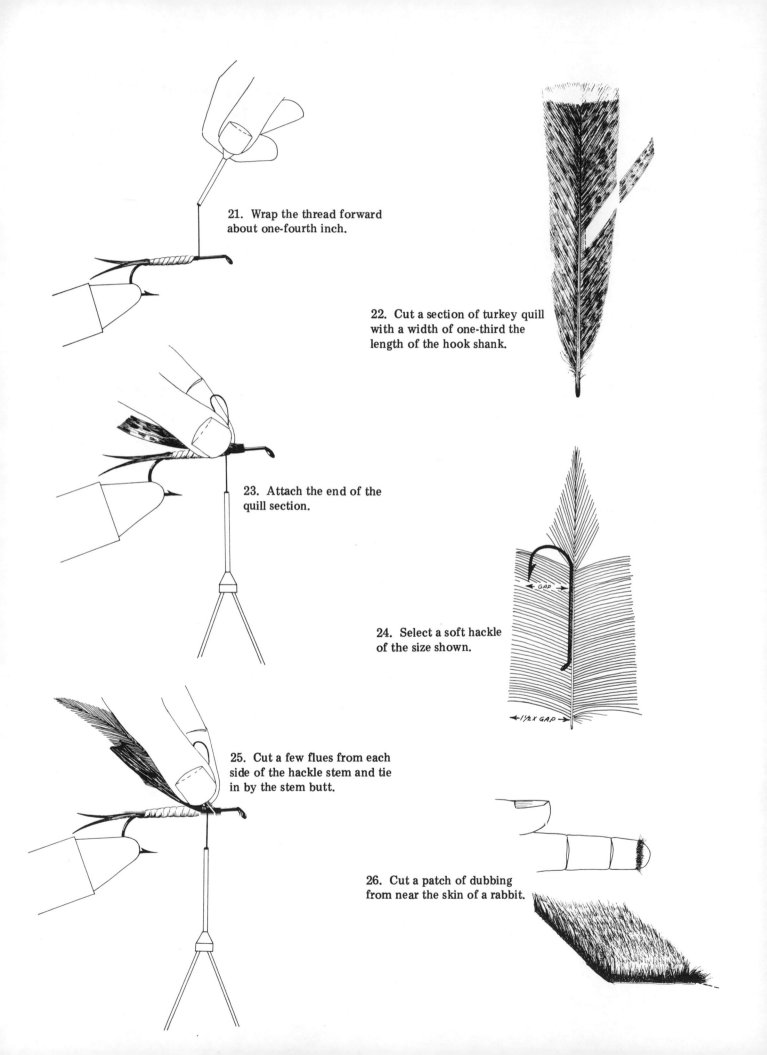

21. Wrap the thread forward about one-fourth inch.

22. Cut a section of turkey quill with a width of one-third the length of the hook shank.

23. Attach the end of the quill section.

24. Select a soft hackle of the size shown.

GAP

←1½x GAP→

25. Cut a few flues from each side of the hackle stem and tie in by the stem butt.

26. Cut a patch of dubbing from near the skin of a rabbit.

27. Spread the dubbing along a section of the thread.

28. Hold the dubbing as shown.

29. Spin the fur onto the thread by moving thumb and finger in opposite directions; repeat the spinning technique until a smooth fur "yarn" is formed.

30. Slide the dubbing down the thread to the hook shank.

31. Begin wrapping the dubbing forward.

32. Stop the dubbing at a point one eyewidth back from the eye of the hook.

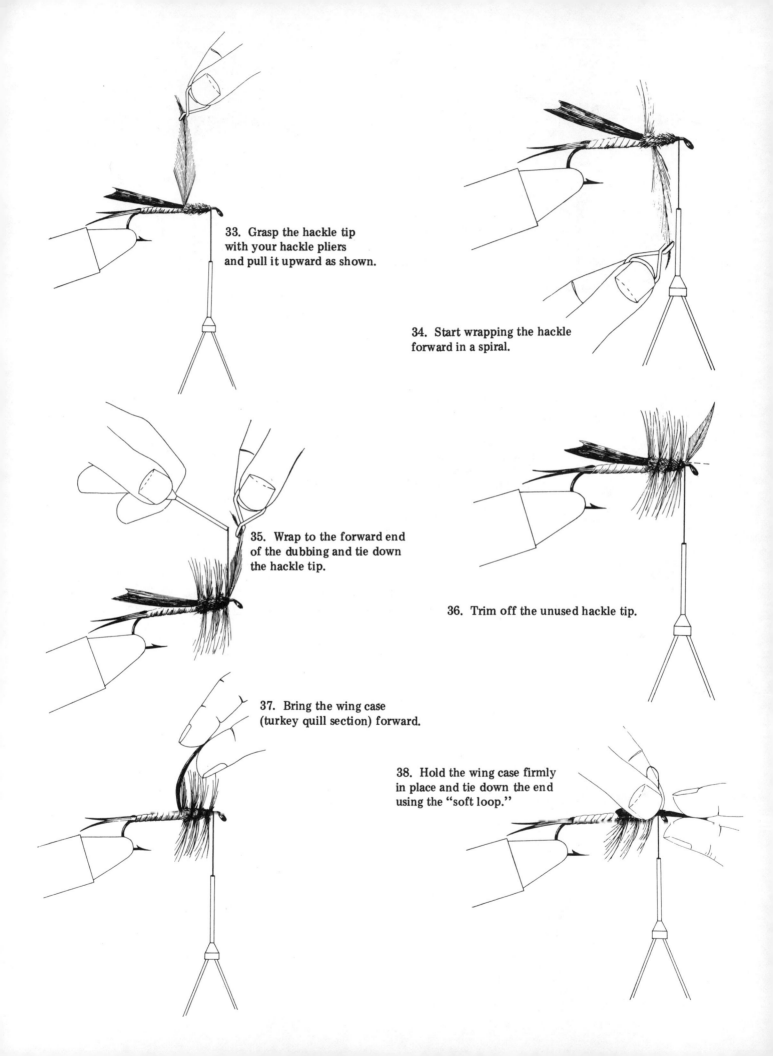

33. Grasp the hackle tip with your hackle pliers and pull it upward as shown.

34. Start wrapping the hackle forward in a spiral.

35. Wrap to the forward end of the dubbing and tie down the hackle tip.

36. Trim off the unused hackle tip.

37. Bring the wing case (turkey quill section) forward.

38. Hold the wing case firmly in place and tie down the end using the "soft loop."

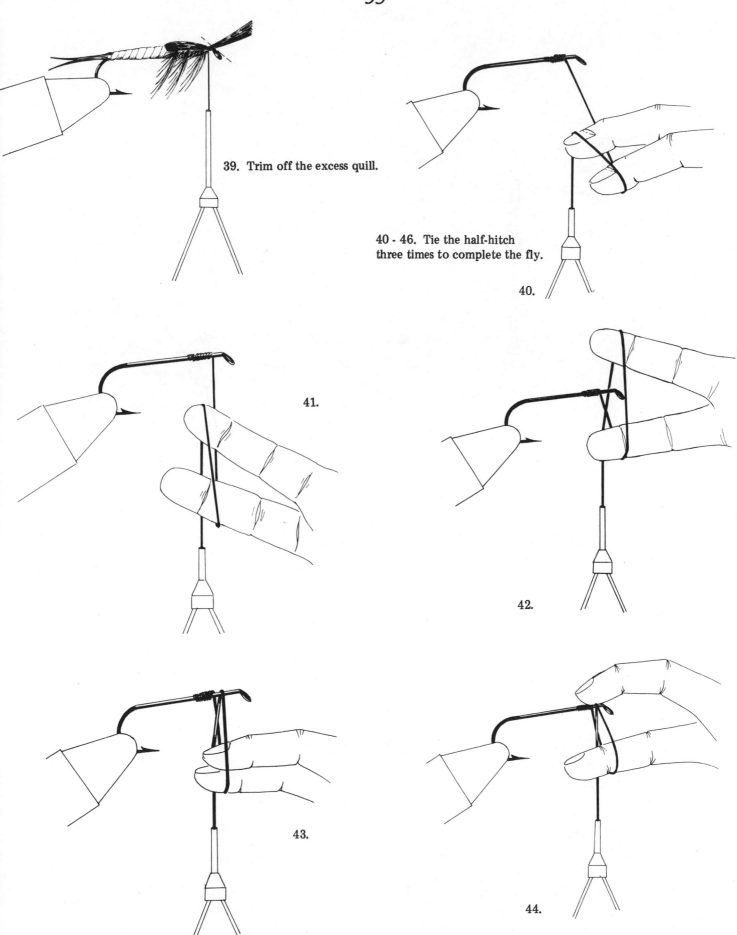

39. Trim off the excess quill.

40 - 46. Tie the half-hitch
three times to complete the fly.

40.

41.

42.

43.

44.

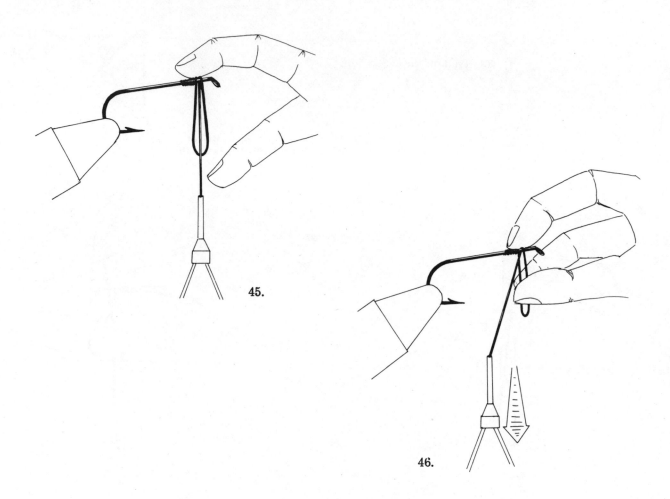

45.

46.

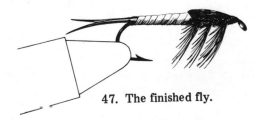

47. The finished fly.

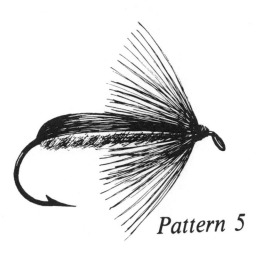

Pattern 5

The pattern that we have selected to present as a caddis-fly pupa imitation was developed by Mr. Bob Good. Although this pattern is not a truly realistic imitation of the insect, it does offer a general appearance of the pupa and is very effective.

The wing case, as we illustrate it, is from a goose quill; the body is wool yarn; and the soft antennae is imitated with a hackle wound at the head. The wing case could also be made from turkey quill section, a section of pheasant tail, or even a strip of floss. You could use dubbing for the body, but peacock would work, and so would many other materials. Instead of a wound hackle at the head, you might choose to use a throat hackle or very small hackle tips tied in on either side of the hook to represent emerging wings.

This is the first time that you will be winding hackle, so pay particular attention to the steps involved. Be especially aware of the correct proportion for the hackle: the hackle should have fibers that are one and a half times the gap of the hook; to easily make this measurement, hold the hackle across the underside of the hook and flare the hackle as it will be when wrapped.

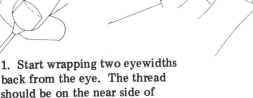

2. Wrap over the top of the hook (away from you) to a point one eyewidth back from the eye.

1. Start wrapping two eyewidths back from the eye. The thread should be on the near side of the hook.

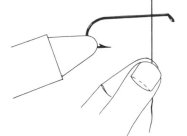

3. Wrap the thread back over itself to the start of the wrap.

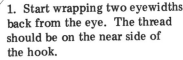

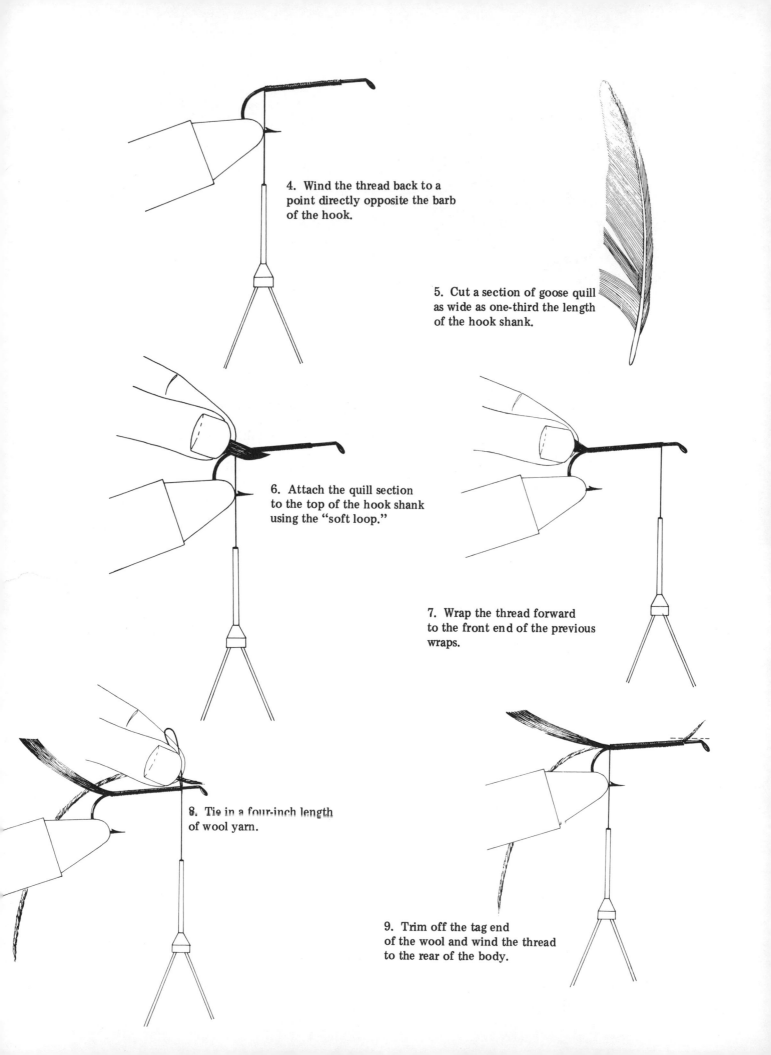

4. Wind the thread back to a point directly opposite the barb of the hook.

5. Cut a section of goose quill as wide as one-third the length of the hook shank.

6. Attach the quill section to the top of the hook shank using the "soft loop."

7. Wrap the thread forward to the front end of the previous wraps.

8. Tie in a four-inch length of wool yarn.

9. Trim off the tag end of the wool and wind the thread to the rear of the body.

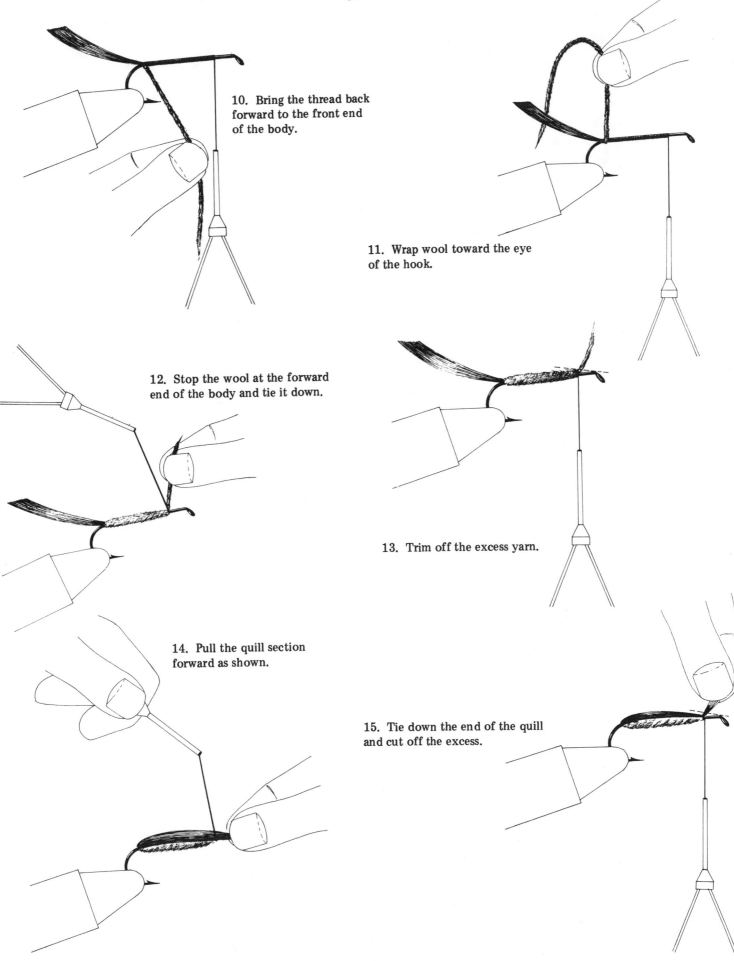

10. Bring the thread back forward to the front end of the body.

11. Wrap wool toward the eye of the hook.

12. Stop the wool at the forward end of the body and tie it down.

13. Trim off the excess yarn.

14. Pull the quill section forward as shown.

15. Tie down the end of the quill and cut off the excess.

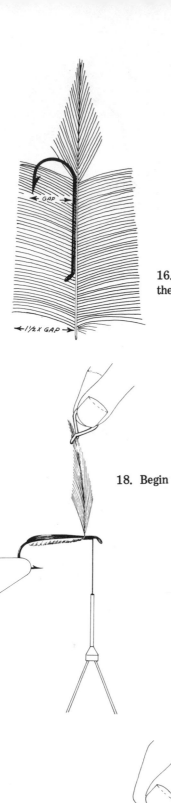

16. Select a hackle of the proper proportion.

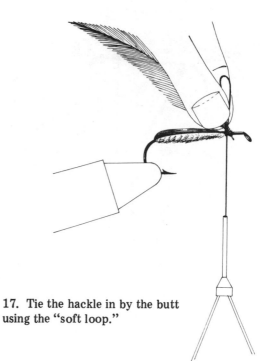

17. Tie the hackle in by the butt using the "soft loop."

18. Begin wrapping the hackle.

19. Wind the hackle to within one eyewidth of the eye and tie it down.

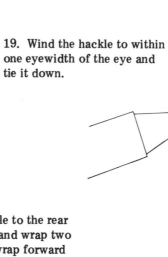

20. Flare the hackle to the rear with the left hand and wrap two turns back on it; wrap forward to form the head and tie the half-hitch three times. Lacquer the head.

21. The finished fly.

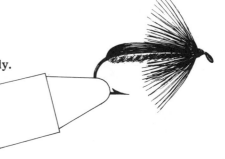

Pattern 6

The midge (Diptera) pupa imitation should look familiar to you; it is basically the same fly that we tied as an imitation of the Diptera larva. Since we want to represent the pupal stage though, we have added a wing case. For the wing case we have chosen a turkey quill section, but as we mentioned in the stone-fly nymph, pheasant or goose quill will work equally well. A latex strip or a bunch of soft hair might be used also. The tail on the larval imitation that we illustrated was soft hackle fibers, as was the throat. For this pattern you might use soft hair or fibers from a duck flank feather or a soft body feather such as partridge. Just as in the larval imitation, the size range should be from #16 to #24, but you should practice first with a size 12.

1. Start wrapping two eyewidths back from the eye. The thread should be on the near side of the hook.

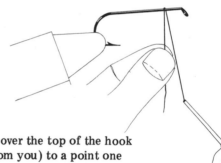

2. Wrap over the top of the hook (away from you) to a point one eyewidth back from the eye.

3. Wrap the thread back over itself to the start of the wrap.

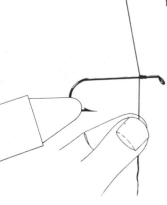

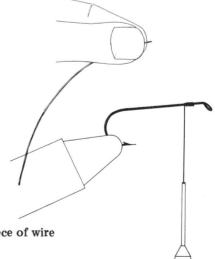

4. Hold a four-inch piece of wire in your left hand.

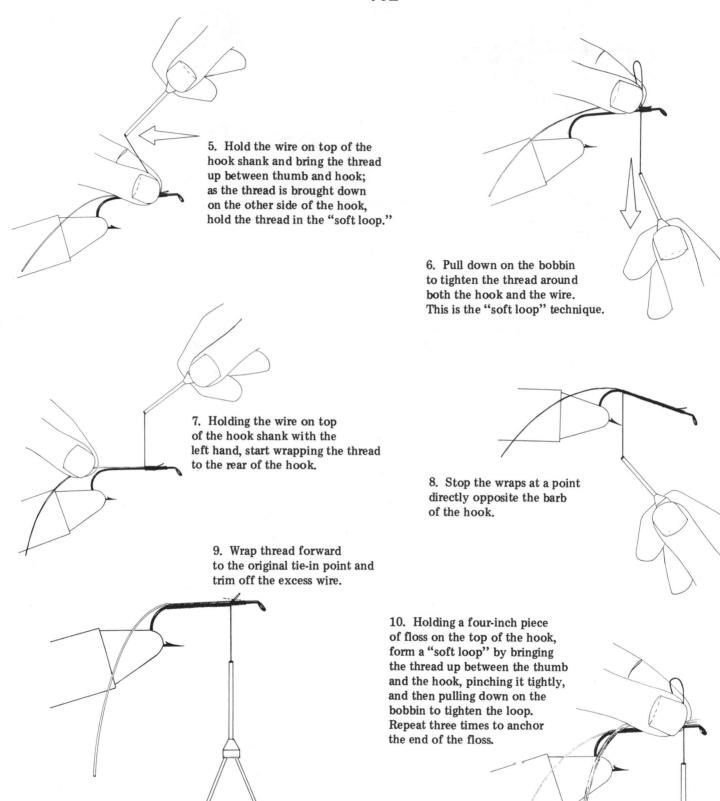

5. Hold the wire on top of the hook shank and bring the thread up between thumb and hook; as the thread is brought down on the other side of the hook, hold the thread in the "soft loop."

6. Pull down on the bobbin to tighten the thread around both the hook and the wire. This is the "soft loop" technique.

7. Holding the wire on top of the hook shank with the left hand, start wrapping the thread to the rear of the hook.

8. Stop the wraps at a point directly opposite the barb of the hook.

9. Wrap thread forward to the original tie-in point and trim off the excess wire.

10. Holding a four-inch piece of floss on the top of the hook, form a "soft loop" by bringing the thread up between the thumb and the hook, pinching it tightly, and then pulling down on the bobbin to tighten the loop. Repeat three times to anchor the end of the floss.

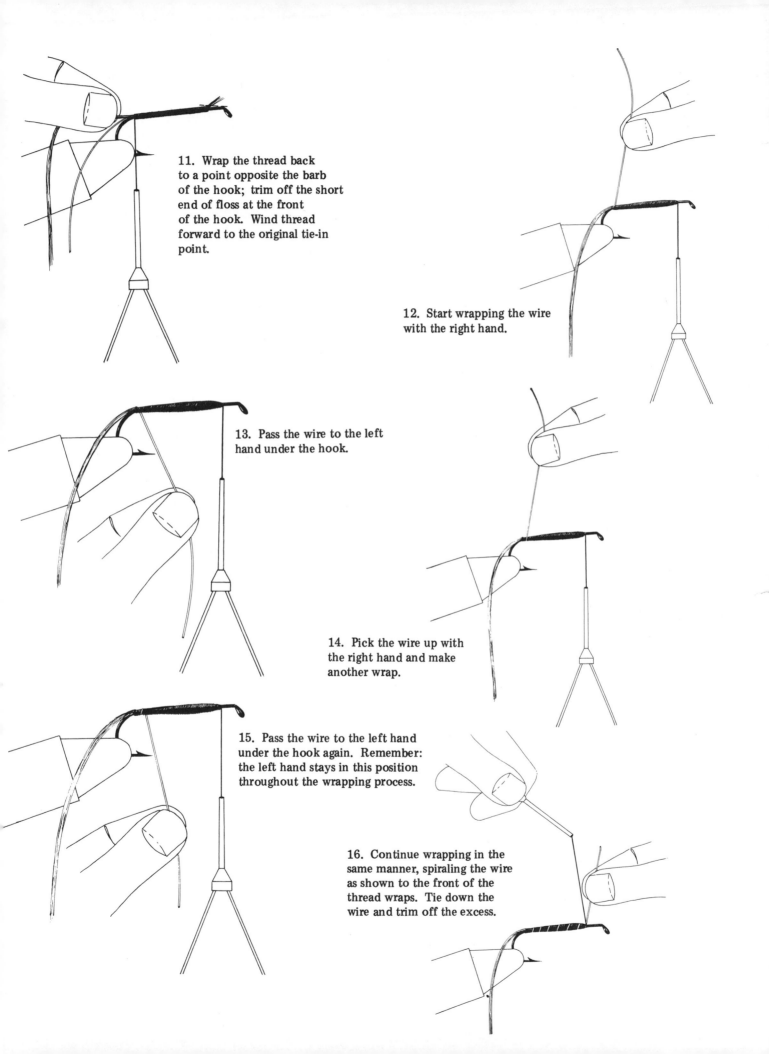

11. Wrap the thread back to a point opposite the barb of the hook; trim off the short end of floss at the front of the hook. Wind thread forward to the original tie-in point.

12. Start wrapping the wire with the right hand.

13. Pass the wire to the left hand under the hook.

14. Pick the wire up with the right hand and make another wrap.

15. Pass the wire to the left hand under the hook again. Remember: the left hand stays in this position throughout the wrapping process.

16. Continue wrapping in the same manner, spiraling the wire as shown to the front of the thread wraps. Tie down the wire and trim off the excess.

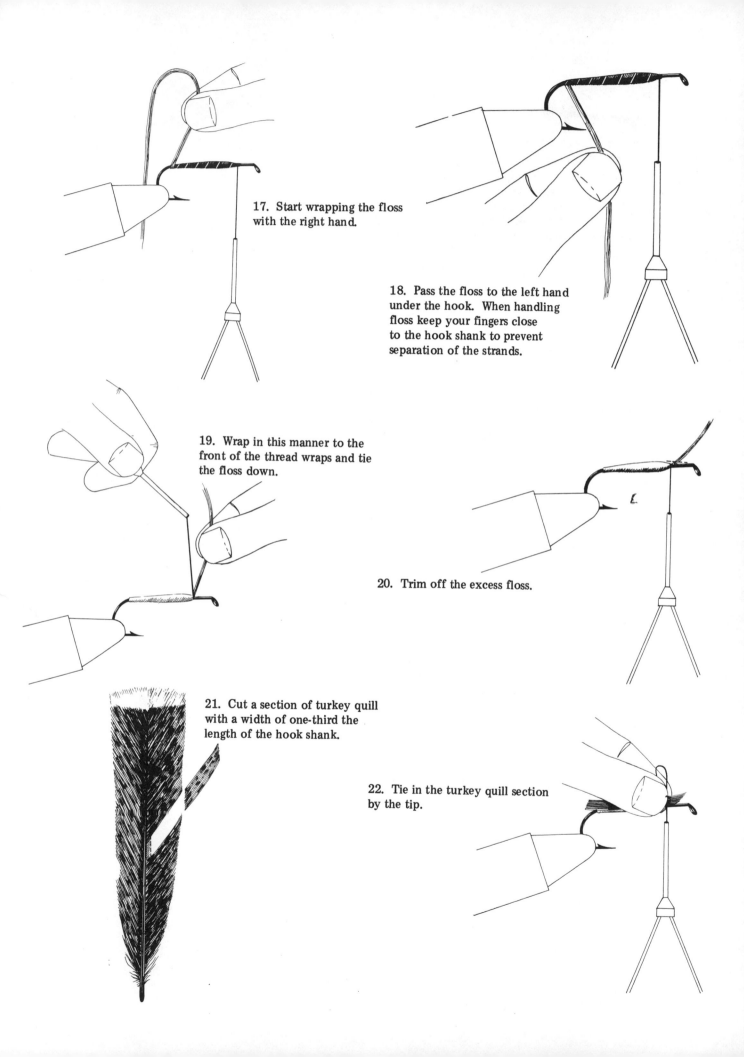

17. Start wrapping the floss with the right hand.

18. Pass the floss to the left hand under the hook. When handling floss keep your fingers close to the hook shank to prevent separation of the strands.

19. Wrap in this manner to the front of the thread wraps and tie the floss down.

20. Trim off the excess floss.

21. Cut a section of turkey quill with a width of one-third the length of the hook shank.

22. Tie in the turkey quill section by the tip.

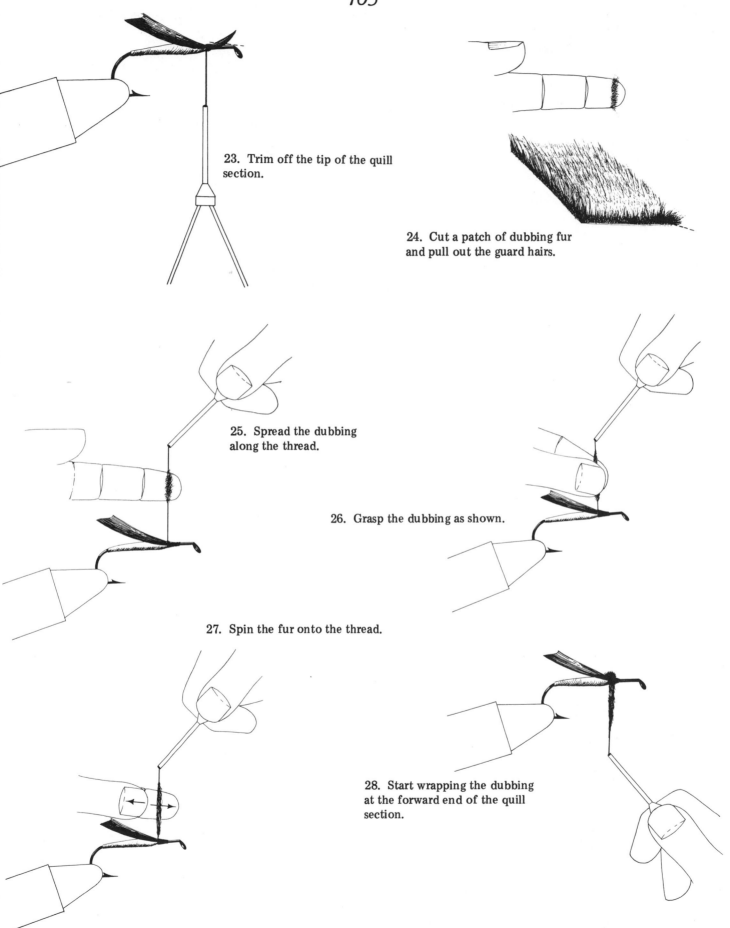

23. Trim off the tip of the quill section.

24. Cut a patch of dubbing fur and pull out the guard hairs.

25. Spread the dubbing along the thread.

26. Grasp the dubbing as shown.

27. Spin the fur onto the thread.

28. Start wrapping the dubbing at the forward end of the quill section.

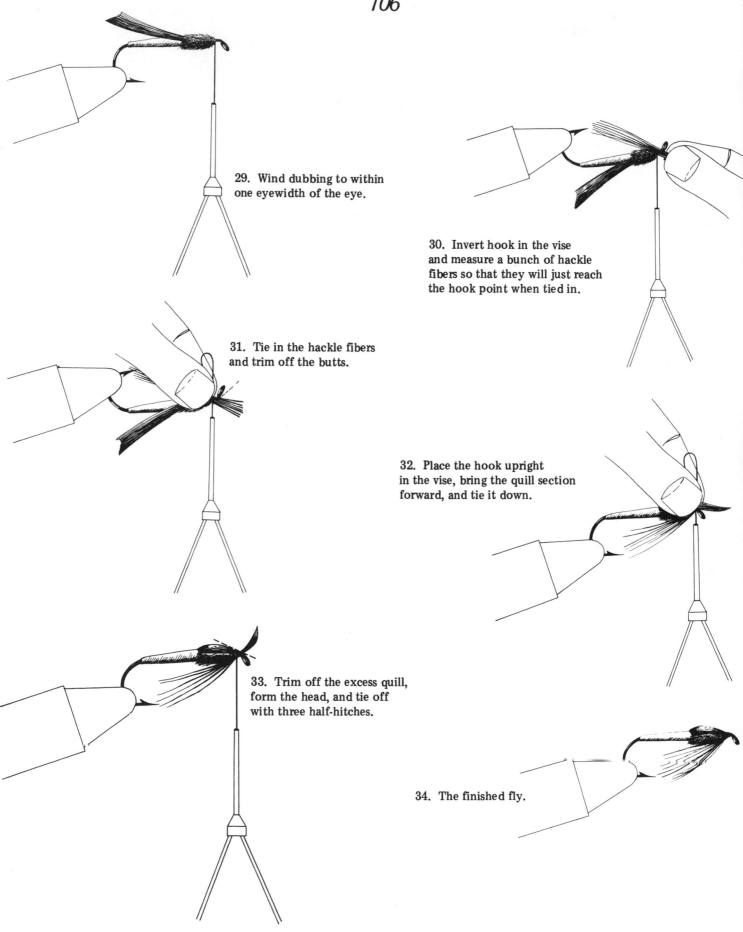

29. Wind dubbing to within one eyewidth of the eye.

30. Invert hook in the vise and measure a bunch of hackle fibers so that they will just reach the hook point when tied in.

31. Tie in the hackle fibers and trim off the butts.

32. Place the hook upright in the vise, bring the quill section forward, and tie it down.

33. Trim off the excess quill, form the head, and tie off with three half-hitches.

34. The finished fly.

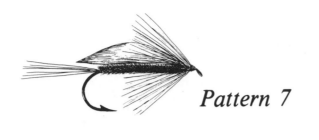

Pattern 7

For an imitation of a mayfly (Ephemeroptera) emerger we have chosen a typical wet-fly pattern. You'll remember that as the mayfly nymph begins its trip to the surface to emerge, the wings may be starting to unfurl, and this is displayed by the quill wing on this pattern. The tail is a bunch of soft hackle fibers, the body is peacock, the wing is made from sections of duck quill, and soft hackle is used to represent the legs and antennae.

There are many wet-fly patterns that are tied in the same basic manner as this one. Some use floss for the body, some use dubbing. Chenille and wool are also used.

Tying a quill wing such as we are using here is often the most difficult technique for the beginner to learn. We can't overemphasize the importance of holding the wing FIRMLY in place as you tie the soft loops to anchor it. Make two soft loops around the quill sections before relaxing your hold on the wings. Another common problem is the tendency to use quill sections that are too wide; each section should be about one-third as wide as the hook shank is long.

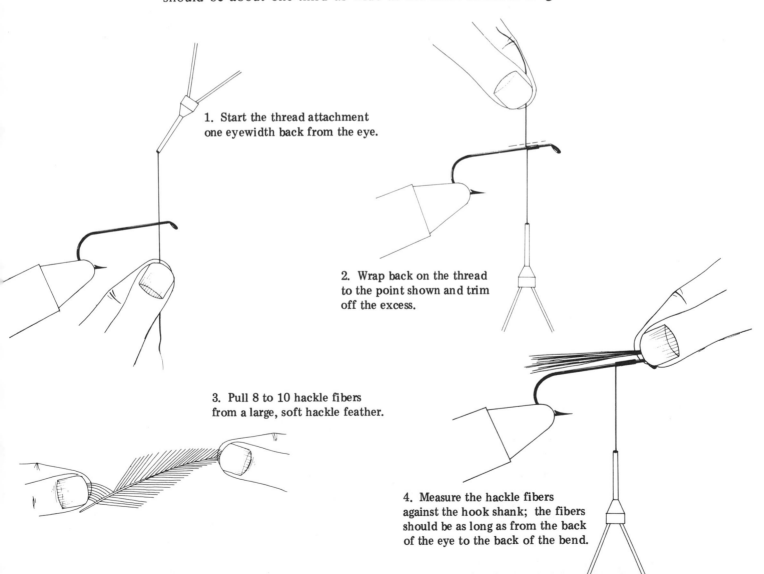

1. Start the thread attachment one eyewidth back from the eye.

2. Wrap back on the thread to the point shown and trim off the excess.

3. Pull 8 to 10 hackle fibers from a large, soft hackle feather.

4. Measure the hackle fibers against the hook shank; the fibers should be as long as from the back of the eye to the back of the bend.

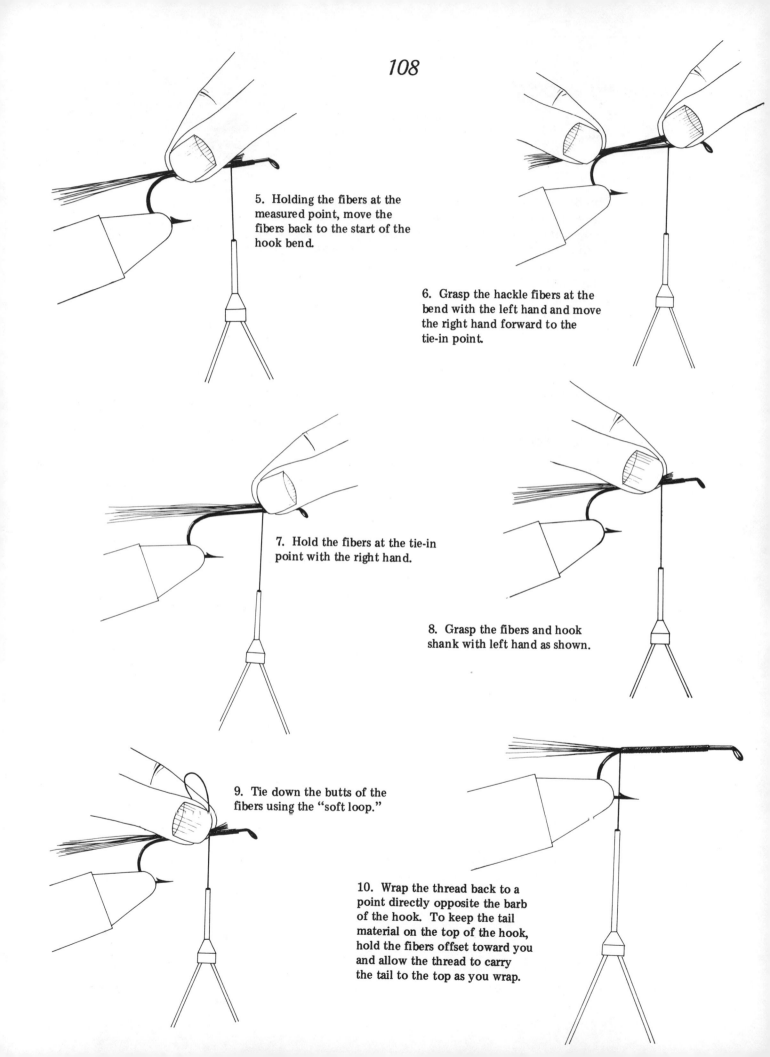

5. Holding the fibers at the measured point, move the fibers back to the start of the hook bend.

6. Grasp the hackle fibers at the bend with the left hand and move the right hand forward to the tie-in point.

7. Hold the fibers at the tie-in point with the right hand.

8. Grasp the fibers and hook shank with left hand as shown.

9. Tie down the butts of the fibers using the "soft loop."

10. Wrap the thread back to a point directly opposite the barb of the hook. To keep the tail material on the top of the hook, hold the fibers offset toward you and allow the thread to carry the tail to the top as you wrap.

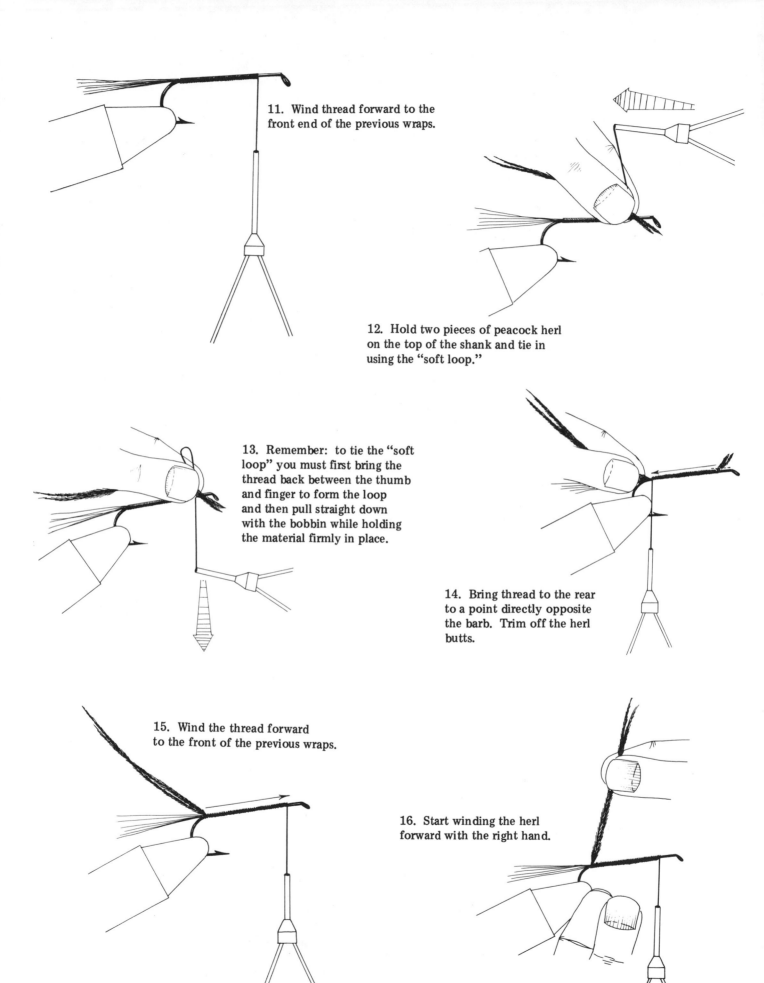

11. Wind thread forward to the front end of the previous wraps.

12. Hold two pieces of peacock herl on the top of the shank and tie in using the "soft loop."

13. Remember: to tie the "soft loop" you must first bring the thread back between the thumb and finger to form the loop and then pull straight down with the bobbin while holding the material firmly in place.

14. Bring thread to the rear to a point directly opposite the barb. Trim off the herl butts.

15. Wind the thread forward to the front of the previous wraps.

16. Start winding the herl forward with the right hand.

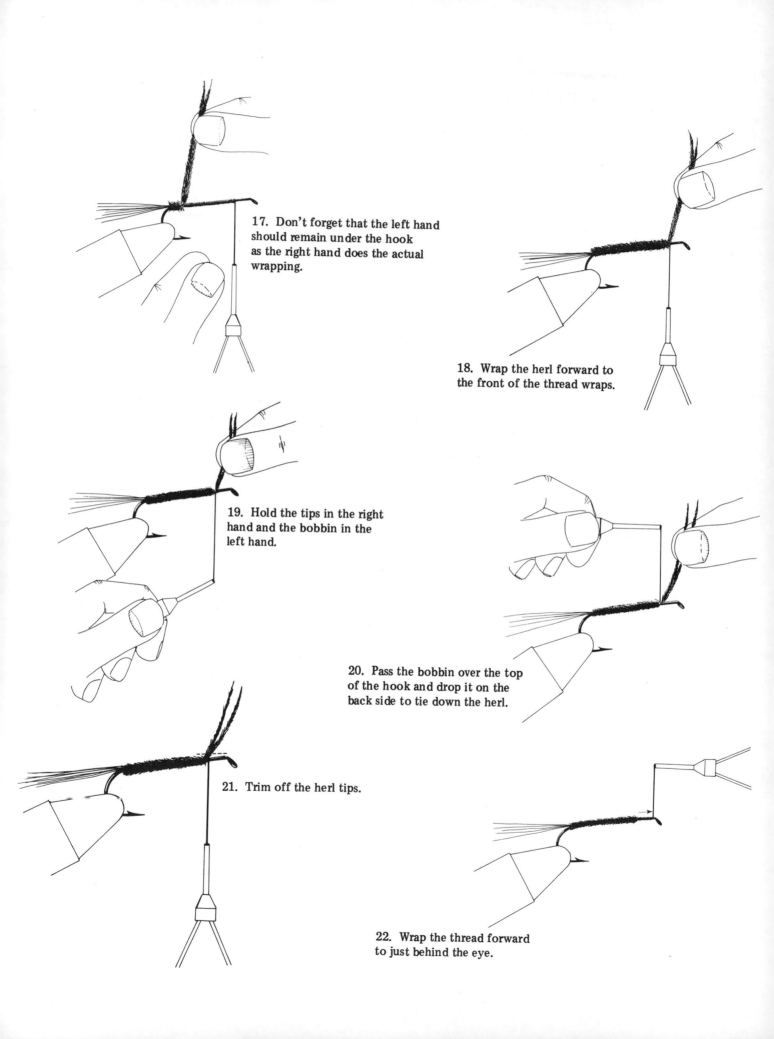

17. Don't forget that the left hand should remain under the hook as the right hand does the actual wrapping.

18. Wrap the herl forward to the front of the thread wraps.

19. Hold the tips in the right hand and the bobbin in the left hand.

20. Pass the bobbin over the top of the hook and drop it on the back side to tie down the herl.

21. Trim off the herl tips.

22. Wrap the thread forward to just behind the eye.

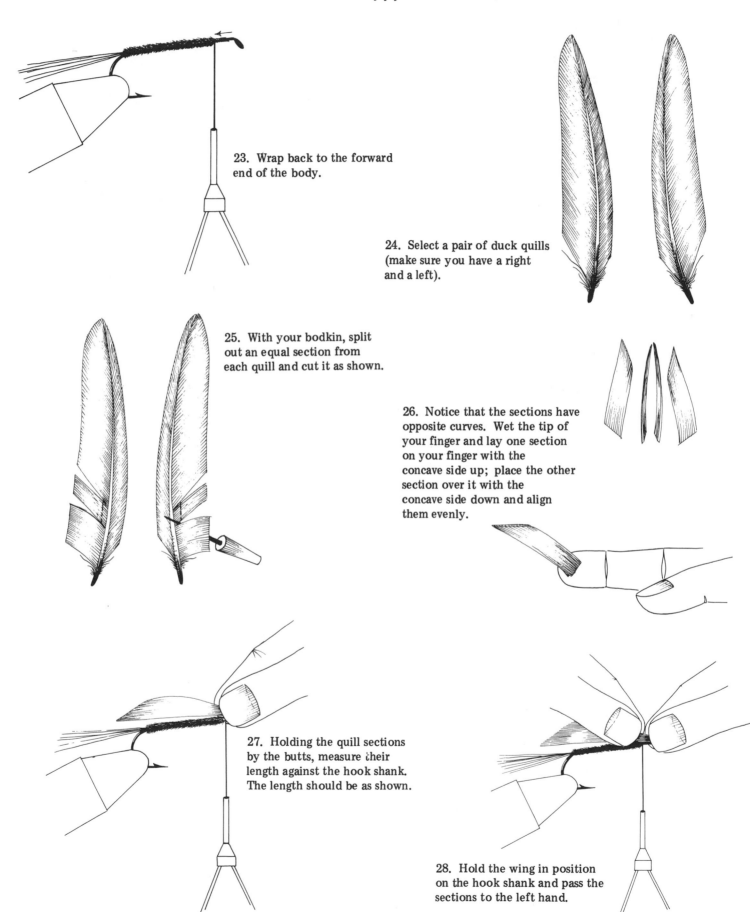

23. Wrap back to the forward end of the body.

24. Select a pair of duck quills (make sure you have a right and a left).

25. With your bodkin, split out an equal section from each quill and cut it as shown.

26. Notice that the sections have opposite curves. Wet the tip of your finger and lay one section on your finger with the concave side up; place the other section over it with the concave side down and align them evenly.

27. Holding the quill sections by the butts, measure their length against the hook shank. The length should be as shown.

28. Hold the wing in position on the hook shank and pass the sections to the left hand.

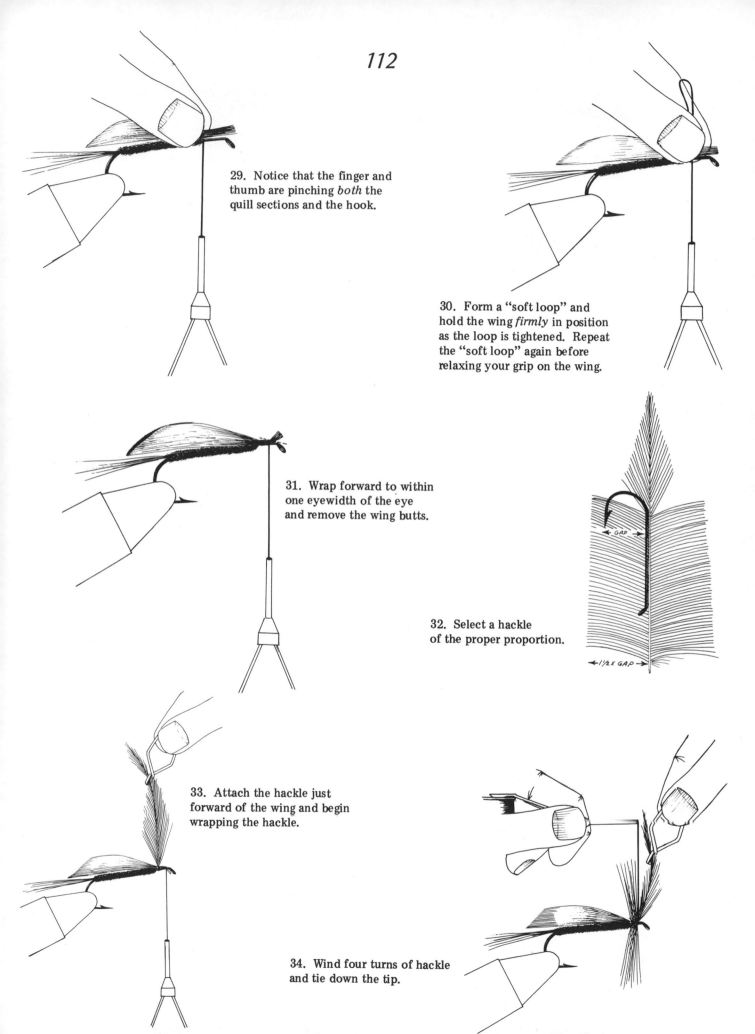

29. Notice that the finger and thumb are pinching *both* the quill sections and the hook.

30. Form a "soft loop" and hold the wing *firmly* in position as the loop is tightened. Repeat the "soft loop" again before relaxing your grip on the wing.

31. Wrap forward to within one eyewidth of the eye and remove the wing butts.

32. Select a hackle of the proper proportion.

33. Attach the hackle just forward of the wing and begin wrapping the hackle.

34. Wind four turns of hackle and tie down the tip.

35. Trim off the hackle tip.

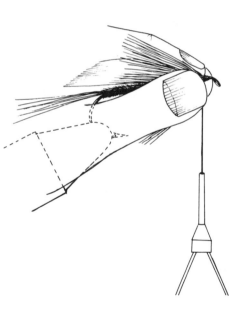

36. Sweep the hackle to the rear with the left hand and wrap back on it so that it remains in this flared position. Form the head, tie off with three half-hitches, and lacquer the head.

37. The finished fly.

Pattern 8

The mayfly (Ephemeroptera) adult imitations are the most used dry flies; for this reason we are going to illustrate how to tie four different types of these flies. The main difference among the types is the method of wing construction.

This pattern is tied using a quill wing such as you used on the mayfly emerger. Watch it, though, for there are some minor changes. Here the quill sections are reversed in reference to each other; for this pattern we want the convex sides of the wings together. Also there is a variation in the tying-in step: notice that the wing is attached *before* the body is wrapped and that it is tied in in the opposite direction.

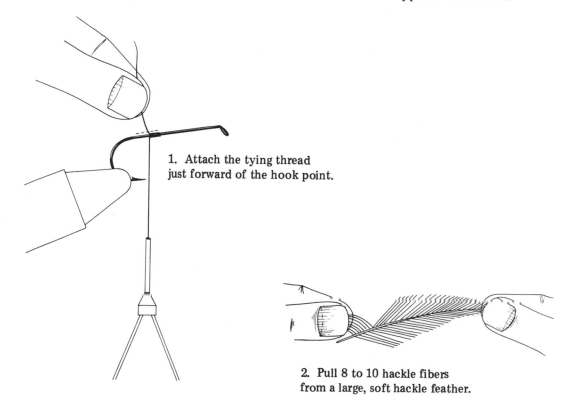

1. Attach the tying thread just forward of the hook point.

2. Pull 8 to 10 hackle fibers from a large, soft hackle feather.

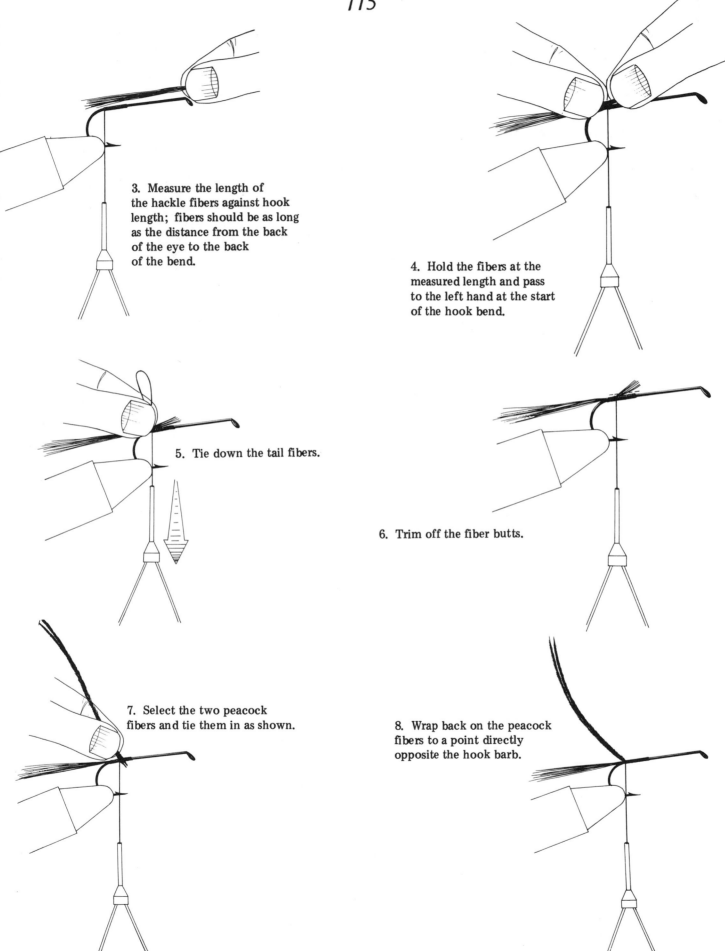

3. Measure the length of the hackle fibers against hook length; fibers should be as long as the distance from the back of the eye to the back of the bend.

4. Hold the fibers at the measured length and pass to the left hand at the start of the hook bend.

5. Tie down the tail fibers.

6. Trim off the fiber butts.

7. Select the two peacock fibers and tie them in as shown.

8. Wrap back on the peacock fibers to a point directly opposite the hook barb.

9. Wind thread forward
to a point two eyewidths
from the eye.

10. Select a pair of duck quills
(make sure you have a right
and a left).

11. With you bodkin, split
out an equal section from
each quill and cut it as shown.

12. Arrange the quill sections
on your wet fingertip; this time
the two convex sides should be
together so that the sections
flare away from each other.

13. Measure the wing length
against the hook shank. The wing
length should be equal to the
distance from the back of the bend
to the back of the eye.

14. Move the paired sections
to the forward end of the thread
and attach them using the
"soft loop."

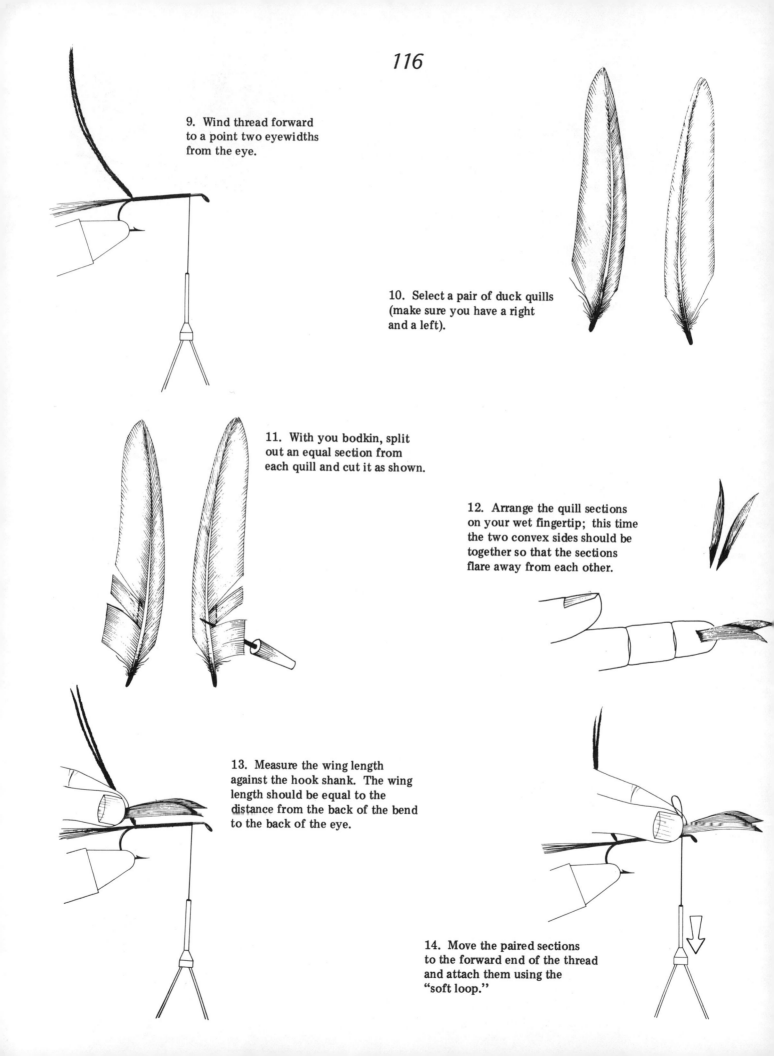

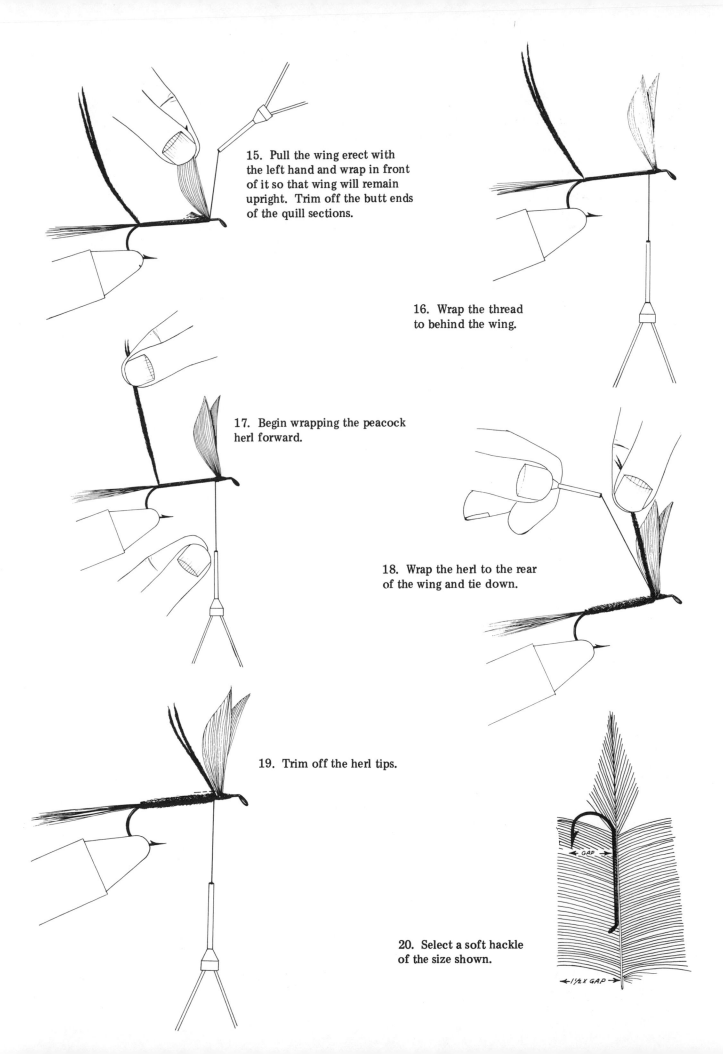

15. Pull the wing erect with the left hand and wrap in front of it so that wing will remain upright. Trim off the butt ends of the quill sections.

16. Wrap the thread to behind the wing.

17. Begin wrapping the peacock herl forward.

18. Wrap the herl to the rear of the wing and tie down.

19. Trim off the herl tips.

20. Select a soft hackle of the size shown.

GAP

1½ X GAP

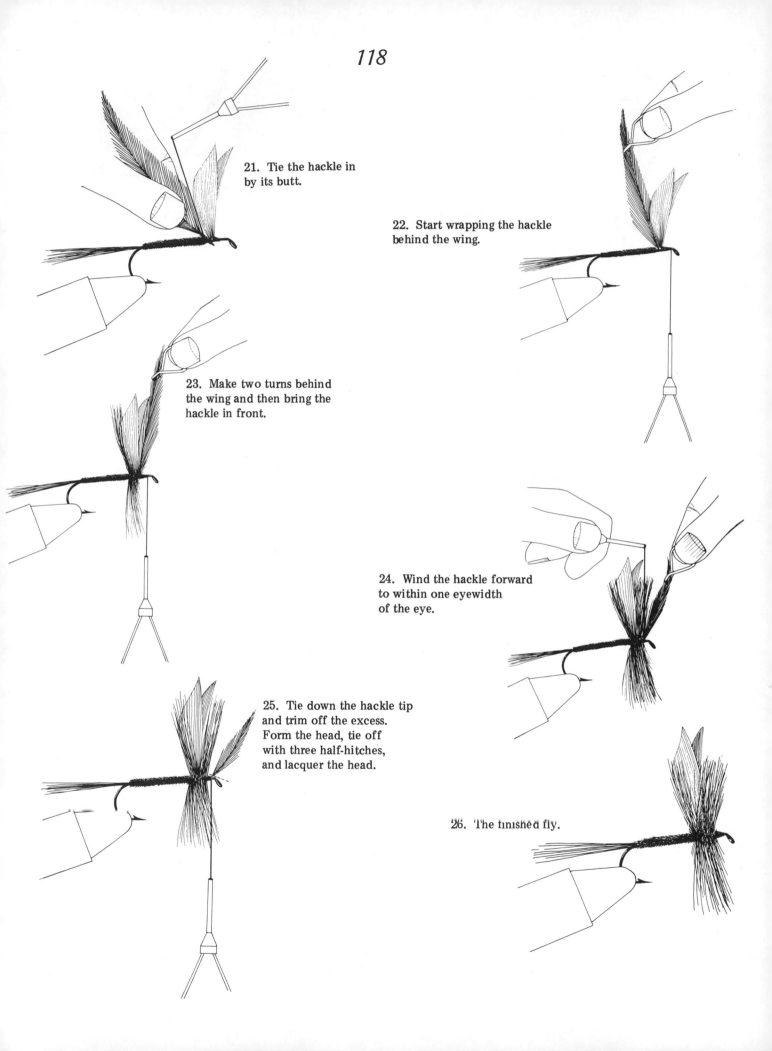

21. Tie the hackle in by its butt.

22. Start wrapping the hackle behind the wing.

23. Make two turns behind the wing and then bring the hackle in front.

24. Wind the hackle forward to within one eyewidth of the eye.

25. Tie down the hackle tip and trim off the excess. Form the head, tie off with three half-hitches, and lacquer the head.

26. The finished fly.

Pattern 9

This is another mayfly imitation, this time using a hackle-tip wing. The hackle-tip wing is easier for most people to tie than the quill wing, and it is more durable.

There is one seemingly illogical point about a hackle-tip wing: the smaller the fly that you are tying, the larger the hackle that you select the wing from. Since we need a shorter wing for the smaller flies, we have to cut it from nearer the tip of the hackle. A small hackle is so slim at the tip that a section cut from it will be too narrow for the fly. By cutting the tip from a larger hackle, it will be wider and better proportioned for use as a wing.

You should be getting the idea by now that there is nothing sacred about a particular arrangement of tail type, body material, or method of wing construction; all the individual parts may be arranged in any manner, and this is what accounts for the tremendous number of patterns that we have today. The only difference between a mosquito and an Adams is the body: one is dubbed and the other is tied with moose mane. There are many pairs like this that are identical except for the type of wing used or the method of tail construction. Tie to imitate insects—not patterns.

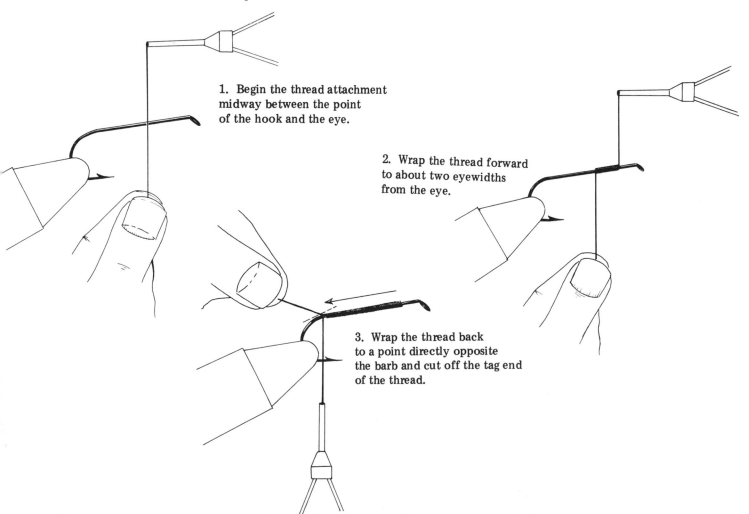

1. Begin the thread attachment midway between the point of the hook and the eye.

2. Wrap the thread forward to about two eyewidths from the eye.

3. Wrap the thread back to a point directly opposite the barb and cut off the tag end of the thread.

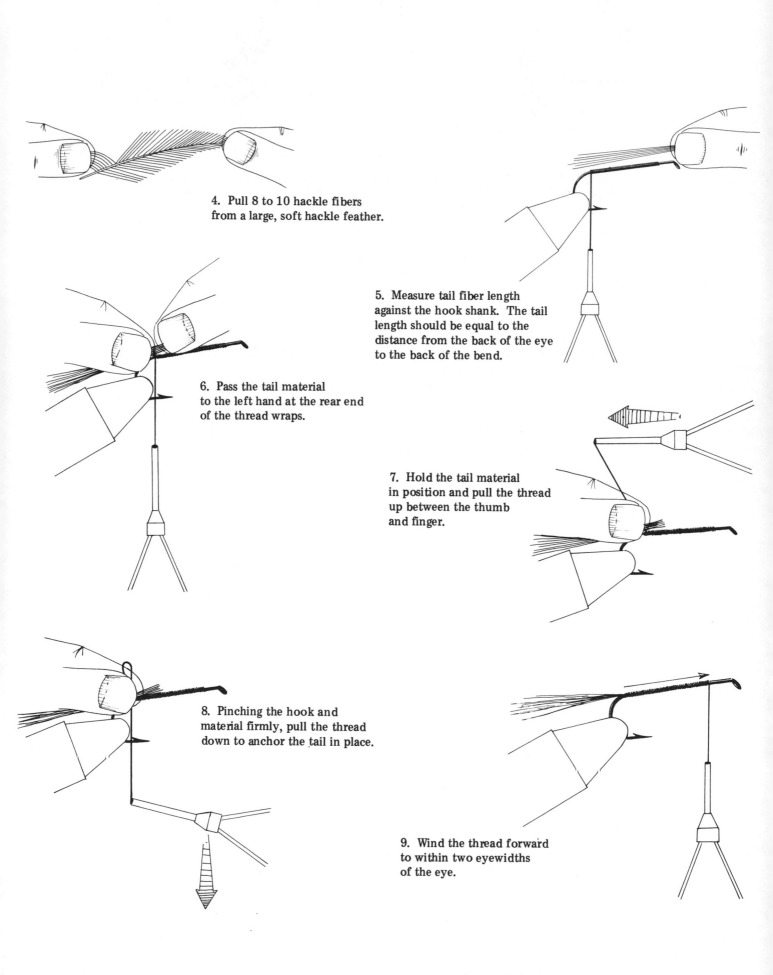

4. Pull 8 to 10 hackle fibers from a large, soft hackle feather.

5. Measure tail fiber length against the hook shank. The tail length should be equal to the distance from the back of the eye to the back of the bend.

6. Pass the tail material to the left hand at the rear end of the thread wraps.

7. Hold the tail material in position and pull the thread up between the thumb and finger.

8. Pinching the hook and material firmly, pull the thread down to anchor the tail in place.

9. Wind the thread forward to within two eyewidths of the eye.

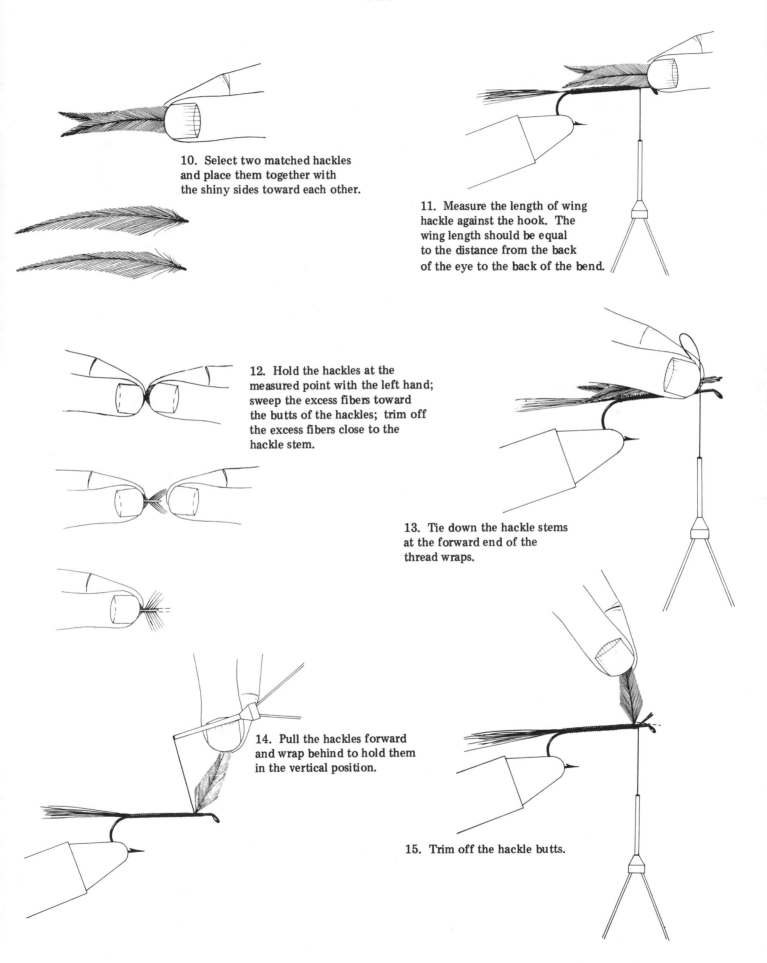

10. Select two matched hackles and place them together with the shiny sides toward each other.

11. Measure the length of wing hackle against the hook. The wing length should be equal to the distance from the back of the eye to the back of the bend.

12. Hold the hackles at the measured point with the left hand; sweep the excess fibers toward the butts of the hackles; trim off the excess fibers close to the hackle stem.

13. Tie down the hackle stems at the forward end of the thread wraps.

14. Pull the hackles forward and wrap behind to hold them in the vertical position.

15. Trim off the hackle butts.

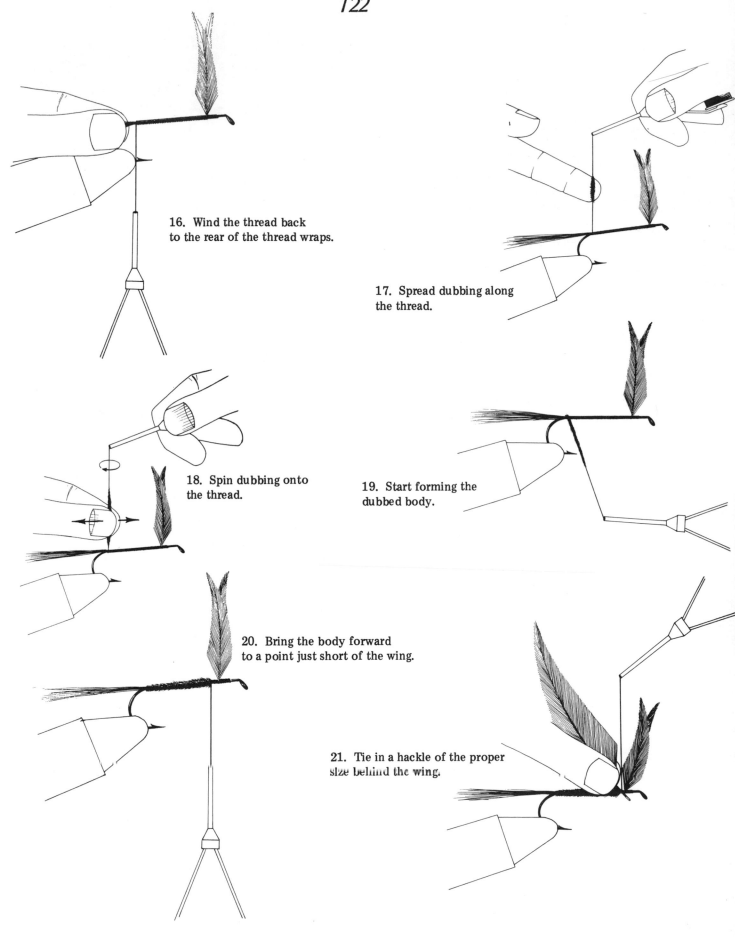

16. Wind the thread back to the rear of the thread wraps.

17. Spread dubbing along the thread.

18. Spin dubbing onto the thread.

19. Start forming the dubbed body.

20. Bring the body forward to a point just short of the wing.

21. Tie in a hackle of the proper size behind the wing.

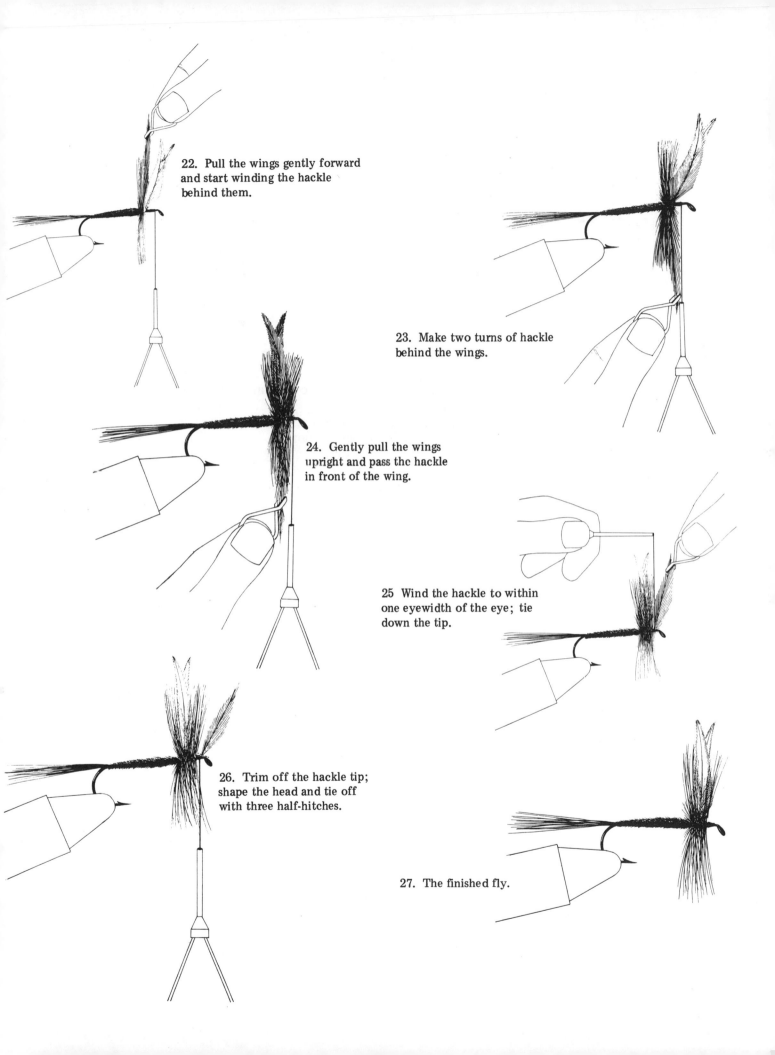

22. Pull the wings gently forward and start winding the hackle behind them.

23. Make two turns of hackle behind the wings.

24. Gently pull the wings upright and pass the hackle in front of the wing.

25 Wind the hackle to within one eyewidth of the eye; tie down the tip.

26. Trim off the hackle tip; shape the head and tie off with three half-hitches.

27. The finished fly.

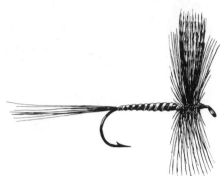

Pattern 10

This is another type of mayfly adult pattern. The method of wing construction that you will be using for this fly is called a rolled wing. As with most procedures used in fly-tying, there are several techniques that may be employed to tie this type of wing. We are using the method that we have found easiest for the beginner to learn.

By now you should realize that proper proportion is critical in order for the finished fly to look right, particularly a dry fly. You will find that as the size of the fly decreases this becomes even more true. The tail should be as long as the distance from the back of the eye to the back of the bend. The hackle needs to be one and one-half times the gap of the hook, and the wing should be twice the gap of the hook.

The body in this pattern is made of the tying thread, which is then wrapped with a stripped peacock herl to provide segmentation; therefore, you must take care as you wrap your thread to produce a smooth body.

The rolled wing provides a very good wing silhouette. Because it is more durable than the quill wing or the hackle-tip wing, we use it more than any other type.

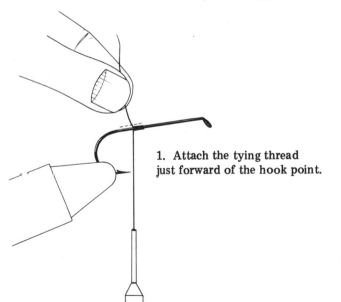

1. Attach the tying thread just forward of the hook point.

2. Pull 8 to 10 hackle fibers from a large, soft hackle feather.

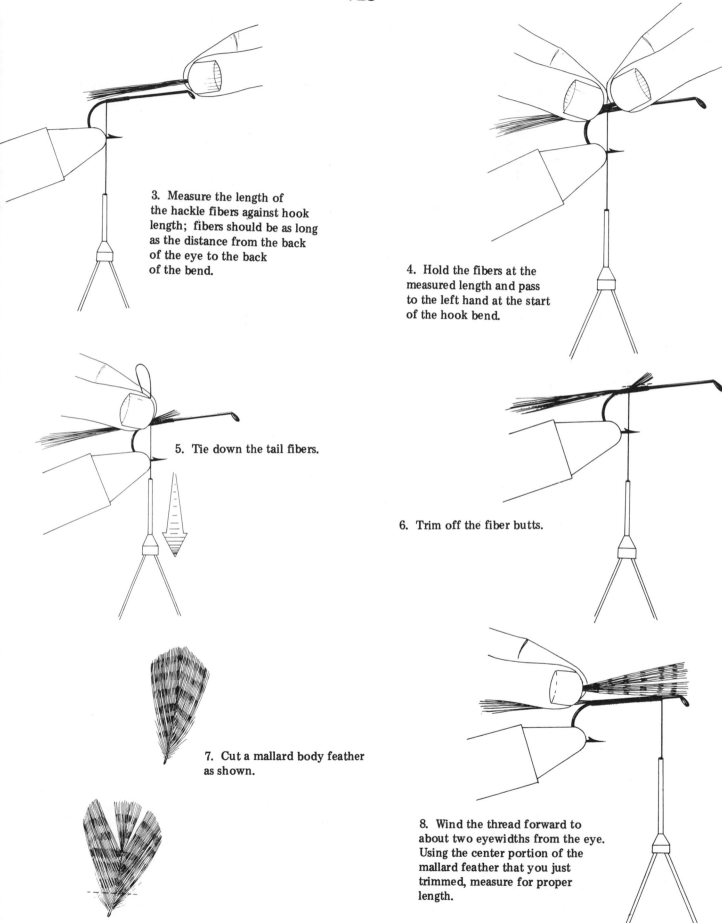

3. Measure the length of the hackle fibers against hook length; fibers should be as long as the distance from the back of the eye to the back of the bend.

4. Hold the fibers at the measured length and pass to the left hand at the start of the hook bend.

5. Tie down the tail fibers.

6. Trim off the fiber butts.

7. Cut a mallard body feather as shown.

8. Wind the thread forward to about two eyewidths from the eye. Using the center portion of the mallard feather that you just trimmed, measure for proper length.

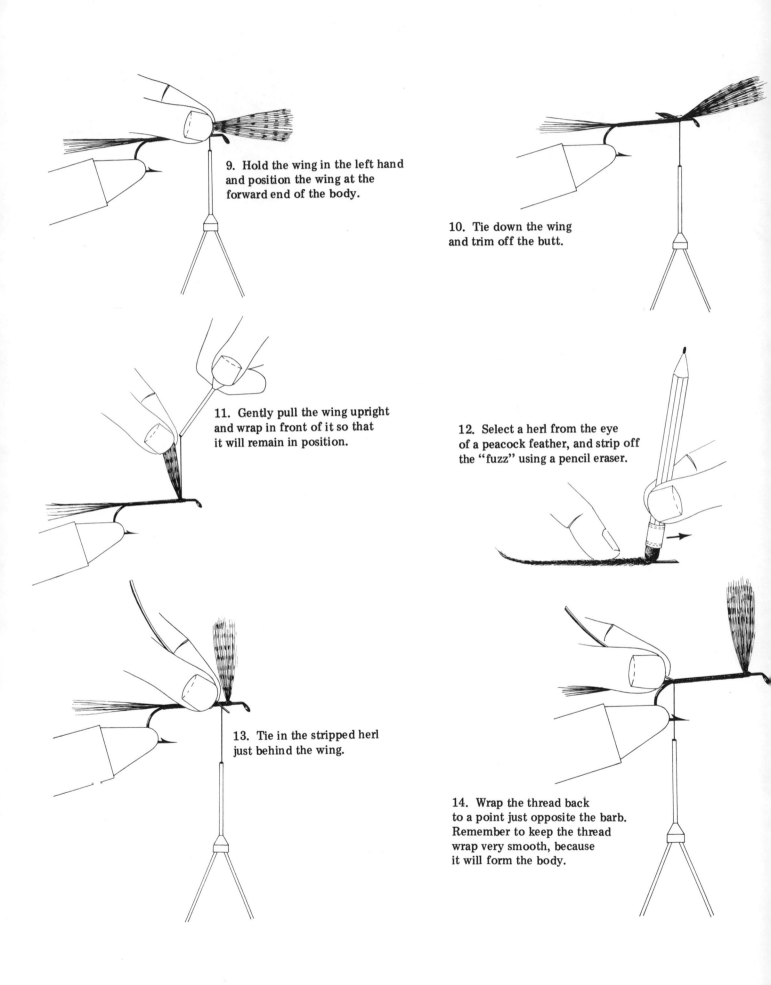

9. Hold the wing in the left hand and position the wing at the forward end of the body.

10. Tie down the wing and trim off the butt.

11. Gently pull the wing upright and wrap in front of it so that it will remain in position.

12. Select a herl from the eye of a peacock feather, and strip off the "fuzz" using a pencil eraser.

13. Tie in the stripped herl just behind the wing.

14. Wrap the thread back to a point just opposite the barb. Remember to keep the thread wrap very smooth, because it will form the body.

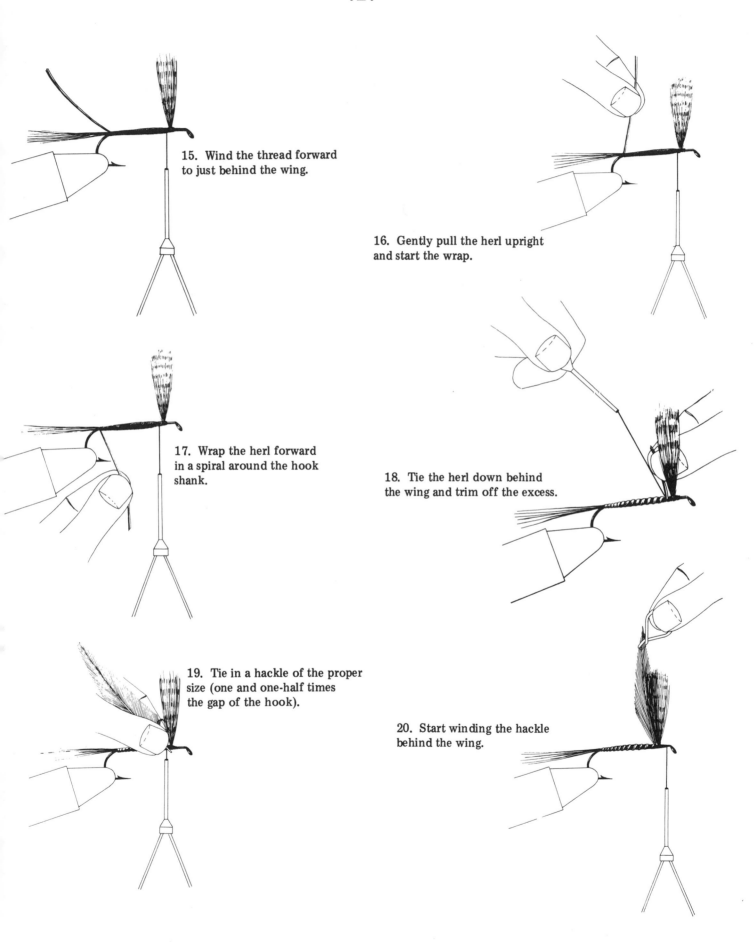

15. Wind the thread forward to just behind the wing.

16. Gently pull the herl upright and start the wrap.

17. Wrap the herl forward in a spiral around the hook shank.

18. Tie the herl down behind the wing and trim off the excess.

19. Tie in a hackle of the proper size (one and one-half times the gap of the hook).

20. Start winding the hackle behind the wing.

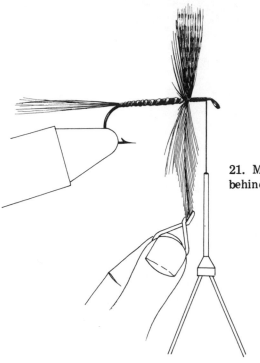

21. Make two turns behind the wing.

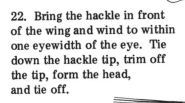

22. Bring the hackle in front of the wing and wind to within one eyewidth of the eye. Tie down the hackle tip, trim off the tip, form the head, and tie off.

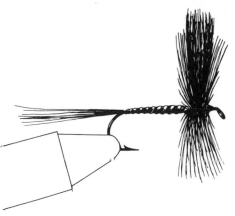

23. The finished fly.

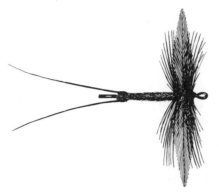

Pattern 11

This pattern is meant to imitate the imago (spinner) stage of the mayfly adult. You'll remember from our discussion of mayflies that they are unique, in that they undergo an additional moult after becoming adults; this is the stage at which mating takes place. After mating has occurred, many of the insects fall to the water in the spent position. For this imitation we have used hackle-tip wings, but a hair wing or hackle fibers could also be used. The body should be dressed a little slimmer than on the emerging adult, and the colors should be somewhat brighter than for the newly emerged adult patterns.

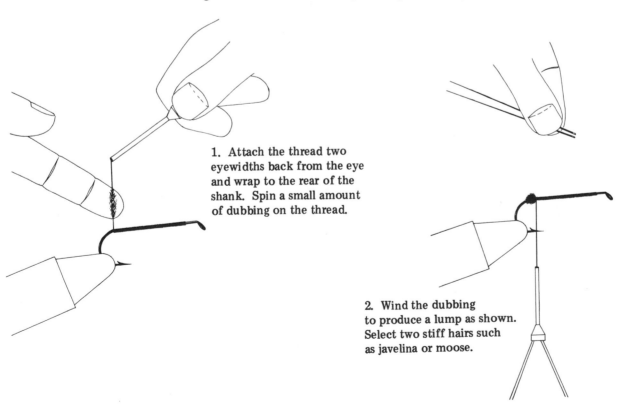

1. Attach the thread two eyewidths back from the eye and wrap to the rear of the shank. Spin a small amount of dubbing on the thread.

2. Wind the dubbing to produce a lump as shown. Select two stiff hairs such as javelina or moose.

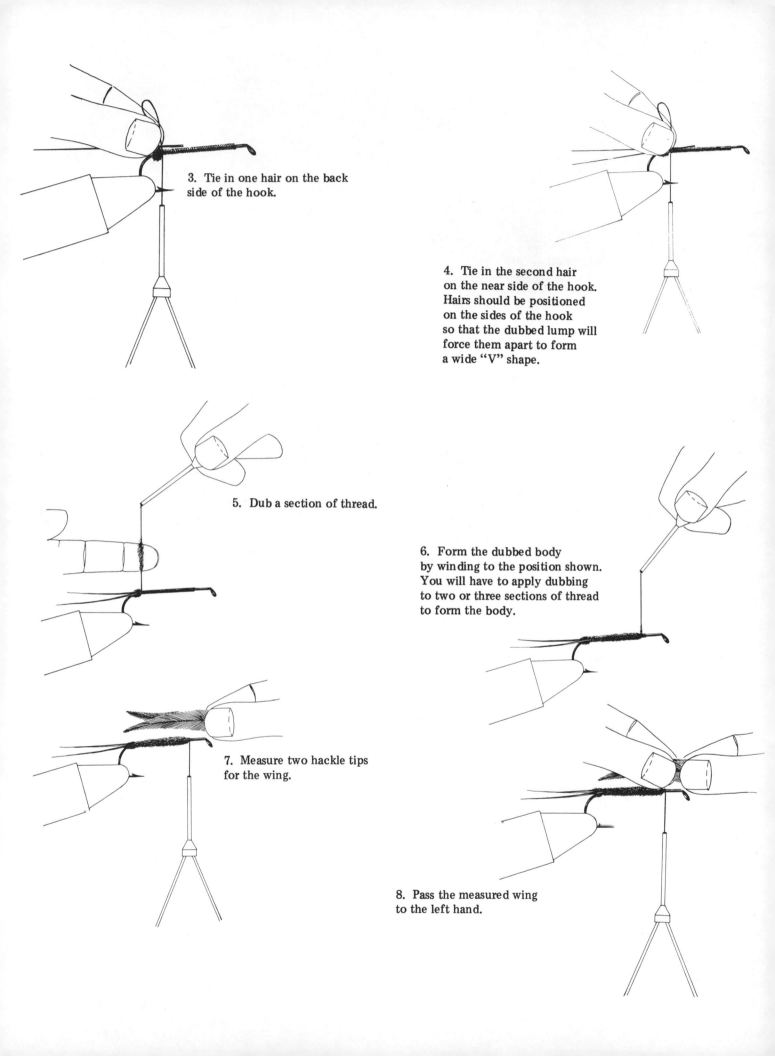

3. Tie in one hair on the back side of the hook.

4. Tie in the second hair on the near side of the hook. Hairs should be positioned on the sides of the hook so that the dubbed lump will force them apart to form a wide "V" shape.

5. Dub a section of thread.

6. Form the dubbed body by winding to the position shown. You will have to apply dubbing to two or three sections of thread to form the body.

7. Measure two hackle tips for the wing.

8. Pass the measured wing to the left hand.

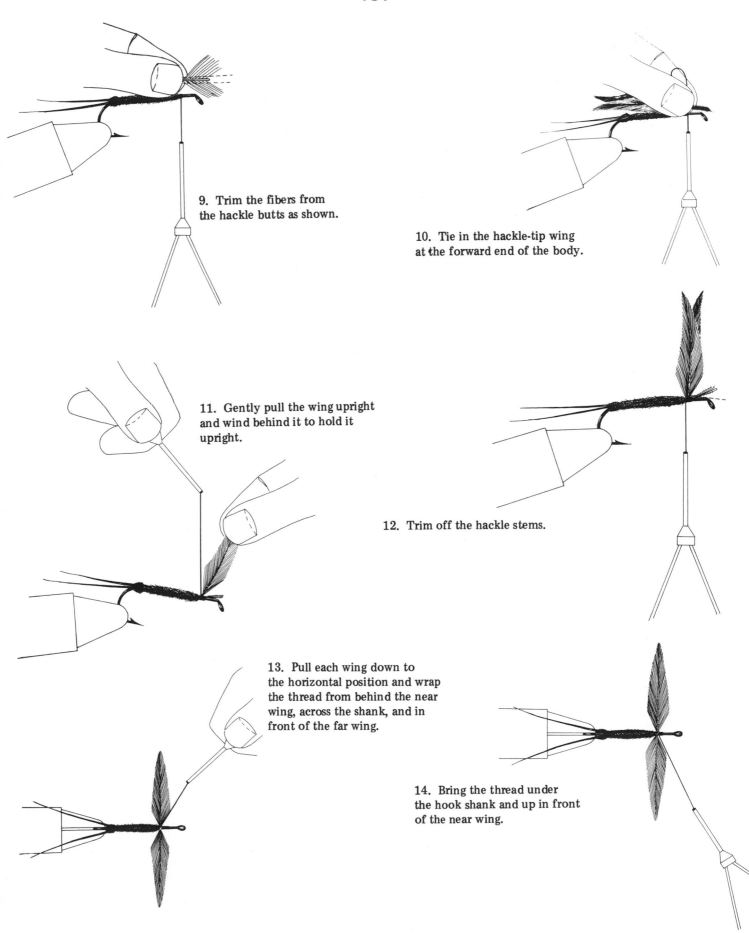

9. Trim the fibers from the hackle butts as shown.

10. Tie in the hackle-tip wing at the forward end of the body.

11. Gently pull the wing upright and wind behind it to hold it upright.

12. Trim off the hackle stems.

13. Pull each wing down to the horizontal position and wrap the thread from behind the near wing, across the shank, and in front of the far wing.

14. Bring the thread under the hook shank and up in front of the near wing.

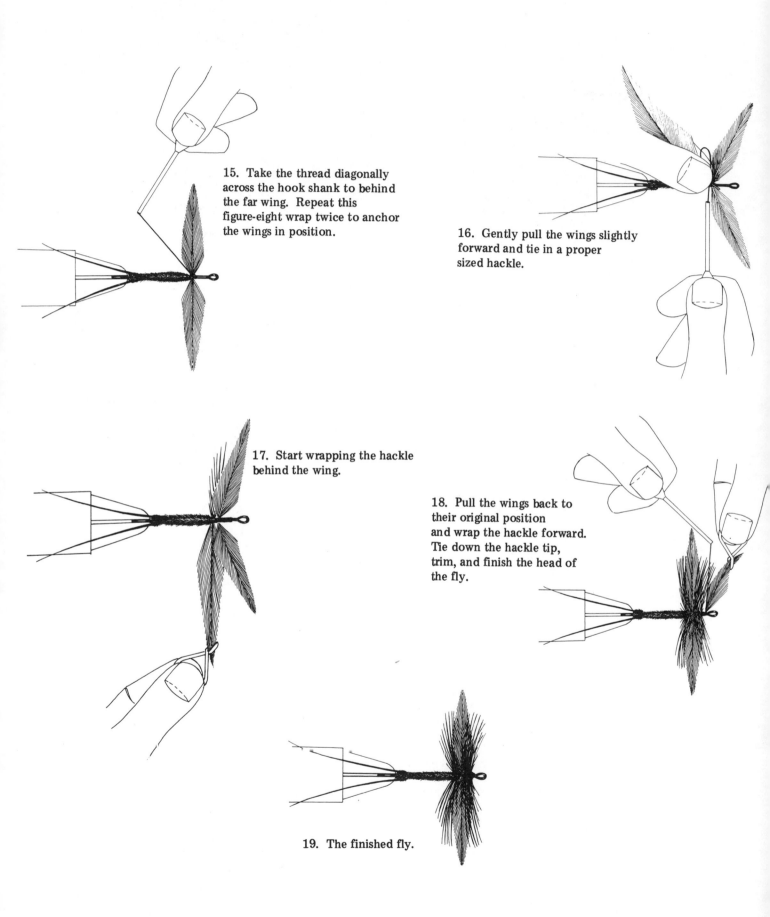

15. Take the thread diagonally across the hook shank to behind the far wing. Repeat this figure-eight wrap twice to anchor the wings in position.

16. Gently pull the wings slightly forward and tie in a proper sized hackle.

17. Start wrapping the hackle behind the wing.

18. Pull the wings back to their original position and wrap the hackle forward. Tie down the hackle tip, trim, and finish the head of the fly.

19. The finished fly.

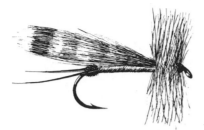

Pattern 12

Because the stone fly (Plecoptera) adult carries its wing in a flat position over its back, it lends itself well to imitation with a hair wing. This is the most durable of the wing types and provides for very good flotation, as the fly rests on the wing in the surface film.

We illustrate this pattern with a split tail, a floss body, a squirrel tail wing, and a double hackle. The winging method and the use of a double hackle are the only new procedures for you to learn as you tie this imitation.

To even the ends of the squirrel tail hairs, follow the illustrations closely. The soft loop must be used at least three times to firmly anchor the hair in place before continuing the wrapping. It is a good idea to apply a drop of head cement to the butts of the wing after it is tied in.

You could substitute a bunch of hackle fibers or hair for the tail, a dubbed body would provide better floatation than the floss, and there are many other hairs that will work for the wing—badger, for instance. Since the stone fly is a long-bodied insect this imitation should be tied on a 2X or 3X long shank hook. We use these in sizes from #4 to #14, and they are deadly when cast up into a fast run and allowed to sweep down into the head of a pool.

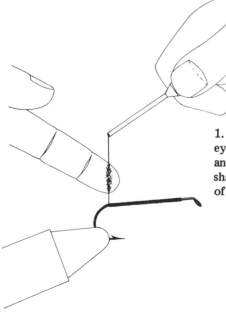

1. Attach the thread two eyewidths back from the eye and wrap to the rear of the shank. Spin a small amount of dubbing on the thread.

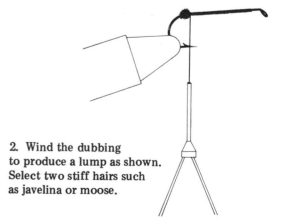

2. Wind the dubbing to produce a lump as shown. Select two stiff hairs such as javelina or moose.

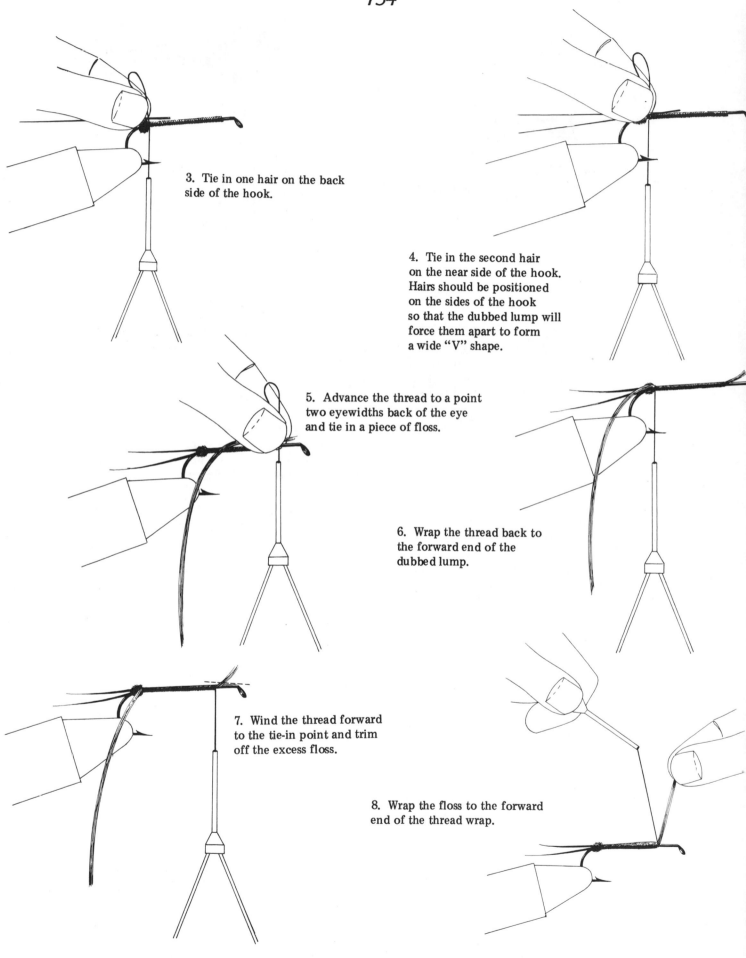

3. Tie in one hair on the back side of the hook.

4. Tie in the second hair on the near side of the hook. Hairs should be positioned on the sides of the hook so that the dubbed lump will force them apart to form a wide "V" shape.

5. Advance the thread to a point two eyewidths back of the eye and tie in a piece of floss.

6. Wrap the thread back to the forward end of the dubbed lump.

7. Wind the thread forward to the tie-in point and trim off the excess floss.

8. Wrap the floss to the forward end of the thread wrap.

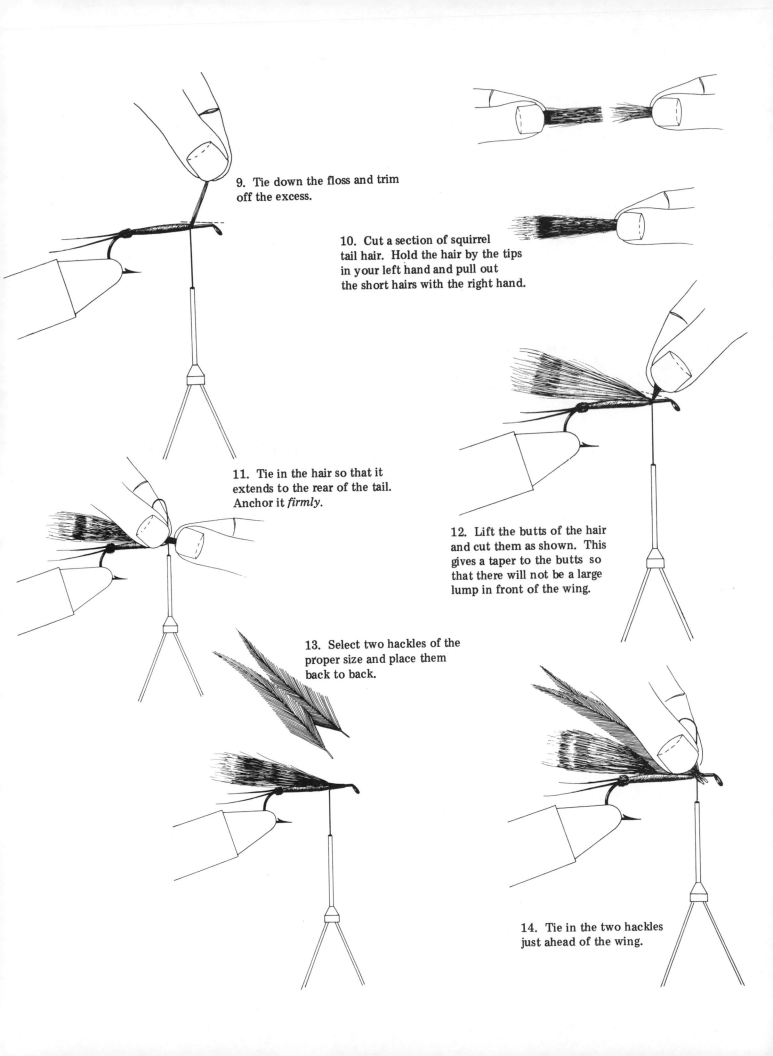

9. Tie down the floss and trim off the excess.

10. Cut a section of squirrel tail hair. Hold the hair by the tips in your left hand and pull out the short hairs with the right hand.

11. Tie in the hair so that it extends to the rear of the tail. Anchor it *firmly*.

12. Lift the butts of the hair and cut them as shown. This gives a taper to the butts so that there will not be a large lump in front of the wing.

13. Select two hackles of the proper size and place them back to back.

14. Tie in the two hackles just ahead of the wing.

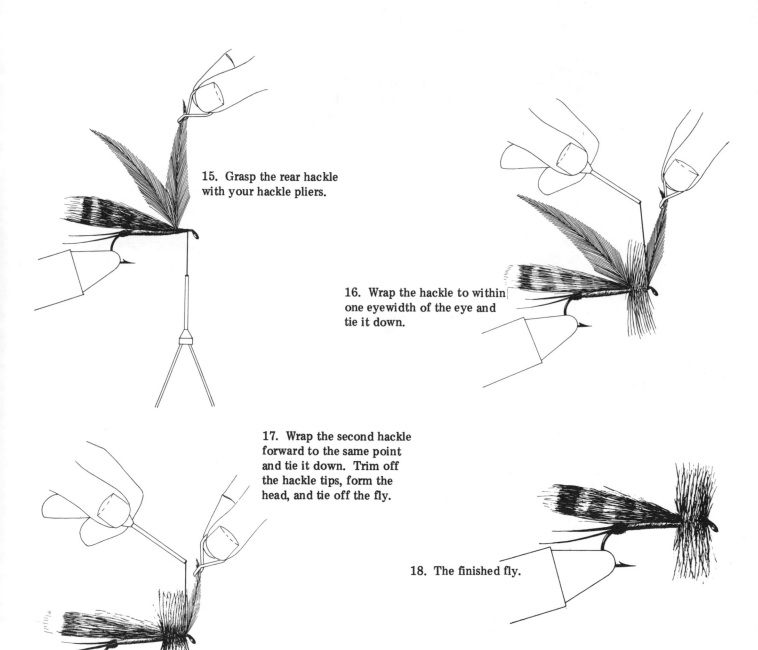

15. Grasp the rear hackle with your hackle pliers.

16. Wrap the hackle to within one eyewidth of the eye and tie it down.

17. Wrap the second hackle forward to the same point and tie it down. Trim off the hackle tips, form the head, and tie off the fly.

18. The finished fly.

Pattern 13

This Trichoptera (caddis fly) adult imitation was developed by Mr. George Bodmer and has become one of the most popular adult caddis imitations in Colorado.

This pattern was chosen because it *is* a good producer and because it will require many of the procedures that we have covered.

This imitation is used in sizes from #10 to #20, and since the adult caddis has a long body, you should use a 2X long shank hook.

The hair used for the wing of this pattern is traditionally elk, but fine deer, carabou, or antelope may be substituted. The body is of wool yarn, although dubbing would work just as well. Notice that the palmered hackle is proportioned the same as if it were used at the head of the fly—one and one-half times the gap of the hook. The wing should extend from just behind the eye to a point halfway between the bend of the hook and the end of the tail.

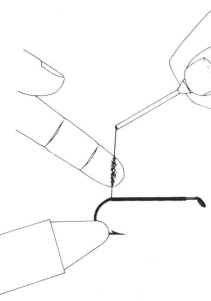

1. Attach the thread two eyewidths back from the eye and wrap to the rear of the shank. Spin a small amount of dubbing on the thread.

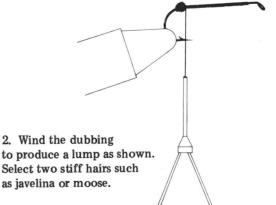

2. Wind the dubbing to produce a lump as shown. Select two stiff hairs such as javelina or moose.

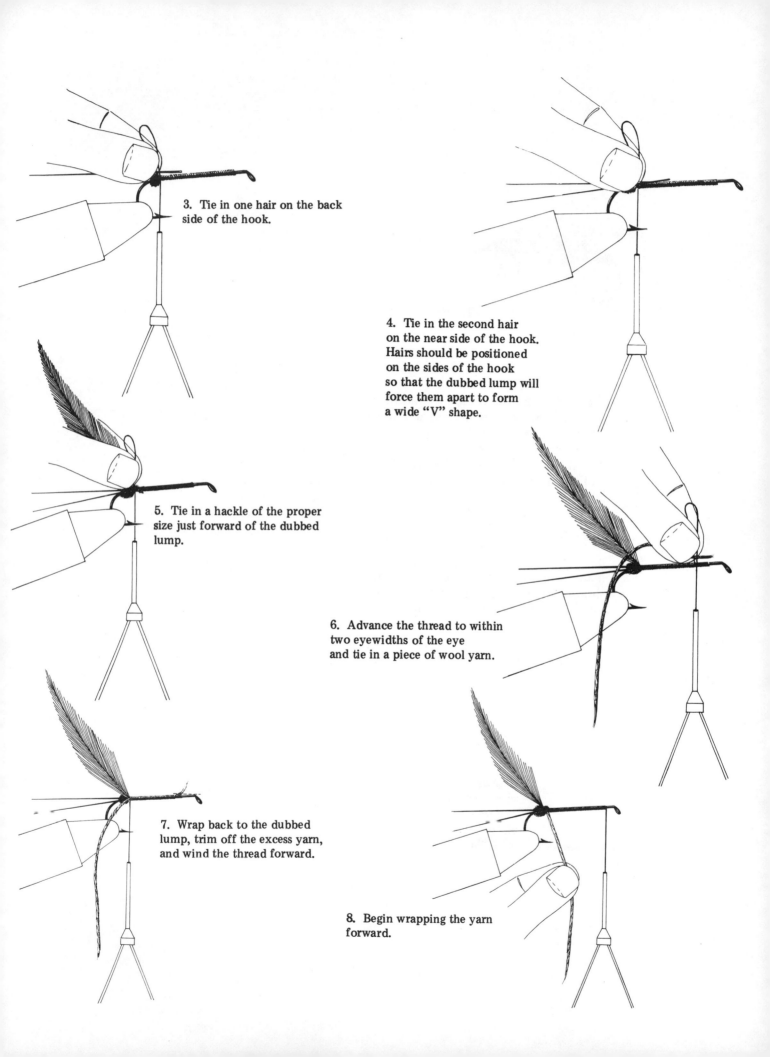

3. Tie in one hair on the back side of the hook.

4. Tie in the second hair on the near side of the hook. Hairs should be positioned on the sides of the hook so that the dubbed lump will force them apart to form a wide "V" shape.

5. Tie in a hackle of the proper size just forward of the dubbed lump.

6. Advance the thread to within two eyewidths of the eye and tie in a piece of wool yarn.

7. Wrap back to the dubbed lump, trim off the excess yarn, and wind the thread forward.

8. Begin wrapping the yarn forward.

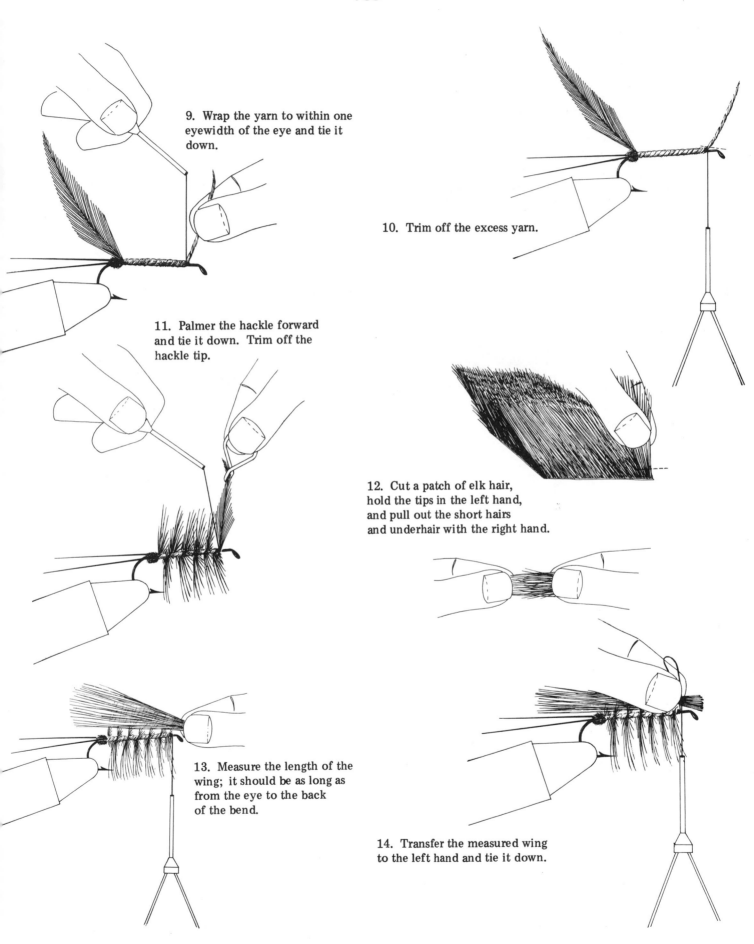

9. Wrap the yarn to within one eyewidth of the eye and tie it down.

10. Trim off the excess yarn.

11. Palmer the hackle forward and tie it down. Trim off the hackle tip.

12. Cut a patch of elk hair, hold the tips in the left hand, and pull out the short hairs and underhair with the right hand.

13. Measure the length of the wing; it should be as long as from the eye to the back of the bend.

14. Transfer the measured wing to the left hand and tie it down.

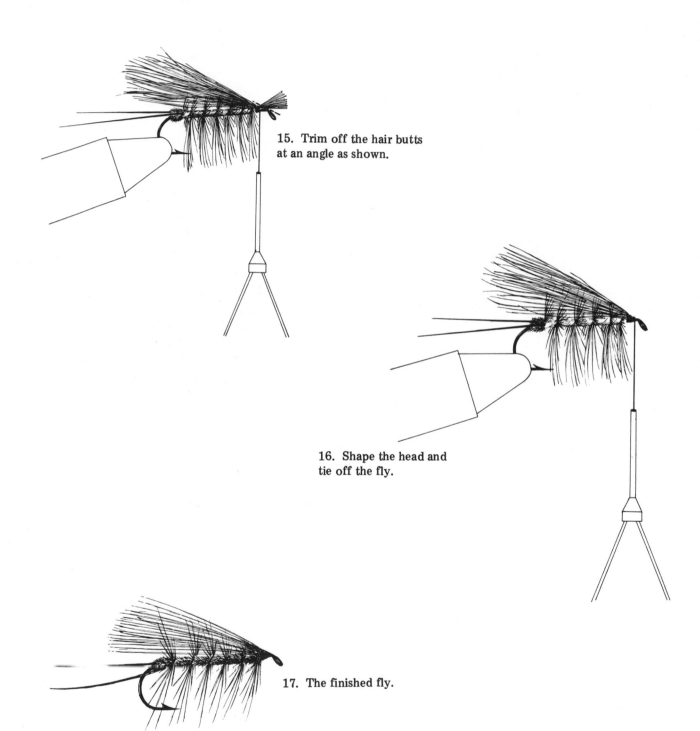

15. Trim off the hair butts at an angle as shown.

16. Shape the head and tie off the fly.

17. The finished fly.

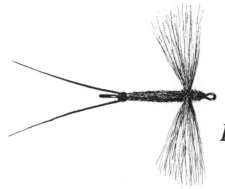

Pattern 14

The adult midge (Diptera) carries its wings either in a spent position or in a flat "V." We are tying a spent-wing type using polypropylene yarn for the winging material. Hackle tips can be used, much as you just did on the spent-wing mayfly. Hackle can be wound and then trimmed top and bottom to leave only the wing shape, or the wing can be fabricated from a bunch of hair tied in on either side of the thorax.

For an imitation of actual insect size, the fly should be dressed on hooks ranging from about #18 to #24 or even smaller, and since the insect has a long, delicate abdomen, a 1X long hook could be used. Midges are found in nearly all colors from white to black, but the whites, greens, and browns are the most common.

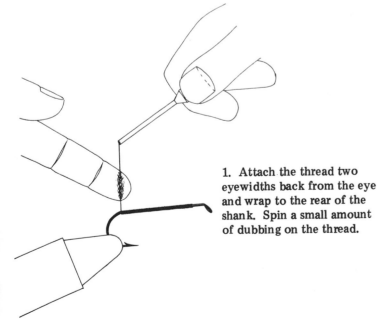

1. Attach the thread two eyewidths back from the eye and wrap to the rear of the shank. Spin a small amount of dubbing on the thread.

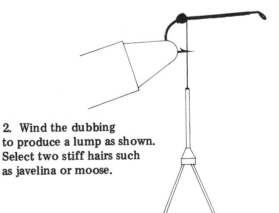

2. Wind the dubbing to produce a lump as shown. Select two stiff hairs such as javelina or moose.

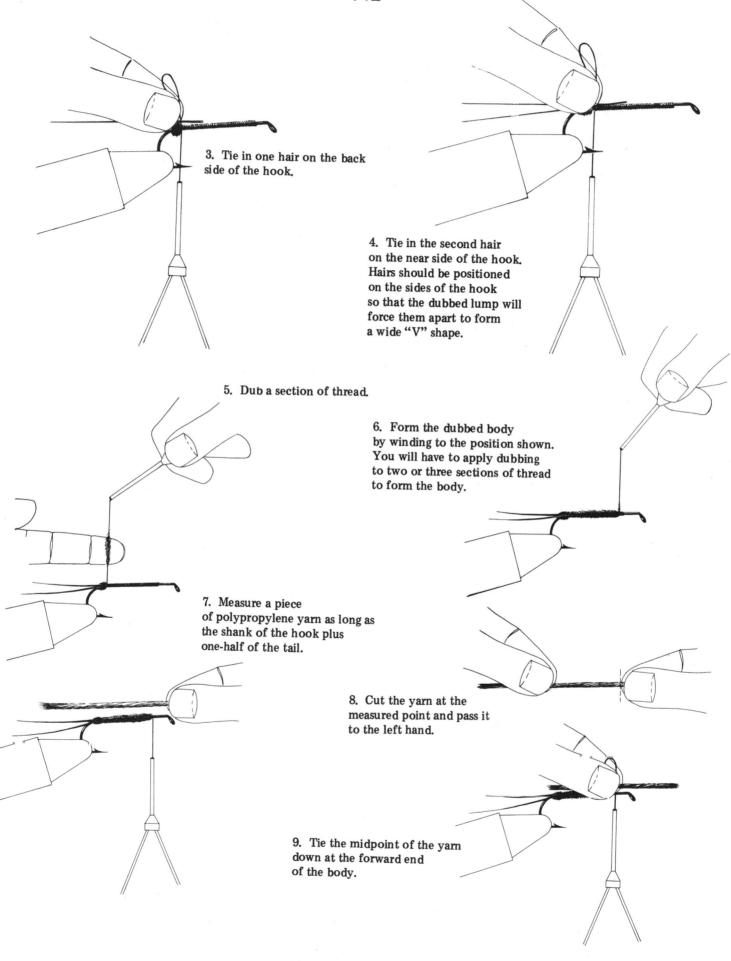

3. Tie in one hair on the back side of the hook.

4. Tie in the second hair on the near side of the hook. Hairs should be positioned on the sides of the hook so that the dubbed lump will force them apart to form a wide "V" shape.

5. Dub a section of thread.

6. Form the dubbed body by winding to the position shown. You will have to apply dubbing to two or three sections of thread to form the body.

7. Measure a piece of polypropylene yarn as long as the shank of the hook plus one-half of the tail.

8. Cut the yarn at the measured point and pass it to the left hand.

9. Tie the midpoint of the yarn down at the forward end of the body.

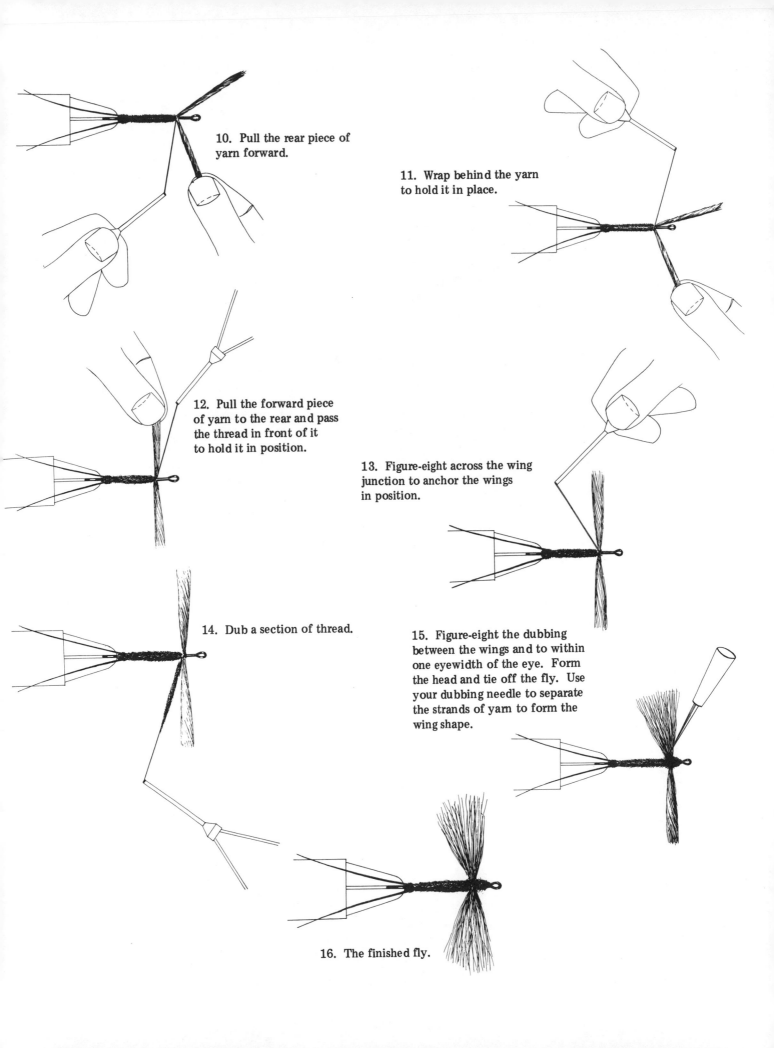

10. Pull the rear piece of yarn forward.

11. Wrap behind the yarn to hold it in place.

12. Pull the forward piece of yarn to the rear and pass the thread in front of it to hold it in position.

13. Figure-eight across the wing junction to anchor the wings in position.

14. Dub a section of thread.

15. Figure-eight the dubbing between the wings and to within one eyewidth of the eye. Form the head and tie off the fly. Use your dubbing needle to separate the strands of yarn to form the wing shape.

16. The finished fly.

Pattern 15

This is the first of four streamer patterns that you are going to tie. This particular pattern is a hairwing streamer, or bucktail, and is meant to imitate a baitfish. The colors used for the wing are variable, depending on the minnow being imitated, but the top bunch of hair should always be darker than the bottom bunch to match the dark dorsal area found on all fish.

In this pattern we are going to have you start tying the whip finish to tie off the head of the fly. This knot is much superior to the half-hitches that you have been using. Follow the illustrations closely the first couple of times and you shouldn't have too much trouble. There are many different ways of tying the whip finish, but we have found this method the easiest to learn.

As you wrap the tinsel body on this fly, keep the edges of the tinsel as close together as possible without overlapping. The reason for wrapping the body in both directions is so there will be tinsel showing through any spaces between wraps.

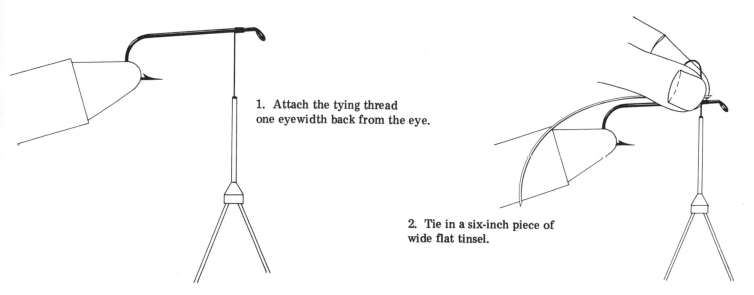

1. Attach the tying thread one eyewidth back from the eye.

2. Tie in a six-inch piece of wide flat tinsel.

144

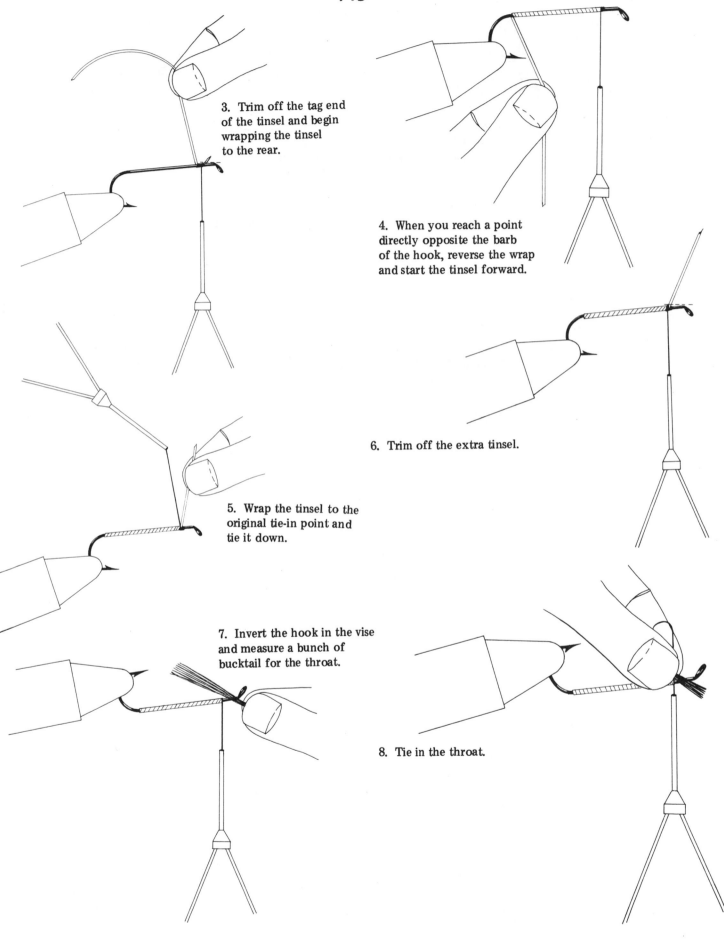

3. Trim off the tag end of the tinsel and begin wrapping the tinsel to the rear.

4. When you reach a point directly opposite the barb of the hook, reverse the wrap and start the tinsel forward.

6. Trim off the extra tinsel.

5. Wrap the tinsel to the original tie-in point and tie it down.

7. Invert the hook in the vise and measure a bunch of bucktail for the throat.

8. Tie in the throat.

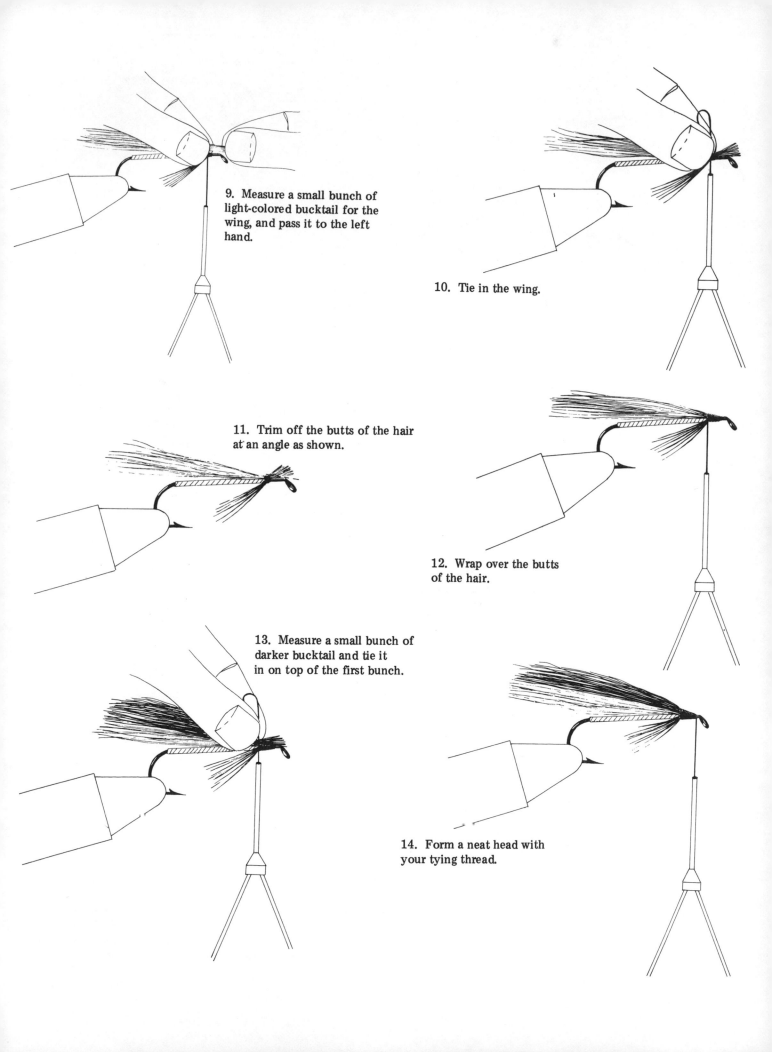

9. Measure a small bunch of light-colored bucktail for the wing, and pass it to the left hand.

10. Tie in the wing.

11. Trim off the butts of the hair at an angle as shown.

12. Wrap over the butts of the hair.

13. Measure a small bunch of darker bucktail and tie it in on top of the first bunch.

14. Form a neat head with your tying thread.

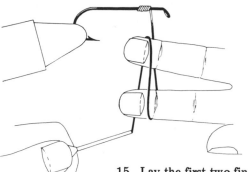

15. Lay the first two fingers of your right hand across the thread (fingernails toward you) and wrap the thread around them as shown.

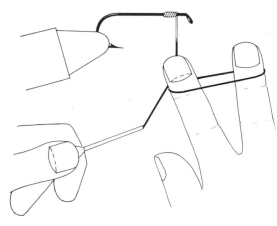

16. Rotate your hand so that your fingers are pointing up (fingernails still towards you).

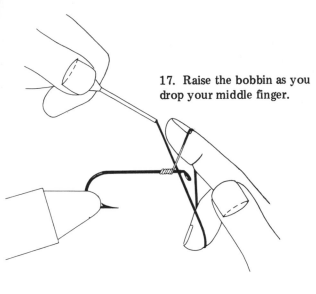

17. Raise the bobbin as you drop your middle finger.

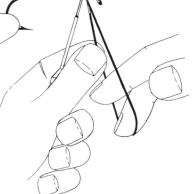

18. Pull the slack from the loop you have formed by lowering your right hand. Grasp the *rear* thread with your left thumb and finger and pull downward.

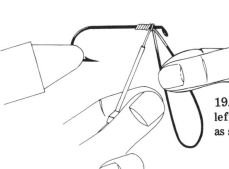

19. Take the thread from your left fingers with the right hand as shown.

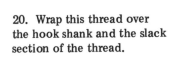

20. Wrap this thread over the hook shank and the slack section of the thread.

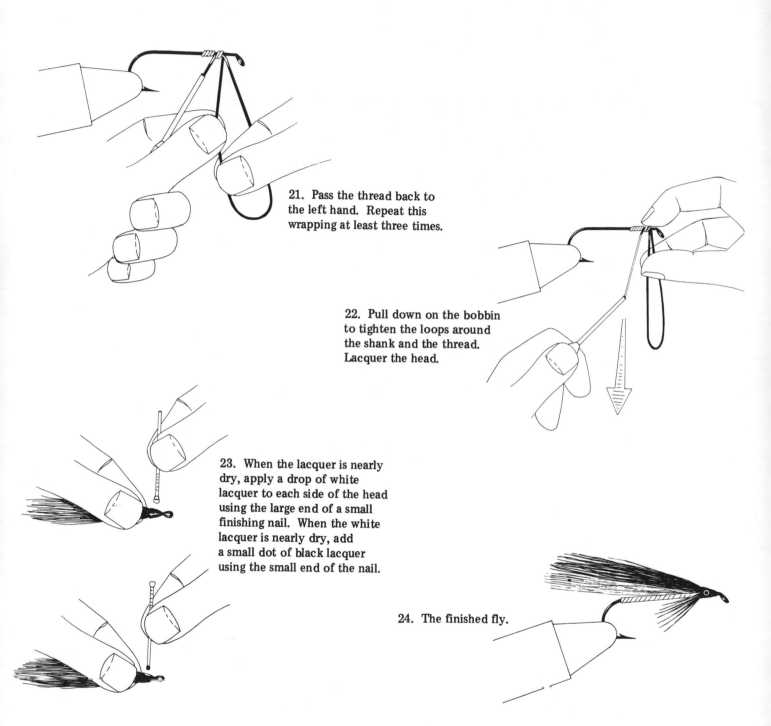

21. Pass the thread back to the left hand. Repeat this wrapping at least three times.

22. Pull down on the bobbin to tighten the loops around the shank and the thread. Lacquer the head.

23. When the lacquer is nearly dry, apply a drop of white lacquer to each side of the head using the large end of a small finishing nail. When the white lacquer is nearly dry, add a small dot of black lacquer using the small end of the nail.

24. The finished fly.

Pattern 16

This streamer is a very simple marabou type. We show it tied with a brass wire body and with two colors of marabou for the wing. You could substitute gold tinsel or Mylar tubing for the body. The wing can be of any color, but we have found this pattern most effective when tied with a white lower wing and a black upper wing. The advantage of the brass wire body is that it adds weight to the fly so that it will really get down in the stream. Since you are tying a streamer, you should use a long shank hook; generally a 4X or 6X long hook is used.

We have no evidence that the painted eyes on the fly contribute to its success, but they certainly make it look better to the fisherman, and that is justification enough for putting the eyes on. If you want a really good-looking head on your streamers, you must take care when shaping it. If you use two or three coats of black lacquer instead of clear on the head before applying the eyes, the fly will have a real professional look.

The trick to handling the marabou is to keep it wet after cutting the fibers from the feather. The wet marabou clings together and can be handled as a single piece of material instead of a group of soft fibers that want to go every which way.

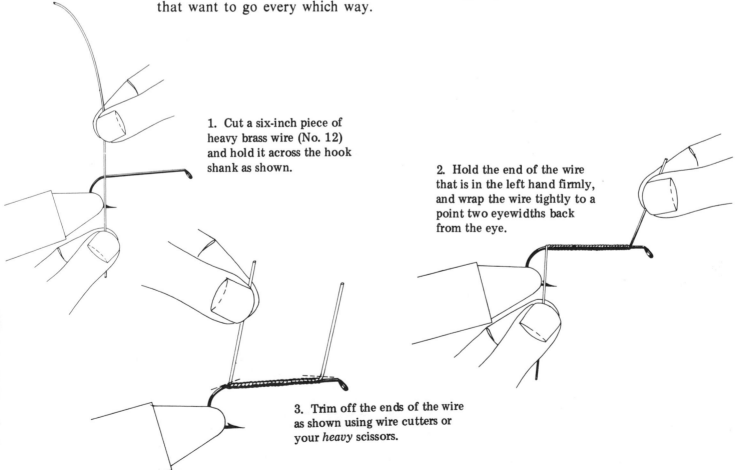

1. Cut a six-inch piece of heavy brass wire (No. 12) and hold it across the hook shank as shown.

2. Hold the end of the wire that is in the left hand firmly, and wrap the wire tightly to a point two eyewidths back from the eye.

3. Trim off the ends of the wire as shown using wire cutters or your *heavy* scissors.

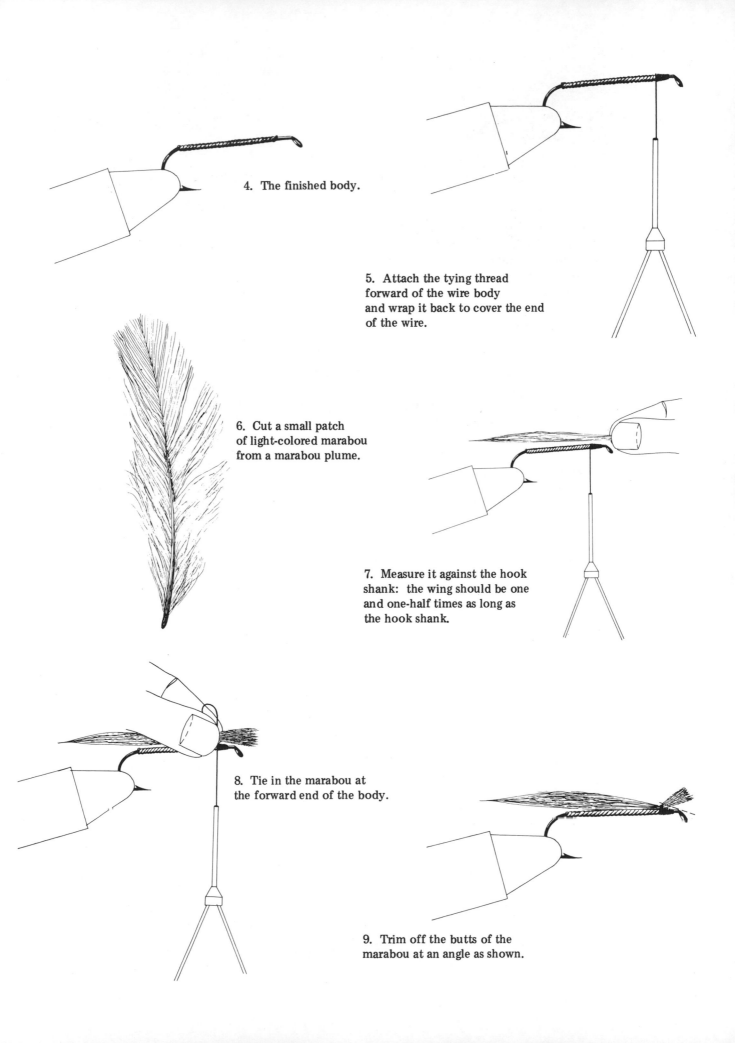

4. The finished body.

5. Attach the tying thread forward of the wire body and wrap it back to cover the end of the wire.

6. Cut a small patch of light-colored marabou from a marabou plume.

7. Measure it against the hook shank: the wing should be one and one-half times as long as the hook shank.

8. Tie in the marabou at the forward end of the body.

9. Trim off the butts of the marabou at an angle as shown.

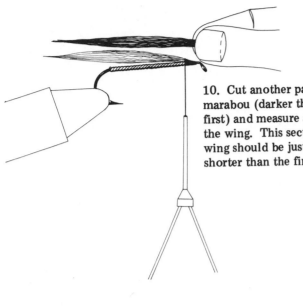

10. Cut another patch of marabou (darker than the first) and measure against the wing. This section of wing should be just slightly shorter than the first section.

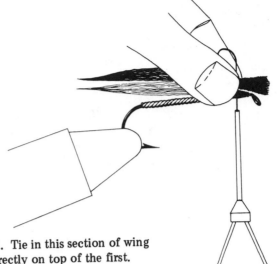

11. Tie in this section of wing directly on top of the first.

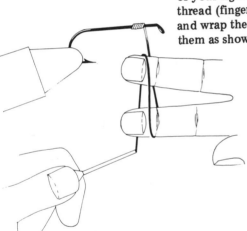

12. Lay the first two fingers of your right hand across the thread (fingernails toward you) and wrap the thread around them as shown.

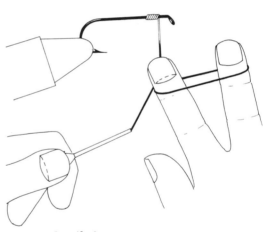

13. Rotate your hand so that your fingers are pointing up (fingernails still towards you).

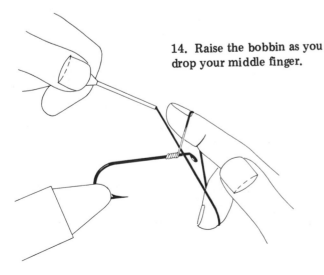

14. Raise the bobbin as you drop your middle finger.

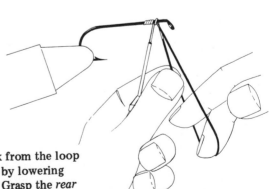

15. Pull the slack from the loop you have formed by lowering your right hand. Grasp the *rear* thread with your left thumb and finger and pull downward.

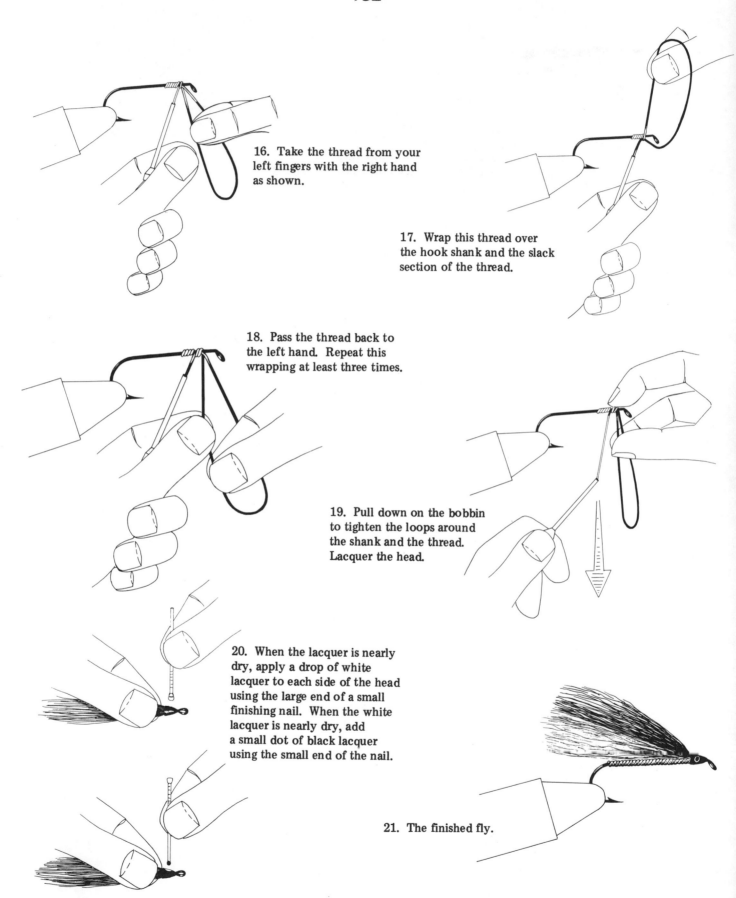

16. Take the thread from your left fingers with the right hand as shown.

17. Wrap this thread over the hook shank and the slack section of the thread.

18. Pass the thread back to the left hand. Repeat this wrapping at least three times.

19. Pull down on the bobbin to tighten the loops around the shank and the thread. Lacquer the head.

20. When the lacquer is nearly dry, apply a drop of white lacquer to each side of the head using the large end of a small finishing nail. When the white lacquer is nearly dry, add a small dot of black lacquer using the small end of the nail.

21. The finished fly.

Pattern 17

The type of streamer tied here uses hackle as the wing material. This is one area where saddle hackle really comes into its own: they give a long slim silhouette and move enticingly in the water. Saddle hackle is also the best choice for the hackle at the head of this fly, since you will be winding the hackle with your fingers and the extra length will make it easier. This pattern uses a double wing; that is, there are two hackles tied in on each side of the hook shank. This is done so that a combination of colors can be obtained. We tie this most often using a tan body floss, a yellow underwing, and a ginger overwing. The two hackles at the head are of the same colors.

The four-wing hackle can be tied in at one time, but it is very difficult to accomplish this so that the wings are on straight. The easiest method is to tie in the underwings as a pair and then add the overwing one hackle at a time as we have shown.

To wind the two hackles at the head simultaneously, you must hold them in your fingers, because nearly always one hackle will have a thicker stem than the other and will wind faster. By using your fingers instead of hackle pliers, you can allow the faster winding hackle to slip through your fingers as you wrap.

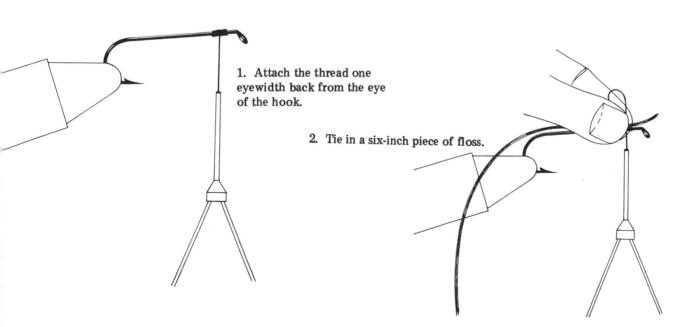

1. Attach the thread one eyewidth back from the eye of the hook.

2. Tie in a six-inch piece of floss.

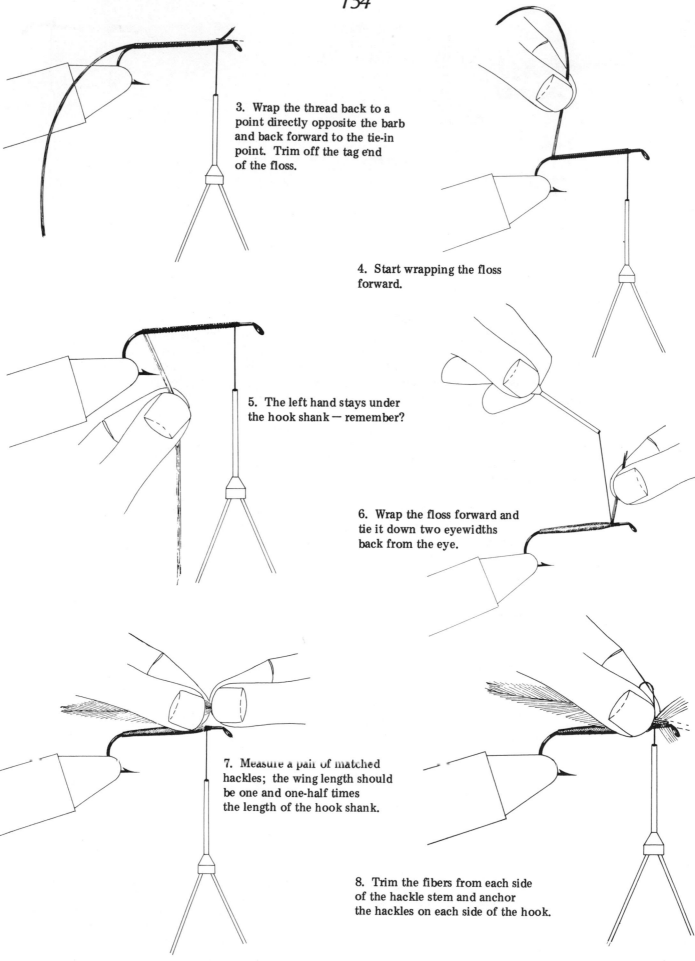

3. Wrap the thread back to a point directly opposite the barb and back forward to the tie-in point. Trim off the tag end of the floss.

4. Start wrapping the floss forward.

5. The left hand stays under the hook shank — remember?

6. Wrap the floss forward and tie it down two eyewidths back from the eye.

7. Measure a pair of matched hackles; the wing length should be one and one-half times the length of the hook shank.

8. Trim the fibers from each side of the hackle stem and anchor the hackles on each side of the hook.

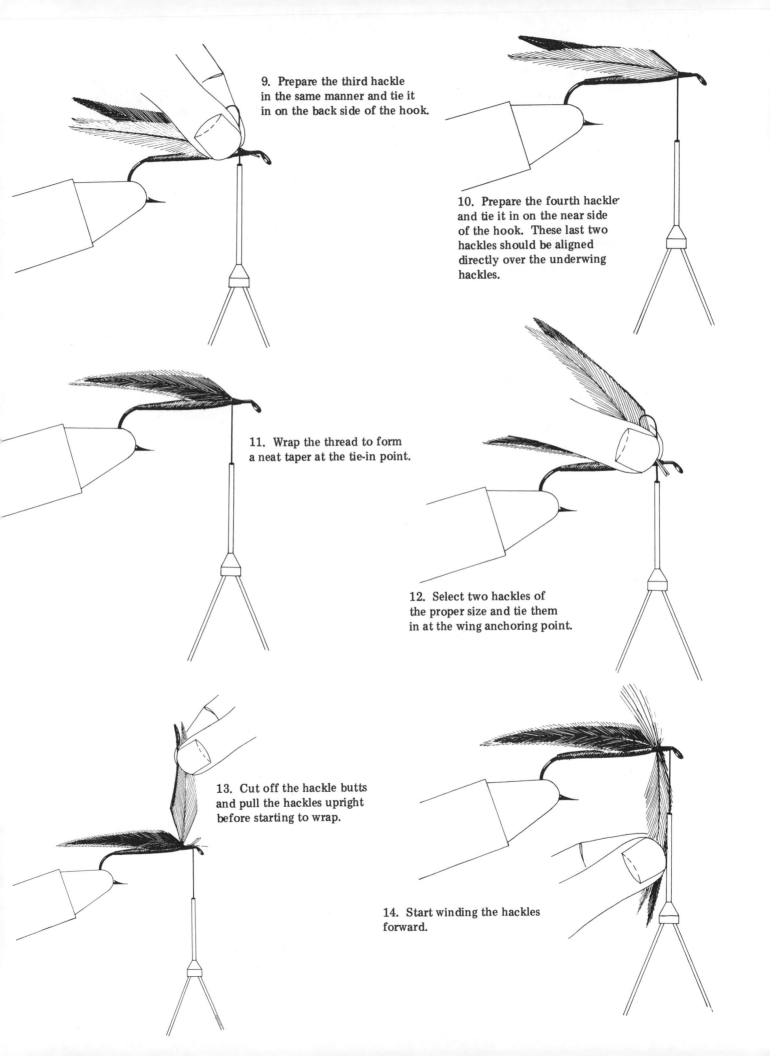

9. Prepare the third hackle in the same manner and tie it in on the back side of the hook.

10. Prepare the fourth hackle and tie it in on the near side of the hook. These last two hackles should be aligned directly over the underwing hackles.

11. Wrap the thread to form a neat taper at the tie-in point.

12. Select two hackles of the proper size and tie them in at the wing anchoring point.

13. Cut off the hackle butts and pull the hackles upright before starting to wrap.

14. Start winding the hackles forward.

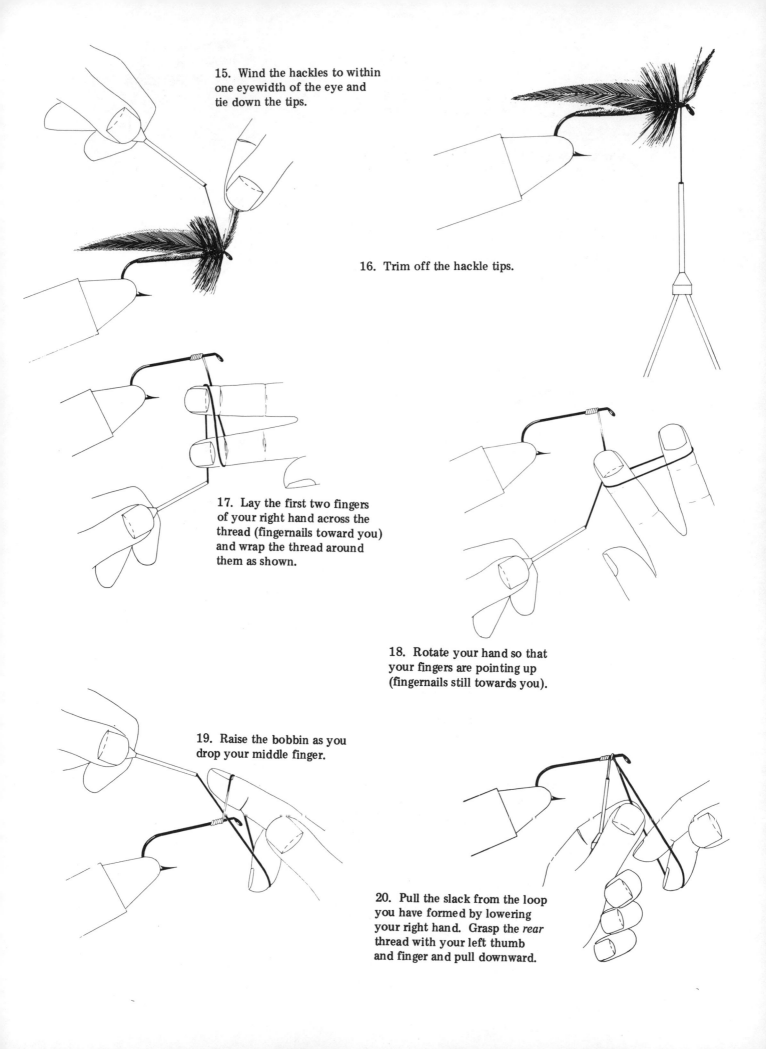

15. Wind the hackles to within one eyewidth of the eye and tie down the tips.

16. Trim off the hackle tips.

17. Lay the first two fingers of your right hand across the thread (fingernails toward you) and wrap the thread around them as shown.

18. Rotate your hand so that your fingers are pointing up (fingernails still towards you).

19. Raise the bobbin as you drop your middle finger.

20. Pull the slack from the loop you have formed by lowering your right hand. Grasp the *rear* thread with your left thumb and finger and pull downward.

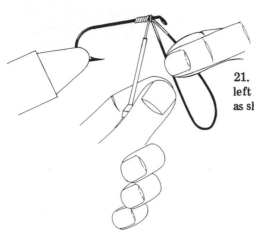

21. Take the thread from your left fingers with the right hand as shown.

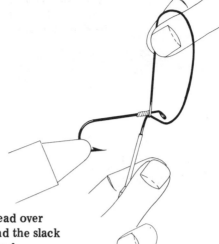

22. Wrap this thread over the hook shank and the slack section of the thread.

23. Pass the thread back to the left hand. Repeat this wrapping at least three times.

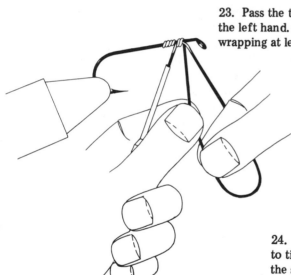

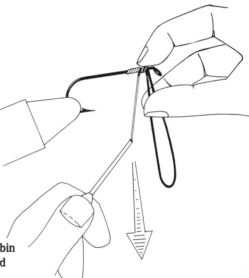

24. Pull down on the bobbin to tighten the loops around the shank and the thread. Lacquer the head.

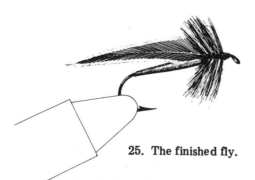

25. The finished fly.

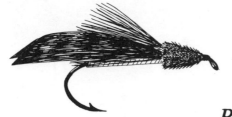

Pattern 18

This pattern is an adaptation of the Muddler Minnow, which is probably the single most useful fly that we will have you tie. When fished deep, it is a superb streamer, and if treated with flotant it is a good cricket or grasshopper imitation. The original pattern calls for a short tail of the same material as the wing, but since the technique for attaching the tail is rather difficult to teach and we don't feel that it adds to the performance of the pattern, we have chosen to illustrate the pattern without it. Many patterns for this fly use squirrel tail for the first bunch of hair ahead of the wing, but we prefer it tied with deer hair so that the butts can be used as part of the head.

The spun deer-hair head causes many beginning tyers (and some experienced tyers) problems. First of all, the hook shank over which you are spinning the hair should be bare; secondly, be sure that you get two loose wraps of thread around the bunch of hair before tightening the loop to spin the hair. There are two tricks to getting a tight smooth surface from spun hair: (1) after spinning each bunch of hair, it must be packed tightly back using the thumb and fingernails; (2) singe the hair with the bottom of a match flame. This not only smooths the hair but also seals the ends and makes the fly more durable.

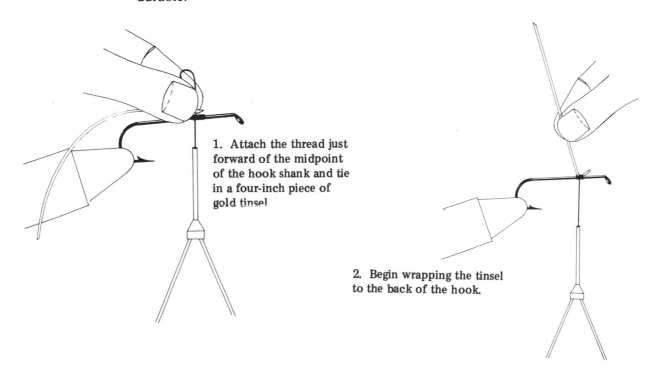

1. Attach the thread just forward of the midpoint of the hook shank and tie in a four-inch piece of gold tinsel

2. Begin wrapping the tinsel to the back of the hook.

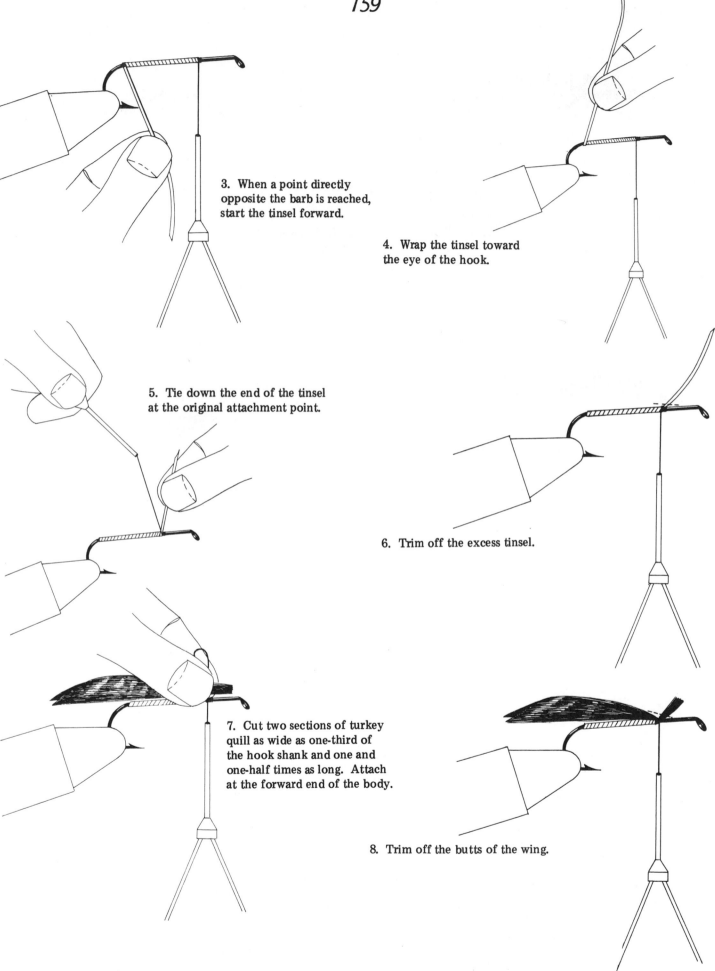

3. When a point directly opposite the barb is reached, start the tinsel forward.

4. Wrap the tinsel toward the eye of the hook.

5. Tie down the end of the tinsel at the original attachment point.

6. Trim off the excess tinsel.

7. Cut two sections of turkey quill as wide as one-third of the hook shank and one and one-half times as long. Attach at the forward end of the body.

8. Trim off the butts of the wing.

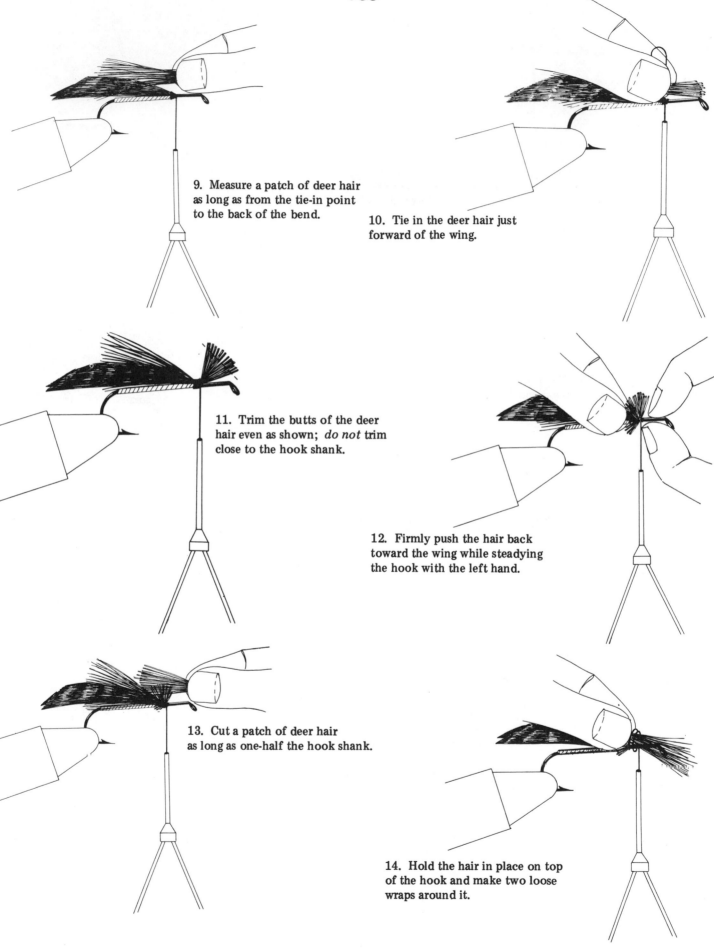

9. Measure a patch of deer hair as long as from the tie-in point to the back of the bend.

10. Tie in the deer hair just forward of the wing.

11. Trim the butts of the deer hair even as shown; *do not* trim close to the hook shank.

12. Firmly push the hair back toward the wing while steadying the hook with the left hand.

13. Cut a patch of deer hair as long as one-half the hook shank.

14. Hold the hair in place on top of the hook and make two loose wraps around it.

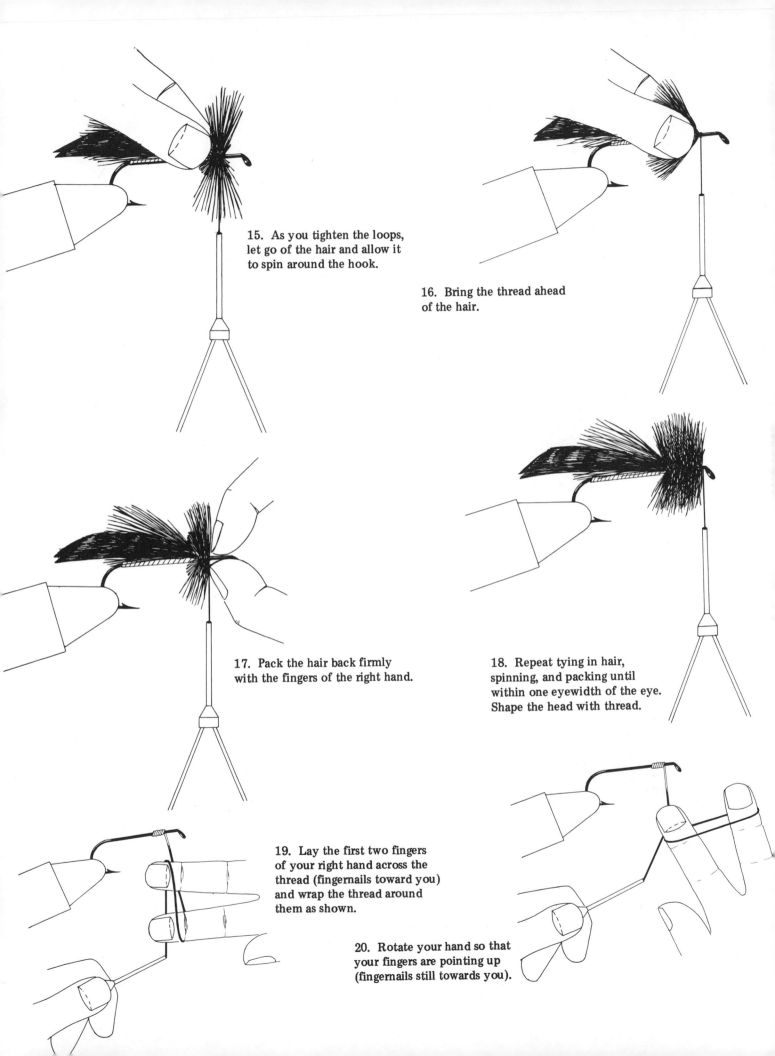

15. As you tighten the loops, let go of the hair and allow it to spin around the hook.

16. Bring the thread ahead of the hair.

17. Pack the hair back firmly with the fingers of the right hand.

18. Repeat tying in hair, spinning, and packing until within one eyewidth of the eye. Shape the head with thread.

19. Lay the first two fingers of your right hand across the thread (fingernails toward you) and wrap the thread around them as shown.

20. Rotate your hand so that your fingers are pointing up (fingernails still towards you).

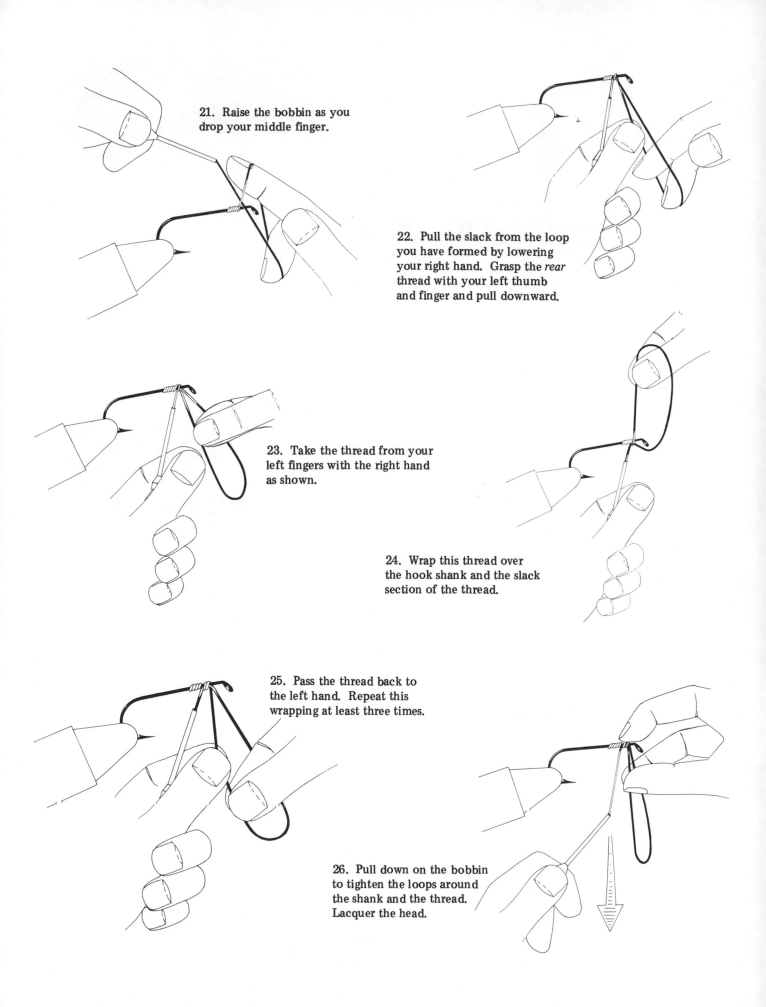

21. Raise the bobbin as you drop your middle finger.

22. Pull the slack from the loop you have formed by lowering your right hand. Grasp the *rear* thread with your left thumb and finger and pull downward.

23. Take the thread from your left fingers with the right hand as shown.

24. Wrap this thread over the hook shank and the slack section of the thread.

25. Pass the thread back to the left hand. Repeat this wrapping at least three times.

26. Pull down on the bobbin to tighten the loops around the shank and the thread. Lacquer the head.

27. Trim the head to shape as shown and singe with the lower edge of a match flame to smooth the deer hair.

28. The finished head shape should be as shown.

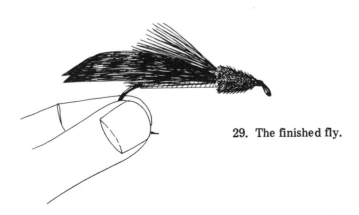

29. The finished fly.

Pattern 19

The pattern that we are going to have you tie next is one of the most used patterns in the West. It is one of the many variation of the hair-bodied flies called Humpies. Of all the dry flies in my fly boxes this is my favorite. It is not a supergood imitation of any particular insect although its upright wing would suggest a mayfly. However, this fly will float through really heavy water where you would drown a normal dry fly in seconds, and that may be its secret—it simply allows you to float a fly where you otherwise wouldn't be able to. Also, in the really heavy, fast water the trout doesn't get as good a look at the imitation because the fly is traveling fast and the water distorts his view.

The only thing a little tough about tying the pattern is getting the hair the right length, since it is used as both the body and the wing. The length of the hair should be equal to the distance from the eye to the back of the tail.

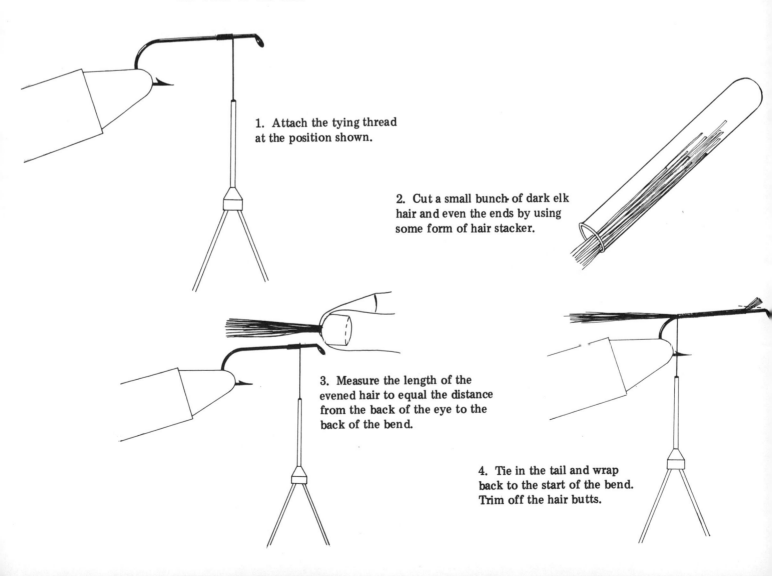

1. Attach the tying thread at the position shown.

2. Cut a small bunch of dark elk hair and even the ends by using some form of hair stacker.

3. Measure the length of the evened hair to equal the distance from the back of the eye to the back of the bend.

4. Tie in the tail and wrap back to the start of the bend. Trim off the hair butts.

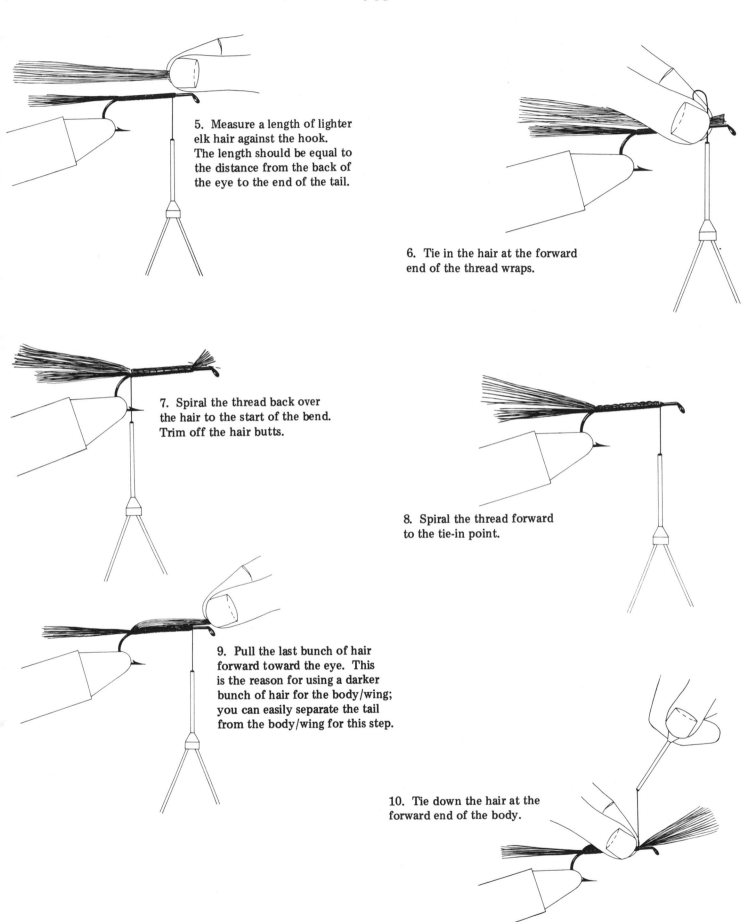

5. Measure a length of lighter elk hair against the hook. The length should be equal to the distance from the back of the eye to the end of the tail.

6. Tie in the hair at the forward end of the thread wraps.

7. Spiral the thread back over the hair to the start of the bend. Trim off the hair butts.

8. Spiral the thread forward to the tie-in point.

9. Pull the last bunch of hair forward toward the eye. This is the reason for using a darker bunch of hair for the body/wing; you can easily separate the tail from the body/wing for this step.

10. Tie down the hair at the forward end of the body.

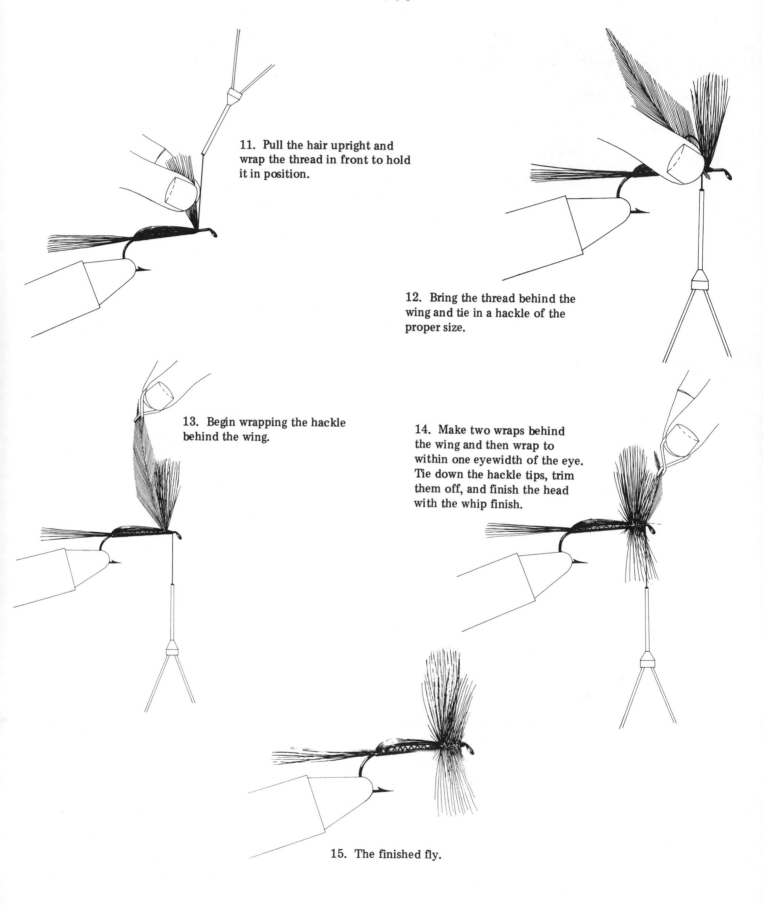

11. Pull the hair upright and wrap the thread in front to hold it in position.

12. Bring the thread behind the wing and tie in a hackle of the proper size.

13. Begin wrapping the hackle behind the wing.

14. Make two wraps behind the wing and then wrap to within one eyewidth of the eye. Tie down the hackle tips, trim them off, and finish the head with the whip finish.

15. The finished fly.

Pattern 20

Show this pattern to a fly fisherman and he will tell you that it is a shrimp imitation, and indeed it could be, but since freshwater shrimp are not very prevalent, it is probably used more often to imitate scuds (Gammarus). Since we are again simulating an underwater form of animal (Crustacea in this case—not an insect), we want to tie this pattern on a wet-fly hook, and since the scuds are relatively short, a regular length hook will best imitate them.

We tie this pattern in two colors: light tan with salmon-colored tail and hackle, and grey with dark-grey hackle and tail. Olive would also be a good choice since some of the scuds are in this color range.

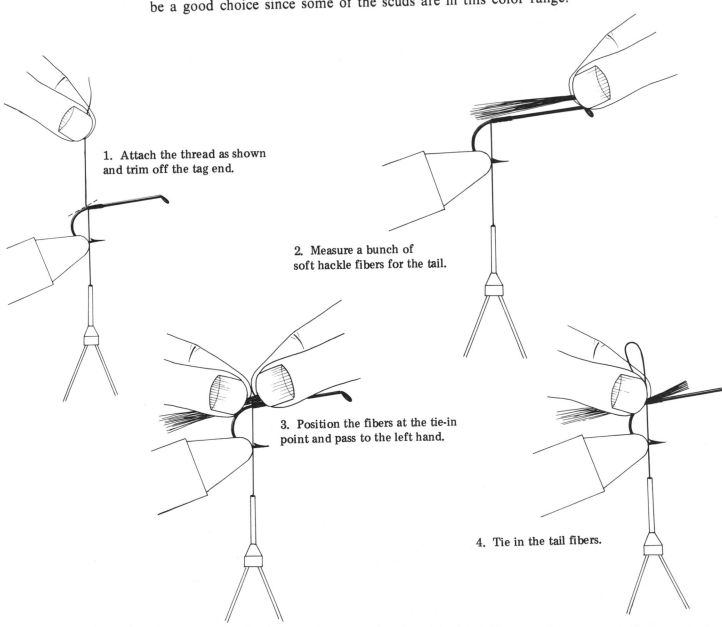

1. Attach the thread as shown and trim off the tag end.

2. Measure a bunch of soft hackle fibers for the tail.

3. Position the fibers at the tie-in point and pass to the left hand.

4. Tie in the tail fibers.

168

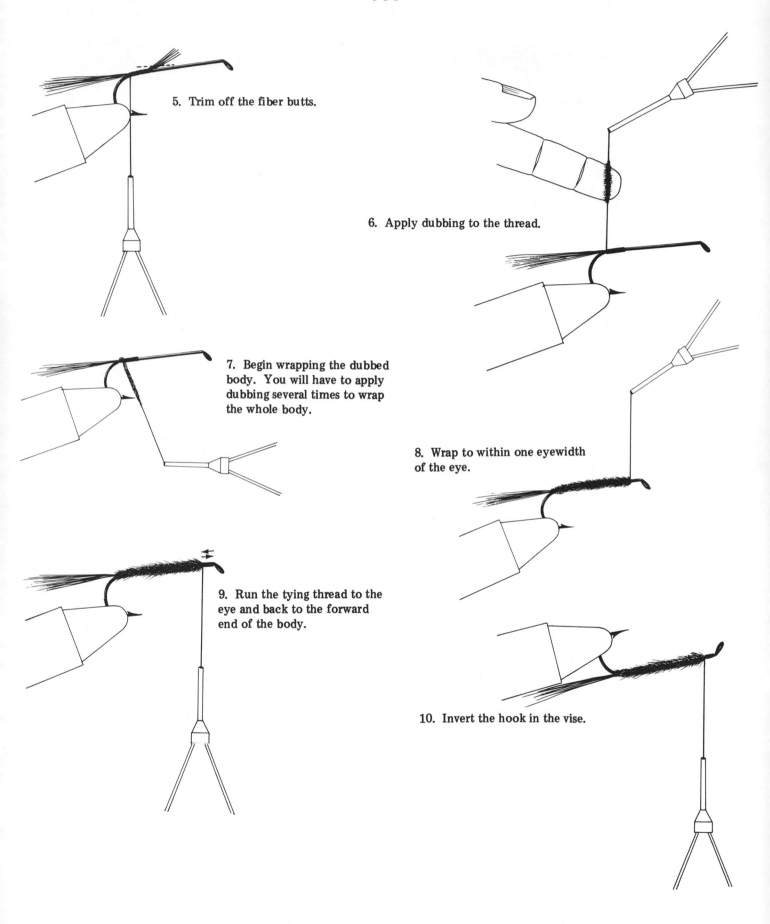

5. Trim off the fiber butts.

6. Apply dubbing to the thread.

7. Begin wrapping the dubbed body. You will have to apply dubbing several times to wrap the whole body.

8. Wrap to within one eyewidth of the eye.

9. Run the tying thread to the eye and back to the forward end of the body.

10. Invert the hook in the vise.

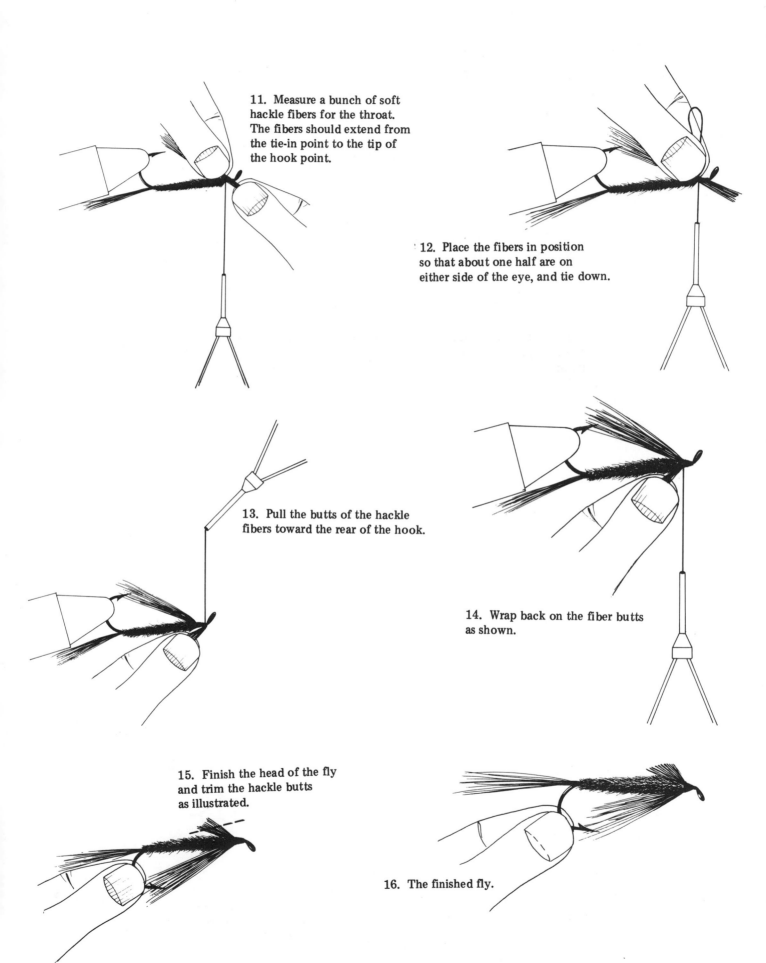

11. Measure a bunch of soft hackle fibers for the throat. The fibers should extend from the tie-in point to the tip of the hook point.

12. Place the fibers in position so that about one half are on either side of the eye, and tie down.

13. Pull the butts of the hackle fibers toward the rear of the hook.

14. Wrap back on the fiber butts as shown.

15. Finish the head of the fly and trim the hackle butts as illustrated.

16. The finished fly.

Pattern 21

The remaining four patterns that we are going to show are attracter patterns. These patterns are intended to give you a review of the techniques that we have already introduced.

The first attracter pattern is a very simple wet-fly pattern that may be effective as a pupal imitation, or perhaps an emerger. It should be tied on a wet-fly hook of standard length.

Your technique should be developed well enough now that you are starting to pay close attention to detail; proportion, neatness, and the finishing of the head in a precise manner are the hallmarks of a good fly-tyer.

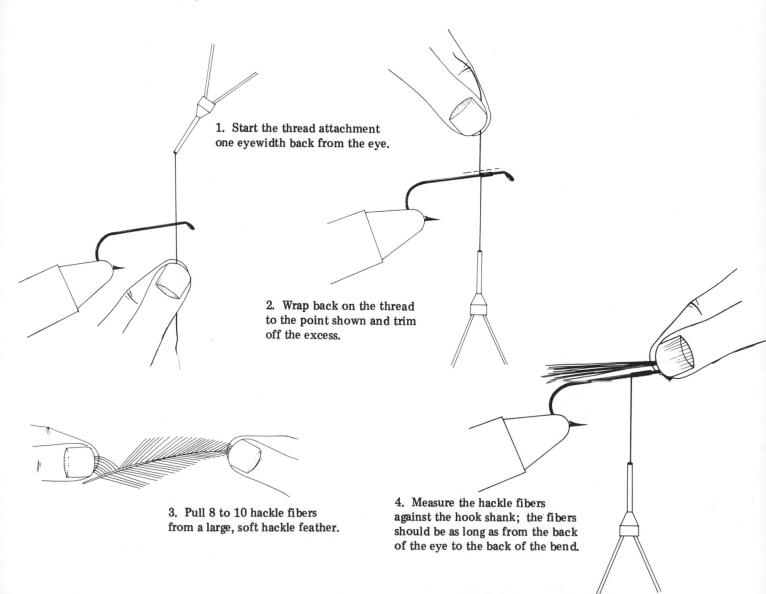

1. Start the thread attachment one eyewidth back from the eye.

2. Wrap back on the thread to the point shown and trim off the excess.

3. Pull 8 to 10 hackle fibers from a large, soft hackle feather.

4. Measure the hackle fibers against the hook shank; the fibers should be as long as from the back of the eye to the back of the bend.

5. Holding the fibers at the measured point, move the fibers back to the start of the hook bend.

6. Grasp the hackle fibers at the bend with the left hand and move the right hand forward to the tie-in point.

7. Hold the fibers at the tie-in point with the right hand.

8. Grasp the fibers and hook shank with left hand as shown.

9. Tie down the butts of the fibers using the "soft loop."

10. Wrap the thread back to a point directly opposite the barb of the hook. To keep the tail material on the top of the hook, hold the fibers offset toward you and allow the thread to carry the tail to the top as you wrap.

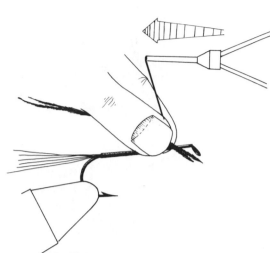

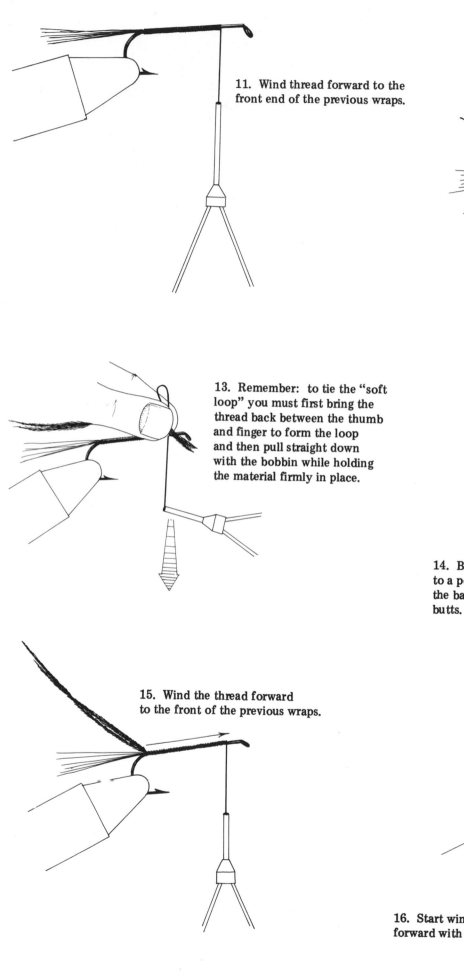

11. Wind thread forward to the front end of the previous wraps.

12. Hold two pieces of peacock herl on the top of the shank and tie in using the "soft loop."

13. Remember: to tie the "soft loop" you must first bring the thread back between the thumb and finger to form the loop and then pull straight down with the bobbin while holding the material firmly in place.

14. Bring thread to the rear to a point directly opposite the barb. Trim off the herl butts.

15. Wind the thread forward to the front of the previous wraps.

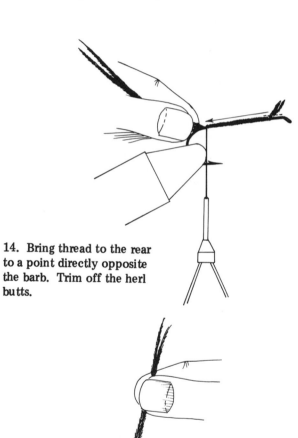

16. Start winding the herl forward with the right hand.

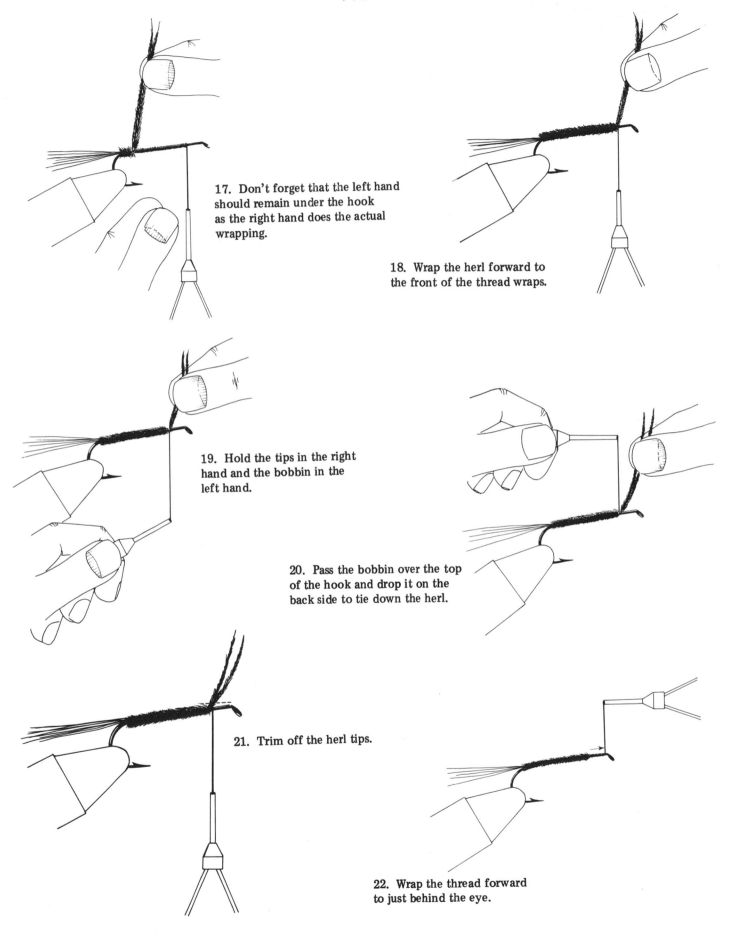

17. Don't forget that the left hand should remain under the hook as the right hand does the actual wrapping.

18. Wrap the herl forward to the front of the thread wraps.

19. Hold the tips in the right hand and the bobbin in the left hand.

20. Pass the bobbin over the top of the hook and drop it on the back side to tie down the herl.

21. Trim off the herl tips.

22. Wrap the thread forward to just behind the eye.

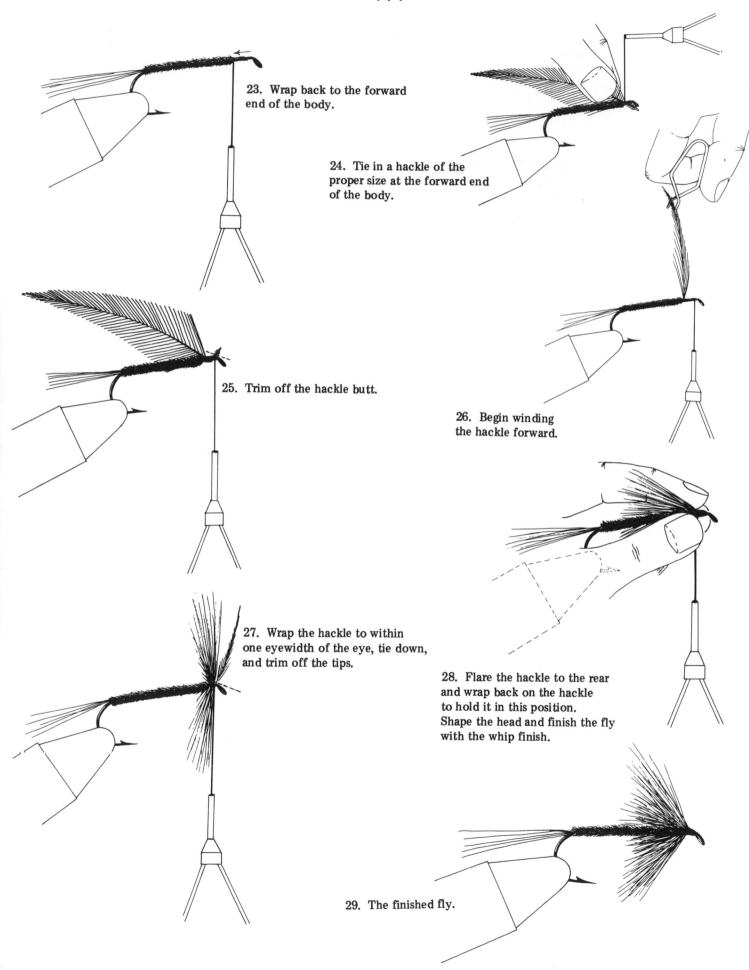

23. Wrap back to the forward end of the body.

24. Tie in a hackle of the proper size at the forward end of the body.

25. Trim off the hackle butt.

26. Begin winding the hackle forward.

27. Wrap the hackle to within one eyewidth of the eye, tie down, and trim off the tips.

28. Flare the hackle to the rear and wrap back on the hackle to hold it in this position. Shape the head and finish the fly with the whip finish.

29. The finished fly.

Pattern 22

This is a dry-fly attracter pattern of the palmered type. We show it tied with a floss body—as it is for the Bloody Butcher (red floss with black hackle) and the Orange Asher (orange floss with ginger hackle)—but the same pattern tied on a long shank hook with a chenille body is a Wooly Worm. The color combinations that you might use are endless.

Flies tied in this manner are very good floaters because of the large amount of hackle used. They can be deadly when caterpillars abound.

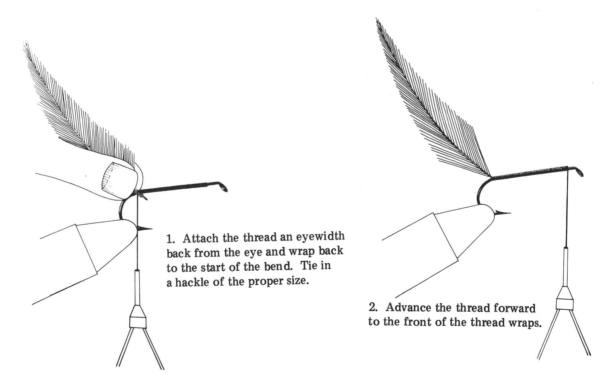

1. Attach the thread an eyewidth back from the eye and wrap back to the start of the bend. Tie in a hackle of the proper size.

2. Advance the thread forward to the front of the thread wraps.

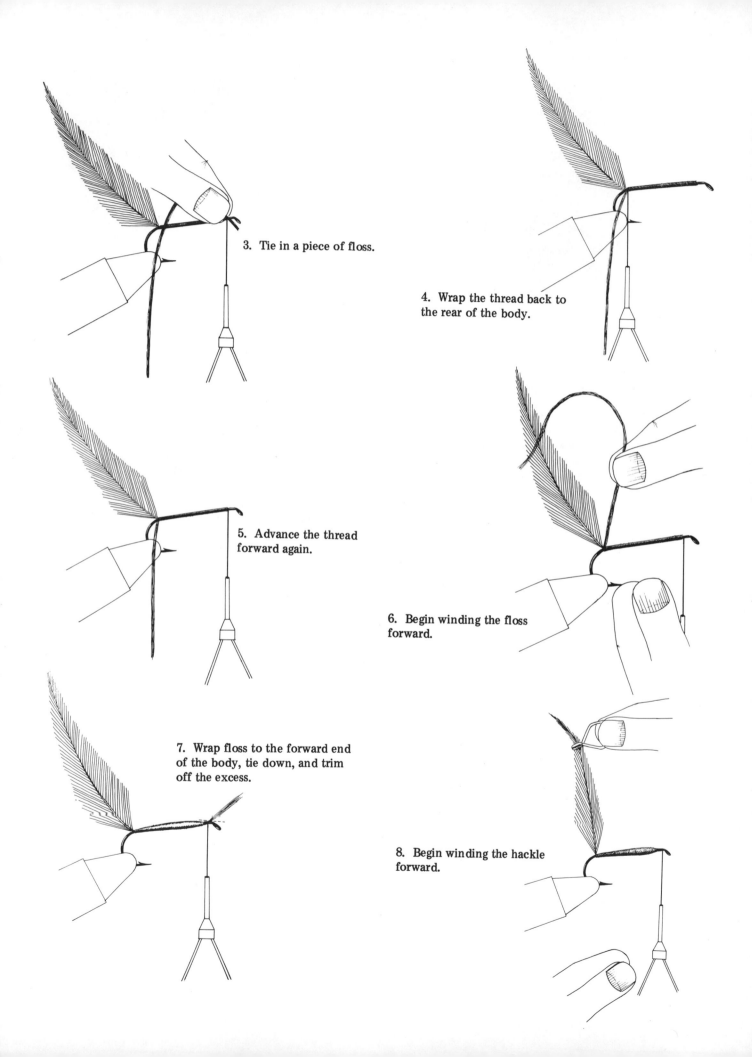

3. Tie in a piece of floss.

4. Wrap the thread back to the rear of the body.

5. Advance the thread forward again.

6. Begin winding the floss forward.

7. Wrap floss to the forward end of the body, tie down, and trim off the excess.

8. Begin winding the hackle forward.

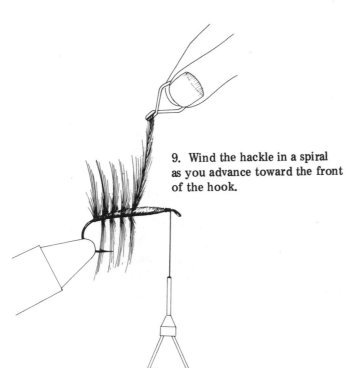

9. Wind the hackle in a spiral as you advance toward the front of the hook.

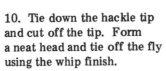

10. Tie down the hackle tip and cut off the tip. Form a neat head and tie off the fly using the whip finish.

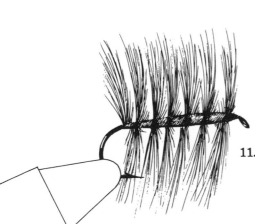

11. The finished fly.

Pattern 23

This is another wet-fly attracter that is a really good producer in the West. It is called a Rio Grande King and is probably effective because it has the shape of an emerging insect.

There are two things you should pick up from tying this pattern. First, notice that the chenille being used for the body has all of the "fuzz" removed from the center thread at the tip so that you can attach it by the thread, so a lump isn't created when you start wrapping. Secondly, pay close attention to the steps involved in preparing the calf tail for the wing. Because calf tail is very curly, it doesn't lend itself well to the use of a hair stacker. The method shown is about the only way to get the hair ends even.

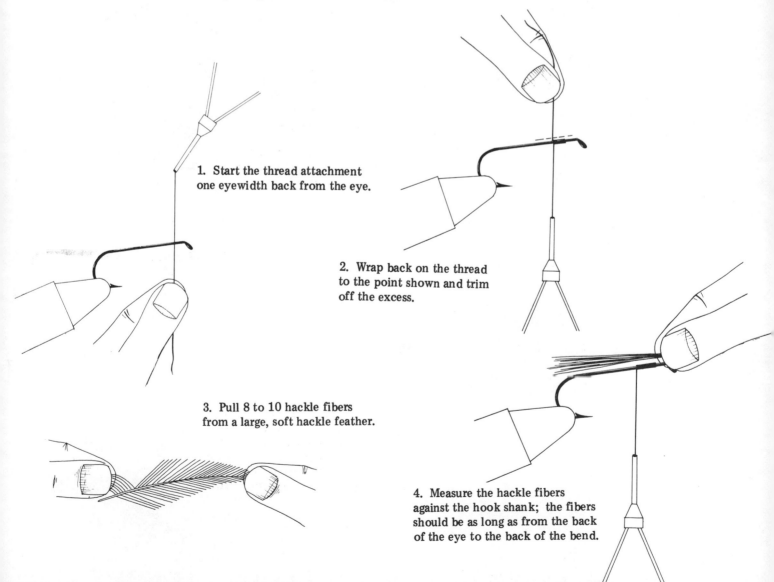

1. Start the thread attachment one eyewidth back from the eye.

2. Wrap back on the thread to the point shown and trim off the excess.

3. Pull 8 to 10 hackle fibers from a large, soft hackle feather.

4. Measure the hackle fibers against the hook shank; the fibers should be as long as from the back of the eye to the back of the bend.

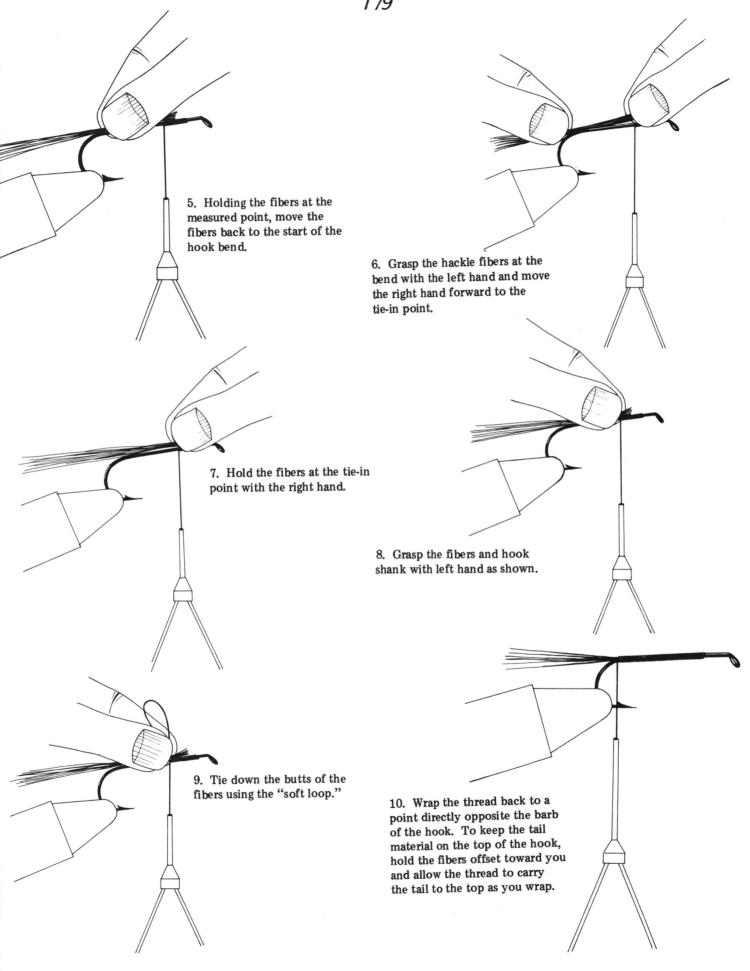

5. Holding the fibers at the measured point, move the fibers back to the start of the hook bend.

6. Grasp the hackle fibers at the bend with the left hand and move the right hand forward to the tie-in point.

7. Hold the fibers at the tie-in point with the right hand.

8. Grasp the fibers and hook shank with left hand as shown.

9. Tie down the butts of the fibers using the "soft loop."

10. Wrap the thread back to a point directly opposite the barb of the hook. To keep the tail material on the top of the hook, hold the fibers offset toward you and allow the thread to carry the tail to the top as you wrap.

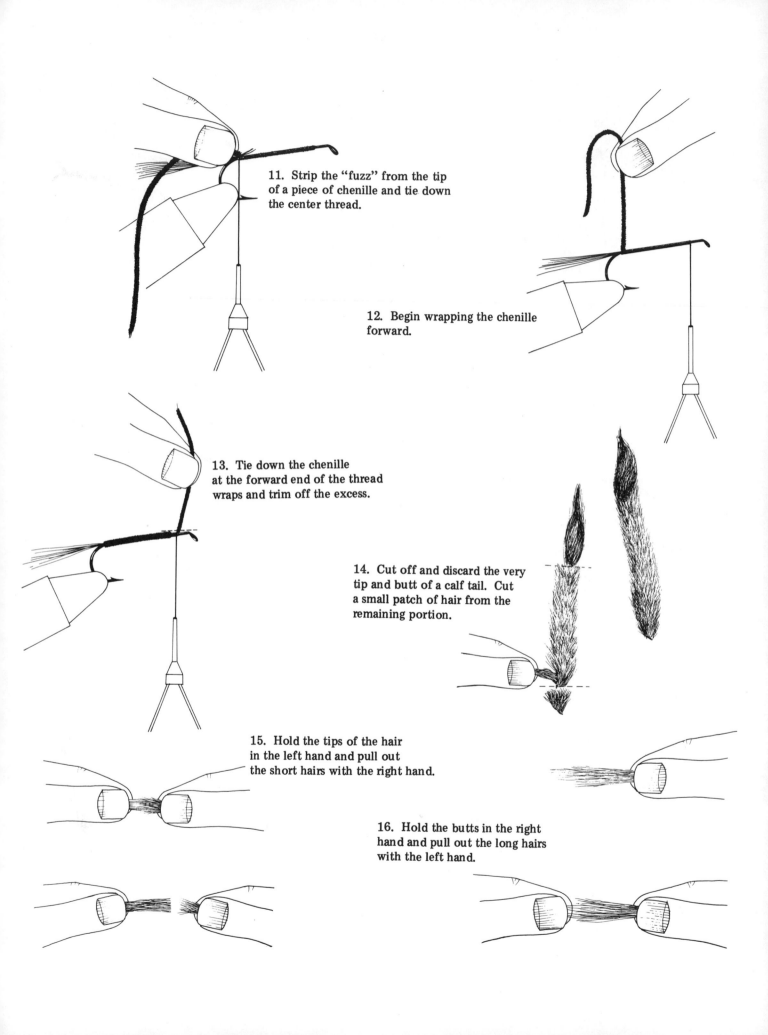

11. Strip the "fuzz" from the tip of a piece of chenille and tie down the center thread.

12. Begin wrapping the chenille forward.

13. Tie down the chenille at the forward end of the thread wraps and trim off the excess.

14. Cut off and discard the very tip and butt of a calf tail. Cut a small patch of hair from the remaining portion.

15. Hold the tips of the hair in the left hand and pull out the short hairs with the right hand.

16. Hold the butts in the right hand and pull out the long hairs with the left hand.

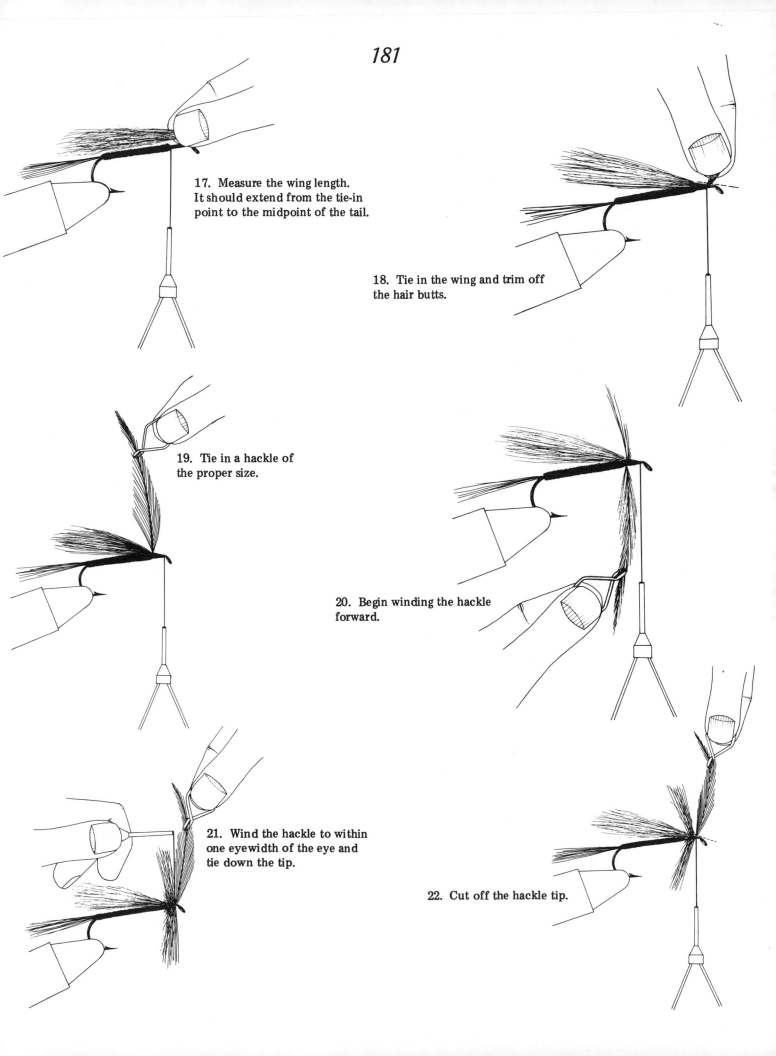

17. Measure the wing length. It should extend from the tie-in point to the midpoint of the tail.

18. Tie in the wing and trim off the hair butts.

19. Tie in a hackle of the proper size.

20. Begin winding the hackle forward.

21. Wind the hackle to within one eyewidth of the eye and tie down the tip.

22. Cut off the hackle tip.

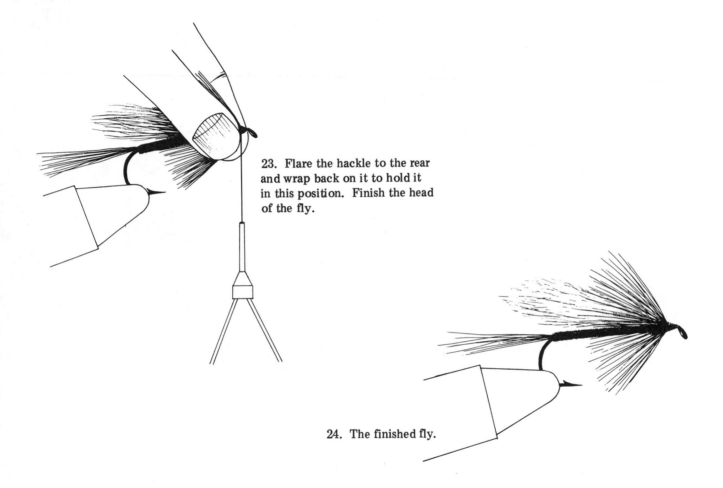

23. Flare the hackle to the rear and wrap back on it to hold it in this position. Finish the head of the fly.

24. The finished fly.

Pattern 24

The last fly that we are going to show you is a very simple wet fly of the classical style. We have chosen this pattern because its simplicity has a certain delicacy that is more difficult to achieve than it would seem. Much like the classic salmon patterns, this fly requires perfect proportion of materials and flawless execution of technique to be tied properly.

Pay particular attention to the taper of the body. This has been shown in many of the previous patterns, but we doubt that you have made a concerted effort to imitate it; very few of our students do so until late in the course. The method of accomplishing it is to start winding the floss flat on the hook shank at the tail and then to begin overlapping the floss wraps as you advance forward, much as you did earlier on the rubber-band-bodied stone-fly nymph.

The flaring of the hackle toward the rear of the hook is another detail that is sometimes hard to get the feel for. Yet this detail counts a lot toward the appearance of the finished fly. To get the desired even flare, try wetting your finger and thumb before pulling the hackle to the rear, start the thumb and finger in front of, and slightly below, the eye, and then follow the shape of the hook with the thumb and finger on either side. The finger and thumb should move slightly upward along the eye and then toward the rear and down following the hook shank as the hackle fibers are picked up and swept back.

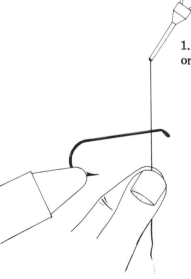

1. Start the thread attachment one eyewidth back from the eye.

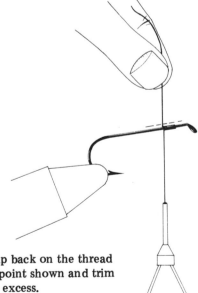

2. Wrap back on the thread to the point shown and trim off the excess.

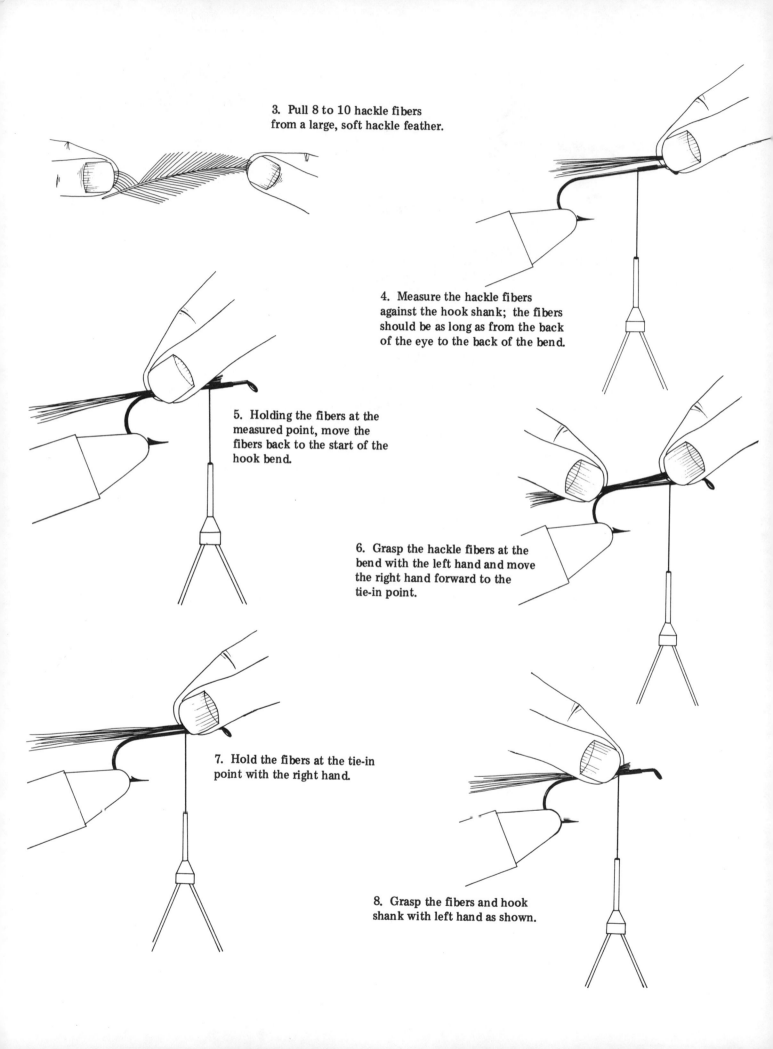

3. Pull 8 to 10 hackle fibers from a large, soft hackle feather.

4. Measure the hackle fibers against the hook shank; the fibers should be as long as from the back of the eye to the back of the bend.

5. Holding the fibers at the measured point, move the fibers back to the start of the hook bend.

6. Grasp the hackle fibers at the bend with the left hand and move the right hand forward to the tie-in point.

7. Hold the fibers at the tie-in point with the right hand.

8. Grasp the fibers and hook shank with left hand as shown.

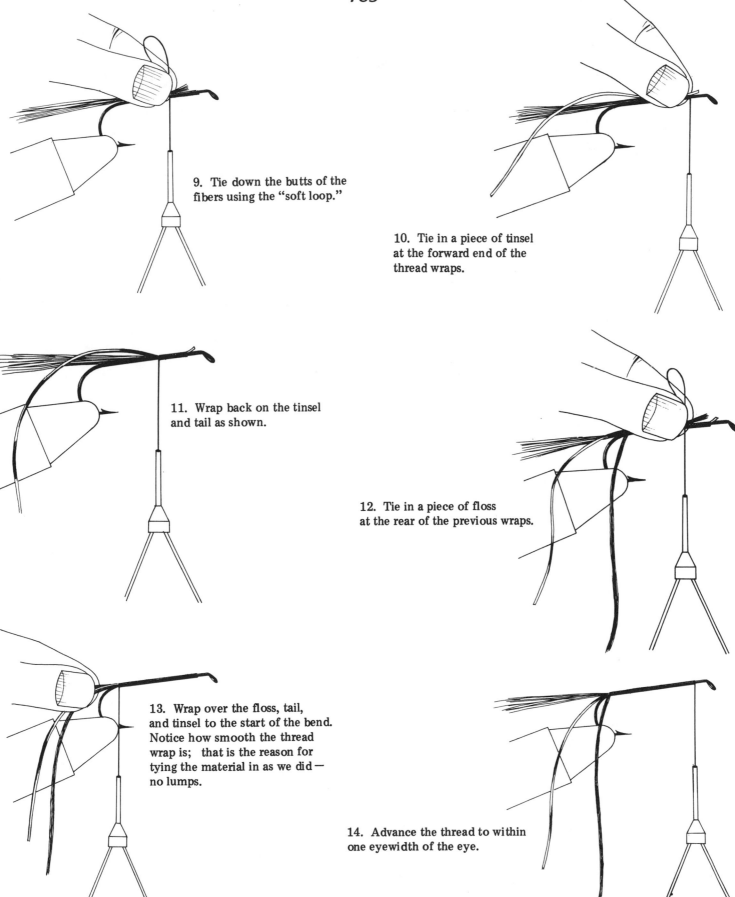

9. Tie down the butts of the fibers using the "soft loop."

10. Tie in a piece of tinsel at the forward end of the thread wraps.

11. Wrap back on the tinsel and tail as shown.

12. Tie in a piece of floss at the rear of the previous wraps.

13. Wrap over the floss, tail, and tinsel to the start of the bend. Notice how smooth the thread wrap is; that is the reason for tying the material in as we did — no lumps.

14. Advance the thread to within one eyewidth of the eye.

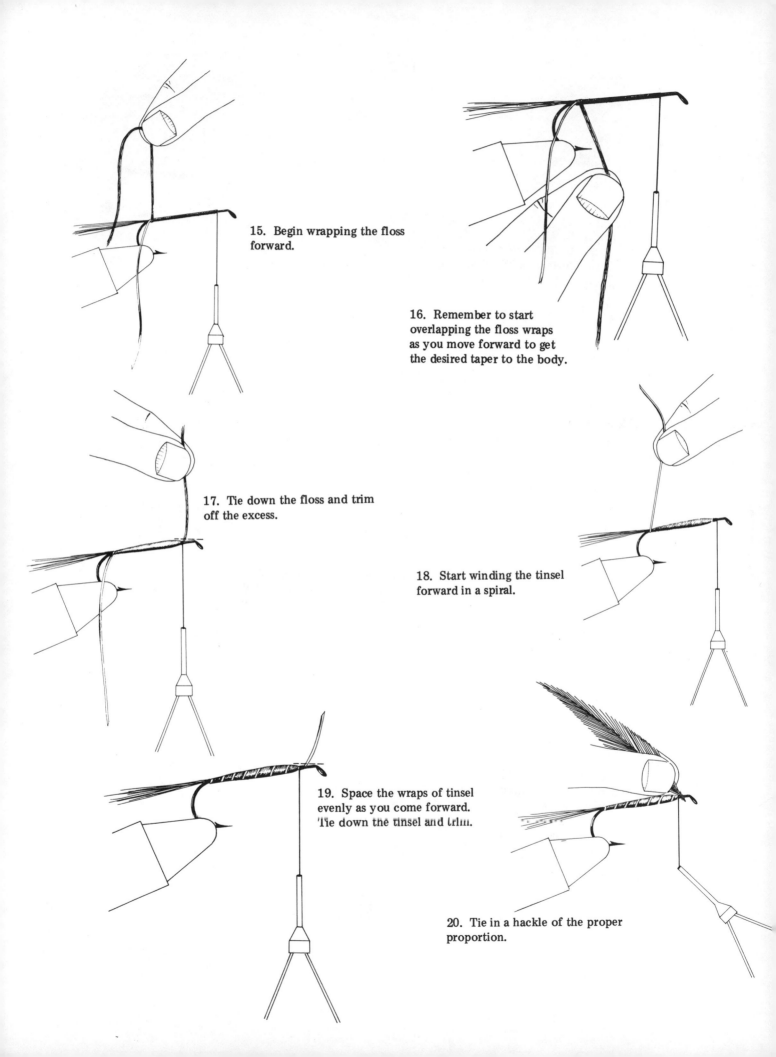

15. Begin wrapping the floss forward.

16. Remember to start overlapping the floss wraps as you move forward to get the desired taper to the body.

17. Tie down the floss and trim off the excess.

18. Start winding the tinsel forward in a spiral.

19. Space the wraps of tinsel evenly as you come forward. Tie down the tinsel and trim.

20. Tie in a hackle of the proper proportion.

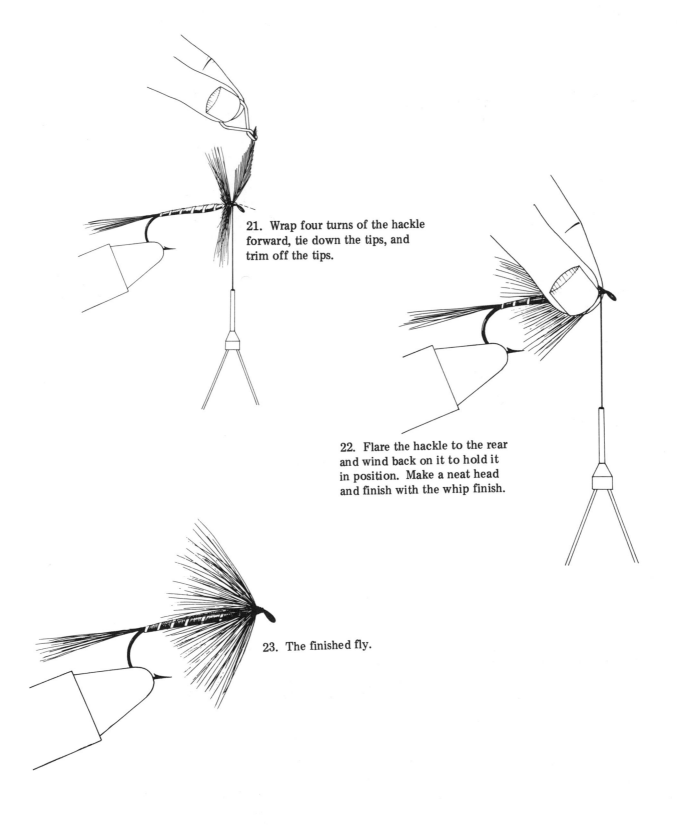

21. Wrap four turns of the hackle forward, tie down the tips, and trim off the tips.

22. Flare the hackle to the rear and wind back on it to hold it in position. Make a neat head and finish with the whip finish.

23. The finished fly.

bibliography

The following books are suggested reading for all fly-tyers. Those marked with an asterisk are works we recommend as the foundation of a fly-tying library.

*Bates, Joseph D., Jr. *Streamer Fly-Tying and Fishing.* Harrisburg, Pa.: The Stackpole Company, 1966.

Bay, Kenneth E. *How to Tie Freshwater Flies.* New York: Winchester Press, 1974.

*Caucci, Al, and Natasi, Bob. *Hatches.* New York: Comparahatch, 1975.

Dennis, Jack H., Jr. *Western Trout Fly Tying Manual.* Jackson Hole, Wyo.: Snake River Books, 1974.

*Flick, Arthur B. *Art Flick's New Streamside Guide.* New York: Crown Publishers, 1969.

——. *Art Flick's Master Fly Tying Guide.* New York: Crown Publishers, 1972.

*Jorgensen, Poul. *Dressing Flies for Fresh and Salt Water.* Rockville Centre, N.Y.: Freshet Press, 1973.

——. *Modern Fly Dressings For the Practical Angler.* New York: Winchester Press, 1976.

LaFontaine, Gary J. *Challenge of the Trout.* Missoula, Mont.: Mountain Press Publishing Company, 1976.

*Leiser, Eric. *Fly-Tying Materials.* New York: Crown Publishers, 1973.

*Schwiebert, Ernest. *Matching the Hatch.* New York: Macmillan Co., 1955.

——. *Nymphs.* New York: Winchester Press, 1973.

Solomon, Larry, and Leiser, Eric. *The Caddis and the Angler.* Harrisburg, Pa.: Stackpole Books, 1977.

*Swisher, Doug, and Richards, Carl. *Selective Trout.* New York: Crown Publishers, 1971.

index